2000 MOST COMMON CHINESE WORDS IN CONTEXT

Get Fluent & Increase Your Chinese Vocabulary with 2000 Chinese Phrases

Chinese Language Lessons

Lingo Mastery

FREE BOOK REVEALS THE 6 STEP BLUEPRINT THAT TOOK STUDENTS **FROM LANGUAGE LEARNERS TO FLUENT IN 3 MONTHS**

- **6 Unbelievable Hacks** that will accelerate your learning curve
- **Mind Training:** why memorizing vocabulary is easy
- **One Hack To Rule Them All:** This <u>secret nugget</u> will blow you away...

Head over to <u>LingoMastery.com/hacks</u>
and claim your free book now!

TABLE OF CONTENT

INTRODUCTION

How many languages are there in the world? There are about 1,500. Chinese (or Mandardin) is one of them, and it is a fascinating, unique, and extremely rich language. Counting roughly 1.3 billion native speakers, it is used by the largest number of people in the world. Not only this, but China's rapid rise as a global superpower is making it an increasingly significant means of communication for people in Asia and beyond. These two reasons should be enough to convince you to learn Chinese, but if not, here are some more!

The study of the Chinese language opens the way to different important fields such as Chinese politics, economy, history or archaeology. To study the Chinese language finally means to study the Chinese culture and the Chinese people. At the heart of Chinese civilization is its rich heritage of novels, short stories, poetry, drama, and, more recently, movies. They contain words, phrases, and expressions that reflect the culturally significant traditions, the values, the ideas, the struggles, the sensibility, the joys and the sorrows that just cannot be expressed correctly through a translation. Through learning Chinese, you'll develop an understanding of all these behind words, phrases, and the characters.

Almost everyone in the world has heard about China's achievements in every aspect and the country's newfound significance in the world economy. Companies aiming at China's market require professionals with an understanding of Chinese culture, language skills, or related knowledge to help them expand their business in China. Learning Chinese will provide you with an excellent opportunity to get ahead of your colleagues and attract the attention of headhunters.

China boasts one of the world's oldest civilizations, richest continuous cultures and an interesting history of over 5,000 years. Learning Chinese will provide you the opportunity to discover the endlessly fascinating lives of over 1.3 billion people. By learning Chinese, you can take one of the most culturally enriching adventures - exploring the populous cities and traditional villages, enjoying delicious foods, and absorb new traditions throughout the country without barriers!

If you've picked this book up, you've already made good progress in learning the language. This book can give you an incredible tool in learning the Chinese language: *vocabulary*. Now you've just got to learn how to use it.

What this book is about and how to use it:

There are hacks to learning every language, but learning the vocabulary is a surefire way of speeding up your learning of a new tongue. Just look at these three amazing stats found in a study done in 1964:

1. *Learning the first thousand (1000) most frequently used words of a language will allow you to understand 76.0% of all non-fiction writing, 79.6% of all fiction writing and an astounding 87.8% of all oral speech.*
2. *Learning the top two thousand (2000) most frequently used words will get you to 84% for non-fiction, 86.1% for fiction, and 92.7% for oral speech.*
3. *Learning the top three thousand (3000) most frequently used words will get you to 88.2% for non-fiction, 89.6% for fiction, and 94.0% for oral speech.*

Just look at those stats and imagine what you could do with this book once you've thoroughly read and practiced what it contains? We're providing you with two thousand of the most frequently used words — equivalent to an understanding of 92.7% of oral speech!

We achieve this not only by giving you a long list of words; there must be context to allow the words to sink in, and we provide that. Each of the terms will be listed with its Chinese Pinyin, translation in English and example sentence with translation, allowing you to study the use of each word in a common, accessible manner. We have ordered the terms in their largest number of occurrences in common media, allowing you to begin with the simplest and most regularly used words first before moving on to the less-used ones.

So now, do you need anything else while reading this book? Yes, you may, as always. There are hundreds of thousands of more words out there, but these will certainly give you a head-start on learning the language and getting closer to mastering it.

Recommendations for readers of 2000 Most Common Words in Chinese:

Although we'd love to begin right away with helping you learn the vocabulary we've provided in this book, we've got a few tips and recommendations for getting the most out of this book:

1. Repetition: The more times you see, hear, say, write a word, the more likely you are to remember it.
2. Concentration: Staying alert when you memorize is vitally important.
3. Application: A word that you find a chance to use in a conversation is more likely to stay with you than one you only study in a book.
4. Movement: Physical movement combined with memorization helps you remember words better. Sway your arms, rock your head, pace the room, do whatever you need to.
5. Associations: Associate a word with something that is memorable, funny, shocking, etc. It may help to associate the Chinese word with some word in your own language that the Chinese word sounds like – the more absurd, the better.

IMPORTANT NOTE:

Chinese has relatively uncomplicated grammar. Unlike Indo-European languages, Chinese has no verb conjugation and no noun declension. For example, while someone learning English has to learn different verb forms like "eat/ ate/ eaten," all you need to do in Chinese is remember one word: 吃(Chi). While in English you have to distinguish between "dog" and "dogs," in Chinese there is only one form: 狗(Gou).

Chinese uses one of four tones for nearly every word in the language. Thus, a syllable pronounced with a high-level intonation is a different word from the same syllable pronounced with a rising intonation, a falling-rising intonation, or a falling intonation. The classic example used to intimidate beginner learners in Chinese is the syllable "ma", which means "mother" when pronounced with a high-level intonation and "horse" when pronounced with a falling-rising intonation. Another classic example is the syllable "en", which expresses hesitation when pronounced with a flat intonation, doubt when pronounced with a rising intonation, rejection when pronounced with a falling-rising intonation and confirmation with a falling intonation.

Learners sometimes feel that they cannot hear tones, but this is not exactly what the problem is. After all, English speakers listen to and use intonation all the time. Consider the difference between a rising tone "Yes?" (as someone answers the door) or a falling tone "Yes!" (as an enthusiastic response to an invitation). The difference between Chinese and English is that in English intonation functions at the sentence level instead of the word level, with the rises and falls of tones, the sentences conveys the emotional impact of the message. The problem for learners is not hearing intonation per se but hearing intonation as part of the pronunciation of a word!

Be wary - the tones mentioned in this book are based on Mandarin, while the writing is based on simplified Chinese characters. However, you may also hear people talking about Cantonese and traditional Chinese characters. Technically, Cantonese is a subset of the Yue language family found in southern China. Both Mandarin and Cantonese refer to spoken languages that are members of the Sinitic linguistic family. They are both tonal languages, though the tones are different and they are not mutually intelligible. As such, they cannot really be referred to as dialects because a Cantonese speaker cannot understand a Mandarin speaker and vice versa. Regarding the writing, both Mandarin and Cantonese shared the same character sets until the 1950s and 1960s when simplified Chinese characters were officially adopted in mainland China in order to increase literacy rates. The traditional characters were retained by Cantonese speakers in Hong Kong and Mandarin speakers in Taiwan, and the writing systems are therefore largely independent of the spoken languages.

THE 2000 MOST COMMON WORDS IN CHINESE

Hello again, reader. As I previously stated in the **Introduction,** the words have been arranged by their frequency of use in common media, such as films, series and books. Feel free to rearrange them during your practice to make things interesting.

You will be provided with a **word, Chinese Pinyin,** a **translation of said word** and **one example with translation** of the term given. It's as easy as that.

Let's begin:

1- 的/de/ – *Adjectival suffix; possessive particle*

这件黑外套是我**的**。

zhè jiàn hēi wài tào shì wǒ **de**.

This black coat is **mine**.

2- 一/yī/ – *One; a, an*

桌面上有**一**个杯子。

zhuō miān shàng yǒu **yī** gè bēi zi.

There is **a** cup on the table.

3- 是/shì/ – *Yes, right; be*

那**是**一本中文书。

nà **shì** yī běn zhōng wén shū.

That **is** a Chinese book.

4- 不/bù/ – *No, not*

我**不**想去看电影。

wǒ **bù** xiǎng qù kàn diàn yǐng.

I do **not** want to go to a movie.

5- 了 /le/ – Particle of completed action

她已经走了。

tā yǐ jīng zǒu **le**.

She has **gone**.

6- 在 /zài/ – At, in, on

他**在**家里睡觉。

tā **zài** jiā lǐ shuì jiào.

He is **at** home sleeping.

7- 人 /rén/ – Man; people

有很多**人**在公园里散步。

yǒu hěn duō **rén** zài gōng yuán lǐ sàn bù.

There are many **people** walking in the park.

8- 有 /yǒu/ – Have, own

她**有**一份不错的工作。

tā **yǒu** yī fèn bù cuò de gōng zuò.

She **has** a nice job.

9- 我 /wǒ/ – I, me

我喜欢打篮球。

wǒ xǐ huān dǎ lán qiú.

I like playing basketball.

10- 他 /tā/ – He, him

他是一位公交车司机。

tā shì yī wèi gōng jiāo chē sī jī.

He is a bus driver.

11- 这 /zhè/ – This, the

我要买**这**本书。

wǒ yāo mǎi **zhè** běn shū.

I'd like to buy **this** book.

12- 个 /gè/ – Measure word for fruits, people, most items, etc.

我早上吃了**一个苹果**。

wǒ zǎo shang chī le **yī gè píng guǒ**.

I ate **an apple** in the morning.

13- 们 /men/ – Adjunct pronoun indicate plural

他们都是从美国来的。

tā men dōu shì cóng měi guó lái de.

They are all from America.

14- 中 /zhōng/ – Center, middle; in the midst of

一个国家的首都通常是文化和政治**中**心。

yī gè guó jiā de shǒu dū tōng cháng shì wén huà hé zhèng zhì **zhōng** xīn.

The capital of a country usually serves as a cultural and political **center**.

15- 来 /lái/ – Come, coming

你先**来**吧，我一会就回。

nǐ xiān **lái** ba, wǒ yī huǐ jiù huí.

You may **come** now; I'll return soon.

16- 上 /shàng/ – Top; go up

山顶**上**很凉快。

shān dǐng **shàng** hěn liáng kuai.

It is cool on the **top** of the hill.

17- 大 /dà/ – Big, large

这件外套太**大**了。

zhè jiàn wài tào tài **dà** le.

This coat is too **big**.

18- 为 /wèi/ – For

我**为**了你才这么做。

wǒ **wèi** le nǐ cái zhè me zuò.

I did it **for** you.

19- 和/hé/ – *And, with*

她不愿意**和**我约会。

tā bù yuàn yì **hé** wǒ yuē huì.

She's unwilling to have a date **with** me.

20- 国/guó/ – *Nation, country*

国与**国**之间的关系很复杂。

guó yǔ **guó** zhī jiān de guān xì hěn fù zá.

The relationship between two **countries** is complicated.

21- 地/dì/ – *Earth; region*

这个**地**方有很多果树。

zhè ge **dì** fāng yǒu hěn duō guǒ shù.

There are many fruit trees in this **region**.

22- 到/dào/ – *Go to, arrive, been to*

你什么时候**到**北京？

nǐ shén me shí hòu **dào** běi jīng?

When will you **arrive** in Beijing?

23- 以/yǐ/ – *Use; therefore; by*

她**以**一首钢琴曲赢得了才艺表演。

tā **yǐ** yī shǒu gāng qín qǔ yíng dé le cái yì biǎo yǎn.

She won the talent show **by** playing the piano.

24- 说/shuō/ – *Speak, say, talk*

她心情不好，所以她什么都不想**说**。

tā xīn qíng bù hǎo, suǒ yǐ tā shén me dōu bù xiǎng **shuō**.

She doesn't want to **say** anything because she's in a bad mood.

25- 时/shí/ – *Time, period*

时间一点点过去，她仍然没有出现。

shí jiān yī diǎn diǎn guò qù, tā réng rán méi yǒu chū xiàn.

Time passed, and still she did not appear.

26- 要 /yào/ – Necessary, essential; want

我想**要**去书店买书。

wǒ xiǎng **yào** qù shū diàn mǎi shū.

I **want** to go to the bookstore to buy some books.

27- 就 /jiù/ – Just, simply

我有一件**就**像这样的外套。

wǒ yǒu yī jiàn **jiù** xiàng zhè yàng de wài tào.

I have a coat **just** like this.

28- 出 /chū/ – Go out, send out

他**出**去了，你一会儿再来吧。

tā **chū** qù le, nǐ yī huǐ er zài lái ba.

He **went out**; You can come back later.

29- 会 /huì/ – Can; meet together; meeting

我马上要去开个**会**。

wǒ mǎ shàng yào qù kāi gè **huì**.

I'm about to have a **meeting**.

30- 可 /kě/ – May, can; possibly

我**可**能感冒了。

wǒ **kě** néng gǎn mào le.

I **may** have caught a cold.

31- 也 /yě/ – Also

他去美国旅游了，我**也**想去。

tā qù měi guó lǚ yóu le, wǒ **yě** xiǎng qù.

He went to America for a sightseeing; I **also** want to go.

32- 你 /nǐ/ – You

你是谁？

nǐ shì shuí?

Who are **you**?

33- 对 /duì/ – Correct, right

我希望你是**对**的。

wǒ xī wàng nǐ shì **duì** de.

I hope you are **right**.

34- 生 /shēng/ – Life, living

他把一**生**都奉献给了科学。

tā bǎ yī **shēng** dōu fèng xiàn gěi le kē xué.

He has devoted all his **life** to science.

35- 能 /néng/ – To be able, can

我**能**用一下你的笔吗？

wǒ **néng** yòng yī xià nǐ de bǐ ma?

Can I use your pen please?

36- 而 /ér/ – But

那不是一棵桃树，**而**是一棵苹果树。

nà bù shì yī kē táo shù, **ér** shì yī kē píng guǒ shù.

This is not a peach tree, **but** an apple tree.

37- 子 /zǐ/ – Son, child, seed

我儿**子**正在上小学。

wǒ ér **zǐ** zhèng zài shàng xiǎo xué.

My **son** is studying in the elementary school.

38- 那 /nà/ – That, those

从**那**时起我就爱上了她。

cóng **nà** shí qǐ wǒ jiù ài shàng le tā.

I fell in love with her from **that** moment.

39- 得 /dé/ – Obtain, get, gain

去年生日我**得**到了一辆崭新的自行车。

qù nián shēng rì wǒ **dé** dào le yī liàng zhǎn xīn de zì xíng chē.

I **got** a new bike on my birthday last year.

40- 于 /yú/ – In, at, from, than

他的收入高**于**我。

tā de shōu rù gāo **yú** wǒ.

His income is higher **than** mine.

41- 着 /zhe/ – Aspect particle indicating action in progress

他在纸上**写着**什么。

tā zài zhǐ shàng **xiě zhe** shén me.

He **is writing** something on the paper.

42- 下 /xià/ – Under, below, down

我要**下**楼买东西。

wǒ yào **xià** lóu mǎi dōng xī.

I want to go **down**stairs to buy something.

43- 自 /zì/ – Self; from

他给**自**己倒了一杯红酒，然后坐在沙发上。

tā gěi **zì** jǐ dào le yī bēi hóng jiǔ, rán hòu zuò zài shā fā shàng.

He poured him**self** a glass of wine and sat down in the sofa.

44- 之 /zhī/ – Archaic equivalent of structural particle 的

他们做得是对还是错，这是**争议之处**。

tā men zuò dé shì duì hái shì cuò, zhè shì **zhēng yì zhī chù**.

It is **a matter of dispute** whether they did the right thing.

45- 年 /nián/ – Year

新**年**快乐！

xīn **nián** kuài lè!

Happy new **year**!

46- 过 /guò/ – Pass, go across

我顺利通**过**了考试。

wǒ shùn lì tōng **guò** le kǎo shì.

I **passed** the exam successfully.

47- 发/fā/ – Issue, send out

路边有个人在**发**传单。

lù biān yǒu gè rén zài **fā** chuán dān.

A person on the road is **sending out** leaflets.

48- 后/hòu/ – After, behind

你下班**后**做什么？

nǐ xià bān **hòu** zuò shén me?

What do you do **after** work?

49- 作/zuò/ – Writings, works; write, compose

这本书收录了他的**作**品。

zhè běn shū shōu lù le tā de **zuò** pǐn.

His **works** are included in this book.

50- 里/lǐ/ – Inside; unit of distance

钱包**里**面有张折起来的纸片。

qián bāo **lǐ** miàn yǒu zhāng zhé qǐ lái de zhǐ piàn.

Inside the wallet was a folded slip of paper.

51- 用/yòng/ – Use

我能**用**一下你的手机吗？

wǒ néng **yòng** yī xià nǐ de shǒu jī ma?

May I **use** your phone please?

52- 道/dào/ – Path, road, way

走这条**道**能去公园。

zǒu zhè tiáo **dào** néng qù gōng yuán.

This is the **way** to the park.

53- 行/xíng/ – Travel, move; go, walk

我喜欢旅**行**。

wǒ xǐ huān lǚ **xíng**.

I like to **travel**.

54- 所 /suǒ/ – Place, area

公共场**所**禁止吸烟。

gōng gòng chǎng **suǒ** jìn zhǐ xī yān.

Smoking is strictly prohibited in public **areas**.

55- 自然 /zì rán/ – Nature; natural

他怨恨你是很**自然**的事。

tā yuàn hèn nǐ shì hěn **zì rán** de shì.

It is only **natural** that he should resent you.

56- 家 /jiā/ – Home; family

你几点会在**家**?

nǐ jǐ diǎn huì zài **jiā**?

When will you be at **home**?

57- 种 /zhòng/ – To plant; seed, race

我上周日**种**了一棵树。

wǒ shàng zhōu rì **zhòng** le yī kē shù.

I **planted** a tree last Sunday.

58- 事 /shì/ – Affair, matter, business

这不关你的**事**。

zhè bù guān nǐ de **shì**.

This is none of your **business**.

59- 成 /chéng/ – Completed, finished, accomplished

任务完**成**!

rèn wù wán **chéng**!

Mission **accomplished**!

60- 方 /fāng/ – Square

这既不是圆的也不是**方**的。

zhè jì bù shì yuán de yě bù shì **fāng** de.

This is neither round nor **square**.

61- 多 /duō/ – Much, many; more than, over

今天晚上有**多**少人来？

jīn tiān wǎn shàng yǒu **duō** shǎo rén lái?

How **many** people will come tonight?

62- 经验 /jīng yàn/ – Pass through; experience

这位顾问有各个方面的管理**经验**。

zhè wèi gù wèn yǒu gè ge fāng miàn de guǎn lǐ **jīng yàn**.

This consultant has managerial **experience** in every aspect.

63- 什么 /shén me/ – Used to form interrogative

这是**什么**？

zhè shì **shén me**?

What is this?

64- 去 /qù/ – Go away, leave, depart

我明天要**去**纽约。

wǒ míng tiān yào **qù** niǔ yuē.

I'm **leaving** for New York tomorrow.

65- 法 /fǎ/ – Law

人人都应遵纪守**法**。

rén rén dōu yīng zūn jì shǒu **fǎ**.

Everyone should abide by the **law**.

66- 学 /xué/ – To learn

彼得正在**学**中文。

bǐ dé zhèng zài **xué** zhōng wén.

Peter is **learning** Chinese.

67- 如 /rú/ – If; like, as

如你所愿。

rú nǐ suǒ yuàn.

As you wish.

68- 都 /dōu/ – *All*

这片建筑**都**是那个富商的。

zhè piàn jiàn zhú **dōu** shì nà gè fù shāng de.

All these buildings belong to the rich businessman.

69- 同 /tóng/ – *Same; together with*

我有一件衬衫和你的相**同**。

wǒ yǒu yī jiàn chèn shān hé nǐ de xiāng **tóng**.

I have a shirt that is the **same** as yours.

70- 现 /xiàn/ – *Appear; now*

从**现**在开始你自由了。

cóng **xiàn** zài kāi shǐ nǐ zì yóu le.

From **now** on you are free.

71- 当 /dāng/ – *When*

当我还小的时候，我爱听收音机，等着那些我喜欢的歌。

dāng wǒ hái xiǎo de shí hòu, wǒ ài tīng shōu yīn jī, děng zhe nà xiē wǒ xǐ huān de gē.

When I was young, I'd listen to the radio waiting for my favorite songs.

72- 没 /méi/ – *Have not*

你去过北京吗？ —我**没**去过。

nǐ qù guò běi jīng ma? wǒ **méi** qù guò.

Have you been to Beijing? —No, I **haven't**.

73- 动 /dòng/ – *Move*

不要**动**!

bù yào **dòng**!

Don't **move**!

74- 面 /miàn/ – *Surface, face*

立方体有六个**面**。

lì fāng tǐ yǒu liù gè **miàn**.

A cube has six **surfaces**.

75- 起/qǐ/ – *Stand up, rise; together*

我们曾一**起**骑自行车长途旅行。

wǒ men céng yī **qǐ** qí zì xíng chē cháng tú lǚ xíng.

We went on long bicycle rides **together**.

76- 看/kàn/ – *Look, see*

我能**看**一下吗？

wǒ néng **kàn** yī xià ma?

May I have a **look** please?

77- 定/dìng/ – *Settle, decide*

就这么**定**了。

jiù zhè me **dìng** le.

That's **settled**.

78- 天/tiān/ – *Day, sky*

我们这周休息三**天**。

wǒ men zhè zhōu xiū xī sān **tiān**.

We have three **days** off this week.

79- 分/fēn/ – *Point; minute; to distribute*

学生们喊着口号，**分**发着传单。

xué shēng men hǎn zhe kǒu hào, **fēn** fā zhe chuán dān.

Students shouted slogans and **distributed** leaflets.

80- 还/hái/ – *Still*

新体系**还**处于规划阶段。

xīn tǐ xì **hái** chǔ yú guī huà jiē duàn.

The new system is **still** in the planning stage.

81-进/jìn/ – *Come in*

我可以**进**来吗？

wǒ kě yǐ **jìn** lái ma?

May I **come in**?

82- 好 /hǎo/ – Good

他似乎是个**好**人。

tā sì hū shì gè **hǎo** rén.

He seems to be a **good** person.

83- 小 /xiǎo/ – Small, tiny

这双鞋子太**小**了。

zhè shuāng xié zi tài **xiǎo** le.

This pair of shoes is too **small**.

84- 部 /bù/ – Part

尊重在任何关系中都是非常重要的**部**分。

zūn zhòng zài rèn hé guān xì zhōng dōu shì fēi cháng zhòng yào de **bù** fèn.

Respect is a very important **part** of any relationship.

85- 其 /qí/ – Third person singular or plural

她刚一收到现金就将**其**存入银行。

tā gāng yī shōu dào xiàn jīn jiù jiāng **qí** cún rù yín háng.

She banked the cash as soon as she received **it**.

86- 些 /xiē/ – Some

你能借我一**些**钱吗？

nǐ néng jiè wǒ yī **xiē** qián ma?

Could you please lend me **some** money?

87- 主 /zhǔ/ – Main

我**主**要关心的就是保护环境。

wǒ **zhǔ** yào guān xīn de jiù shì bǎo hù huán jìng.

My **main** concern now is to protect the environment.

88- 样 /yàng/ – Sample; shape, appearance

你能给我寄些**样**品过来吗？

nǐ néng gěi wǒ jì xiē **yàng** pǐn guò lái ma?

Can you send me some **samples**?

89- 理/lǐ/ – Reason; to manage

他这么做的**理**由是什么？

tā zhè me zuò de **lǐ** yóu shì shén me?

What is his **reason** for doing this?

90- 心/xīn/ – Heart

她的话让我**心**感自豪。

tā de huà ràng wǒ **xīn** gǎn zì háo.

Her words filled my **heart** with pride.

91- 她/tā/ – She

她是一名服务员。

tā shì yī míng fú wù yuán.

She works as a waitress.

92- 本/běn/ – Basis; originally

他原**本**没打算这么做。

tā yuán **běn** méi dǎ suàn zhè me zuò.

He had not **originally** planned to do this.

93- 前/qián/ – Before, in front of

不要站在我**前**面！

bù yào zhàn zài wǒ **qián** miàn!

Don't stand **in front of** me!

94- 开/kāi/ – Open; begin, start

请张**开**嘴。

qǐng zhāng **kāi** zuǐ.

Please **open** your mouth.

95- 但/dàn/ – But, however

艾米丽虽然年轻**但**经验丰富。

ài mǐ lì suī rán nián qīng **dàn** jīng yàn fēng fù.

Emily is young **but** very experienced.

96- 因为/yīn wèi/ – *Because*

我不喜欢你，**因为**你太懒了。

wǒ bù xǐ huān nǐ, **yīn wèi** nǐ tài lǎn le.

I don't like you **because** you are so lazy.

97- 只/zhǐ/ – *Only, but*

我想给她买一份生日礼物，**只**是我没有钱。

wǒ xiǎng gěi tā mǎi yī fèn shēng rì lǐ wù, **zhǐ** shì wǒ méi yǒu qián.

I'd like to buy her a birthday present, **but** I don't have money.

98- 从/cóng/ – *From*

你**从**哪里来？

nǐ **cóng** nǎ lǐ lái?

Where are you **from**?

99- 想/xiǎng/ – *Think, want*

我儿子**想**去动物园。

wǒ ér zi **xiǎng** qù dòng wù yuán.

My son **wants** to go to the zoo.

100- 实/shí/ – *Real; honest*

爸爸是我见过的最诚**实**的人。

bà ba shì wǒ jiàn guò de zuì chéng **shí** de rén.

My dad was the most **honest** man I ever met.

101- 日/rì/ – *Sun; day; daytime*

今天是我的**生日**。

jīn tiān shì wǒ de shēng **rì**.

Today is my birth**day**.

102- 军/jūn/ – *Army*

我们反对强迫人民参**军**的政策。

wǒ men fǎn duì qiǎng pò rén mín cān **jūn** de zhèng cè.

We oppose the policy of forcing people into the **army**.

103- 者 /zhě/ – -er, -ist

他们甩掉了**追赶者**。

tā men shuǎi diào le **zhuī gǎn zhě**.

They had shaken off their pursu**ers**.

104- 意 /yì/ – Thought, opinion

对于补救措施存在**意**见分歧。

duì yú bǔ jiù cuò shī cún zài **yì** jiàn fēn qí.

There are differences of **opinion** about the remedy.

105- 无 /wú/ – None, no

那次空难**无**人幸存。

nà cì kōng nàn **wú** rén xìng cún.

No one survived the air crash.

106- 力 /lì/ – Power, strength

知识就是**力**量。

zhī shí jiù shì **lì** liàng.

Knowledge is **power**.

107- 它 /tā/ – It

我养了一只猫，**它**喜欢让我抱着。

wǒ yǎng le yī zhī māo, **tā** xǐ huān ràng wǒ bào zhe.

I have a cat; **it** likes to be held by me.

108- 与 /yǔ/ – And, with

你**与**他是好朋友吗？

nǐ **yǔ** tā shì hǎo péng yǒu ma?

Are you a good friend **with** him?

109- 长 /cháng/ – Long; length

她有一头乌黑的**长**发。

tā yǒu yī tóu wū hēi de **cháng** fā.

She has **long** black hair.

110- 把/bǎ/ – Take, hold

不要忘了**把**这个带走。

bù yào wàng le **bǎ** zhè ge dài zǒu.

Don't forget to **take** this away.

111- 机/jī/ – Machine; opportunity

机器运转不正常。

jī qì yùn zhuǎn bù zhèng cháng.

The **machine** is not operating properly.

112- 十/shí/ –Ten

桌子上有**十**个苹果。

zhuō zi shàng yǒu **shí** gè píng guǒ.

There are **ten** apples on the table.

113- 民/mín/ – People, citizen

它将人们视为二等公**民**。

tā jiāng rén men shì wéi èr děng gōng **mín**.

It treats people as second-class **citizens**.

114- 第/dì/ – Prefix indicating ordinal number

我坐在**第**一排。

wǒ zuò zài **dì** yī pái.

I am sitting in the **first** row.

115- 公/gōng/ – Fair; public; duke

这是为了给人们一个**公**平的机会。

zhè shì wèi le gěi rén men yī gè **gōng** píng de jī huì.

It's about giving people a **fair** chance.

116- 此/cǐ/ – This; then

此时，他终于意识到了自己的错误。

cǐ shí, tā zhōng yú yì shí dào le zì jǐ de cuò wù.

At **this** moment, he finally realizes his mistakes.

117- 已/yǐ/ – Already

他已经走了。

tā **yǐ** jīng zǒu le.

He's **already** left.

118- 工/gōng/ – Work, job; worker

我一点也不喜欢我的工作。

wǒ yī diǎn yě bù xǐ huān wǒ de **gōng** zuò.

I don't like my **job** at all.

119- 使/shǐ/ – Make, cause

她的热情使我感到宾至如归。

tā de rè qíng **shǐ** wǒ gǎn dào bīn zhì rú guī.

Her enthusiasm **makes** me feel at home.

120- 情/qíng/ – Feeling, emotion

你对家乡有没有特殊的感情？

nǐ duì jiā xiāng yǒu méi yǒu tè shū de gǎn **qíng**?

Do you have any special **feelings** about your hometown?

121- 明/míng/ – Bright; understand

你明白了吗？

nǐ **míng** bái le ma?

Do you **understand**?

122- 性/xìng/ – Nature, character

这曾是人的本性。

zhè céng shì rén de běn **xìng**.

This was the **nature** of the man.

123- 知/zhī/ – Know

你知道公园在哪里吗？

nǐ **zhī** dào gōng yuán zài nǎ lǐ ma?

Do you **know** where the park is?

124- 全 /quán/ – *All, whole*

我们**全**都通过了考试。

wǒ men **quán** dōu tōng guò le kǎo shì.

We **all** passed the exam.

125- 三 /sān/ – *Three*

我**三**天后回来。

wǒ **sān** tiān hòu huí lái.

I'll be back in **three** days.

126- 又 /yòu/ – *And, also, again*

他**又**一次让我们失望了。

tā **yòu** yī cì ràng wǒ men shī wàng le.

He failed us once **again**.

127- 关 /guān/ – *Close*

你介意**关**一下窗户吗?

nǐ jiè yì **guān** yī xià chuāng hù ma?

Would you mind **closing** the window?

128- 点 /diǎn/ – *Dot, spot, point*

她穿着一件带红**点**的白色棉质连衣裙。

tā chuān zhe yī jiàn dài hóng **diǎn** de bái sè mián zhì lián yī qún.

She was wearing a white cotton dress with red **dots**.

129- 正 /zhèng/ – *Right, correct*

也许这就是**正**确的决定吧。

yě xǔ zhè jiù shì **zhèng** què de jué dìng ba.

Maybe this is the **right** decision.

130- 业 /yè/ – *Business, industry*

现在做什么行**业**最有前途?

xiàn zài zuò shén me háng **yè** zuì yǒu qián tú?

What **industry** is the most promising now?

131-外/wài/ – Out, outside

你能在课堂**外**学到很多东西。

nǐ néng zài kè táng **wài** xué dào hěn duō dōng xī.

You can learn so much **outside** the classroom.

132- 将/jiāng/ – Will, going to

我**将**在两年内环游全国。

wǒ **jiāng** zài liǎng nián nèi huán yóu quán guó.

I'm **going to** travel around the country within two years.

133- 两/liǎng/ – Two, both

他们**两**个都喜欢游泳。

tā men **liǎng** gè dōu xǐ huān yóu yǒng.

Both of them like swimming.

134- 高/gāo/ – High, tall

她喜欢穿**高**跟鞋。

tā xǐ huān chuān **gāo** gēn xié.

She likes to wear **high** heels.

135- 间/jiān/ – Room; between, among

我们之**间**不应该有秘密。

wǒ men zhī **jiān** bù yìng gāi yǒu mì mì.

There should be no secret **between** us.

136- 由/yóu/ – Reason; from

我们**由**此出发向东走。

wǒ men **yóu** cǐ chū fā xiàng dōng zǒu.

We go east **from** here.

137- 问/wèn/ – To ask

我能**问**你一个问题吗？

wǒ néng **wèn** nǐ yī gè wèn tí ma?

May I **ask** you a question please?

138- 很/hěn/ – *Very, quite*

我**很**喜欢这顶帽子。

wǒ **hěn** xǐ huān zhè dǐng mào zi.

I like this hat **very** much.

139- 最/zuì/ – *Most*

你**最**喜欢的电影是什么？

nǐ **zuì** xǐ huān de diàn yǐng shì shén me?

What is your **most** favorite movie?

140- 重/zhòng/ – *Heavy*

这个行李箱太**重**了！

zhè ge xíng lǐ xiāng tài **zhòng** le!

This suitcase is too **heavy**!

141- 并/bìng/ – *And, furthermore*

我不喜欢这件毛衣，**并**且它太贵了。

wǒ bù xǐ huān zhè jiàn máo yī, **bìng** qiě tā tài guì le.

I don't like this sweater. **Furthermore**, it is too expensive.

142- 物/ wù/ – *Thing, object*

他紧盯着地平线上的某一**物**体。

tā jǐn dīng zhe dì píng xiàn shàng de mǒu yī **wù** tǐ.

He is staring at an **object** on the horizon.

143- 手/shǒu/ – *Hand*

举起**手**来！

jǔ qǐ **shǒu** lái!

Hands up!

144-应/yīng/ – *Should*

你**应**该给她道歉。

nǐ **yīng** gāi gěi tā dào qiàn.

You **should** apologize to her.

145- 战/zhàn/ – War, fighting, battle

无数人在**战**争中丧生。

wú shù rén zài **zhàn** zhēng zhōng sàng shēng.

Millions of people lost their lives in **wars**.

146- 向/xiàng/ – Toward, direction

我们正朝着正确的方**向**前进。

wǒ men zhèng cháo zhe zhèng què de fāng **xiàng** qián jìn.

We are going in the right **direction**.

147- 头/tóu/ – Head

我**头**疼。

wǒ **tóu** téng.

I have a **head**ache.

148- 文/wén/ – Literature, culture

我喜欢传统中国**文**化。

wǒ xǐ huān chuán tǒng zhōng guó **wén** huà.

I like traditional Chinese **culture**.

149- 体/tǐ/ – Body

他的身**体**非常强壮。

tā de shēn **tǐ** fēi cháng qiáng zhuàng.

He has a strong **body**.

150- 政/zhèng/ – Government; political

我们最好避免讨论**政**治问题。

wǒ men zuì hǎo bì miǎn tǎo lùn **zhèng** zhì wèn tí.

We'd better avoid discussing **political** issues.

151- 美/měi/ – Beautiful

这里真**美**!

zhè lǐ zhēn **měi**!

What a **beautiful** place!

152- 相/xiāng/ – *Each other*

我们应该**相**互尊重。

wǒ men yīng gāi **xiāng** hù zūn zhòng.

We should respect **each other**.

153- 见/jiàn/ – *See*

明天**见**。

míng tiān **jiàn**.

See you tomorrow.

154- 被/bèi/ – *Indicates passive-voice clauses*

他**被车撞**了。

tā **bèi chē zhuàng** le.

He **was hit by a car**.

155- 利/lì/ – *Profit*

去年的年**利**润是多少?

qù nián de nián **lì** rùn shì duō shǎo?

What was the annual **profit** last year?

156- 什/shén/ – *What*

你叫**什**么名字?

nǐ jiào **shén** me míng zì?

What is your name?

157- 二/èr/ – *Two; second*

这是我第**二**次来中国。

zhè shì wǒ dì **èr** cì lái zhōng guó.

This is my **second** visit to China.

158- 等/děng/ – *Wait*

等一下!

děng yī xià!

Wait a minute!

159- 产 /chǎn/ – *Produce*

这家工厂是生**产**什么的？

zhè jiā gōng chǎng shì shēng **chǎn** shén me de?

What does this factory **produce**?

160- 或 /huò/ – *Or*

你想要哪个，这个**或**那个？

nǐ xiǎng yào nǎ ge, zhè ge **huò** nà gè?

Which one do you prefer, this one **or** that one?

161- 新 /xīn/ – *New*

我买了一双**新**鞋。

wǒ mǎi le yī shuāng **xīn** xié.

I bought a **new** pair of shoes.

162- 己 /jǐ/ – *Self*

我自**己**能行。

wǒ zì **jǐ** néng xíng.

I can do it my**self**.

163- 制 /zhì/ – *System*

这家公司有一套完整的晋升**制**度。

zhè jiā gōng sī yǒu yī tào wán zhěng de jìn shēng **zhì** dù.

This company has a complete promotion **system**.

164- 身 /shēn/ – *Body*

她说他正在抚摸她的**身**体和头部。

tā shuō tā zhèng zài fǔ mō tā de **shēn** tǐ hé tóu bù.

She said he was touching her **body** and her head.

165- 果 /guǒ/ – *Fruit; result*

你最喜欢的水**果**是什么？

nǐ zuì xǐ huān de shuǐ **guǒ** shì shén me?

What is your favorite **fruit**?

166- 加 /jiā/ – Add, plus

一加一等于二。

yī **jiā** yī děng yú èr.

One **plus** one equals two.

167- 西 /xī/ – West

西边的那座房子就是他的家。

xī bian de nà zuò fáng zi jiù shì tā de jiā.

The house in the **west** is his home.

168- 斯 /sī/ – This

有友如**斯**，夫复何求？

yǒu yǒu rú **sī**, fū fù hé qiú?

With a good friend like **this**, I no longer need anything else.

169- 月 /yuè/ – Moon; month

你学中文多久了？—两个**月**。

nǐ xué zhōng wén duō jiǔ le? —liǎng gè **yuè**.

How long have you been learning Chinese? –Two **months**.

170- 话 /huà/ – Talk, speech

他的讲**话**打动了我。

tā de jiǎng **huà** dǎ dòng le wǒ.

His **speech** touched me.

171- 合 /hé/ – Together

你应该与我们**合**作。

nǐ yīng gāi yǔ wǒ men **hé** zuò.

You should work **together** with us.

172- 回 /huí/ – Return

快**回**家去。

kuài **huí** jiā qù.

Return to your home immediately.

173- 特/tè/ – *Special*

我想给你看点**特**别的东西。

wǒ xiǎng gěi nǐ kàn diǎn **tè** bié de dōng xī.

I'd like to show you something **special**.

174- 代/dài/ – *Replace; generation*

没有人能够取**代**你！

méi yǒu rén néng gòu qǔ **dài** nǐ!

No one can **replace** you!

175- 内/nèi/ – *Inside*

你必须走进他的**内**心来让他开口说话。

nǐ bì xū zǒu jìn tā de **nèi** xīn lái ràng tā kāi kǒu shuō huà.

You have to get **inside** him to make him speak.

176- 信/xìn/ – *Trust; letter*

请相**信**我！

qǐng xiāng **xìn** wǒ!

Trust me, Please!

177- 表/biǎo/ – *Watch; express*

我买了一块新的腕**表**。

wǒ mǎi le yī kuài xīn de wàn **biǎo**.

I bought a new wrist**watch**.

178-化/huà/ – *Convert, change*

所有这些都可以通过身体转**化**为脂肪或能量。

suǒ yǒu zhè xiē dōu kě yǐ tōng guò shēn tǐ zhuǎn **huà** wéi zhī fáng huò néng liàng.

All of these can be **converted** by the body into fat or energy.

179- 老/lǎo/ – *Old*

那里有个**老**人在遛狗。

nà li yǒu gè **lǎo** rén zài liù gǒu.

There is an **old** man walking his dog.

180- 给 /gěi/ – Give

把它**给**我。

bǎ tā **gěi** wǒ.

Give it to me.

181- 世 /shì/ – World; era

我想环游**世**界。

wǒ xiǎng huán yóu **shì** jiè.

I want to travel around the **world**.

182- 位 /wèi/ – Seat, position

在这两个航班上我们都没得到预订座**位**。

zài zhè liǎng gè háng bān shàng wǒ men dōu méi dé dào yù dìng zuò **wèi**.

On neither flight did we get our reserved **seats**.

183- 次 /cì/ – Measure word for enumerated events

我一周去体育馆三**次**。

wǒ yī zhōu qù tǐ yù guǎn sān **cì**.

I go to the gym three **times** a week.

184- 度 /dù/ – Degree; system; to spend

我在那里**度**过了一段美好的时光.

wǒ zài nà lǐ **dù** guò le yī duàn měi hǎo de shí guāng.

I **spent** a wonderful time there.

185- 门 /mén/ – Door

请帮我关上**门**。

qǐng bāng wǒ guān shàng **mén**.

Please close the **door** for me.

186- 任命 /rèn/ – To appoint

这家伙不会被正式**任命**为董事会成员。

zhè jiā huo bù huì bèi zhèng shì **rèn mìng** wéi dǒng shì huì chéng yuán.

This guy will not be formally **appointed** to the board.

187- 常 /cháng/ – *Common, normal, regular, often*

我经**常**去这家餐馆吃饭。

wǒ jīng **cháng** qù zhè jiā cān guǎn chī fàn.

I **often** go to this restaurant for meals.

188- 先 /xiān/ – *First*

谁**先**来？

shuí **xiān** lái?

Who will come **first**?

189- 海 /hǎi/ – *Sea, ocean*

她从未见过**海**。

tā cóng wèi jiàn guò **hǎi**.

She has never seen the **sea**.

190- 交通 /jiāo tōng/ – *Traffic*

交通事故减少了。

jiāo tōng shì gù jiǎn shǎo le.

There has been a decrease in **traffic** accidents.

191- 教 /jiāo/ – *Teach*

你能**教**我吗？

nǐ néng **jiāo** wǒ ma?

Can you **teach** me?

192- 儿 /ér/ – *Son*

这是我**儿**子。

zhè shì wǒ **ér** zi.

This is my **son**.

193- 原 /yuán/ – *original*

原本的计划是一周内完成。

yuán běn de jì huà shì yī zhōu nèi wán chéng.

The **original** plan was to finish it within a week.

194- 东 /dōng/ – *East*

东边的那座房子就是我的家。

dōng bian de nà zuò fáng zi jiù shì wǒ de jiā.

The house in the **east** is my home.

195- 声 /shēng/ – *Sound, noise*

彼德听见了枪炮**声**。

bǐ dé tīng jiàn le qiāng pào **shēng**.

Peter heard the **sound** of gunfire.

196- 提 /tí/ – *Mention; to lift*

她并没有**提**到她母亲不在场的事。

tā bìng méi yǒu **tí** dào tā mǔ qīn bù zài chǎng de shì.

She did not **mention** her mother's absence.

197- 立 /lì/ – *Establish*

这家公司是去年设**立**的。

zhè jiā gōng sī shì qù nián shè **lì** de.

This company was **established** last year.

198- 及时 /jí shí/ – *in time*

我会**及**时赶到。

wǒ huì **jí shí** gǎn dào.

I'll be there **in time**.

199- 比 /bǐ/ – *To compare; than*

他**比**我聪明。

tā **bǐ** wǒ cōng míng.

He's cleverer **than** me.

200- 员 /yuán/ – *Member*

她是我们俱乐部的成**员**。

tā shì wǒ men jù lè bù de chéng **yuán**.

She is a **member** of our club.

201- 解/jiě/ – Explain, solve

问题**解**决了。

wèn tí **jiě** jué le.

Problem **solved**.

202- 水/shuǐ/ – Water

请给我一杯**水**。

qǐng gěi wǒ yī bēi **shuǐ**.

Please give me a cup of **water**.

203- 名/míng/ – Name

她叫什么**名**字？

tā jiào shén me **míng** zì?

What is her **name**?

204- 真/zhēn/ – Real

它不是一个梦，它是**真**实的。

tā bù shì yī gè mèng, tā shì **zhēn** shí de.

It wasn't a dream. It was **real**.

205- 讨论/tǎo lùn/ – Discuss

我需要和你**讨论**一下这件事。

wǒ xū yào hé nǐ **tǎo lùn** yī xià zhè jiàn shì.

I need to **discuss** this matter with you.

206- 处/chù/ – Deal with, in a position of

这件事怎么**处**理？

zhè jiàn shì zěn me **chù** lǐ?

How to **deal with** this matter?

207- 走/zǒu/ – Leave, walk

我得**走**了。

wǒ děi **zǒu** le.

I have to **leave**.

208- 义 /yì/ – *Meaning, justice*

他富有正**义**感。

tā fù yǒu zhèng **yì** gǎn.

He has a good sense of **justice**.

209- 各 /gè/ – *Every, each*

我们应该就**各**个问题提出解决方案。

wǒ men yīng gāi jiù **gè** gè wèn tí tí chū jiě jué fāng àn.

We should come up with solutions to **each** problem.

210- 入 /rù/ – *Enter, come in, join*

欢迎加**入**我们。

huān yíng jiā **rù** wǒ men.

Welcome to **join** us.

211- 几 /jǐ/ – *How many, how much, several, a few*

有**几**个人在房间里？

yǒu **jǐ** gè rén zài fáng jiān lǐ?

How many people are in the room?

212- 口 /kǒu/ – *Mouth; entrance*

那是该建筑物的入**口**。

nà shì gāi jiàn zhù wù de rù **kǒu**.

That is the **entrance** to the building.

213- 认 /rèn/ – *Know, recognize*

你**认**识这个人吗？

nǐ **rèn** shì zhè gè rén ma?

Do you **know** this man?

214- 条款 /tiáo kuǎn/ – *Condition, clause*

合同中有一项**条款**使他能分得利润。

hé tóng zhōng yǒu yī xiàng **tiáo kuǎn** shǐ tā néng fēn dé lì rùn.

He has a **clause** in the contract which entitles him to the profits.

215- 平 /píng/ – *Flat; peaceful*

他试图寻求和**平**解决冲突的方案。

tā shì tú xún qiú hé **píng** jiě jué chōng tū de fāng àn.

He has attempted to find a **peaceful** solution to the conflict.

216- 关系 /guān xì/ – *To related to*

轻工业和农业**关系**密切。

qīng gōng yè hé nóng yè **guān xì** mì qiè.

Light industry is closely **related to** agriculture.

217- 气 /qì/ – *Gas, air*

穿堂风有助于空**气**流通。

chuān táng fēng yǒu zhù yú kōng **qì** liú tōng.

Draughts help to circulate **air**.

218- 题 /tí/ – *Theme, topic*

活动的主**题**是什么？

huó dòng de zhǔ **tí** shì shén me?

What is the **theme** of the event?

219- 活 /huó/ – *Alive; to live*

她不知道他是死是**活**。

tā bù zhī dào tā shì sǐ shì **huó**.

She does not know if he is **alive** or dead.

220- 尔 /ěr/ – *You; so, thus*

尔等何人？

ěr děng hé rén?

Who are you?

221- 更 /gèng/ – *More*

那家商店现在**更**受欢迎了。

nà jiā shāng diàn xiàn zài **gèng** shòu huān yíng le.

That store is **more** popular now.

222- 别 /bié/ – Do not; to depart

别动！

bié dòng!

Don't move!

223- 打 /dǎ/ – Hit, beat

她**打**了我。

tā **dǎ** le wǒ.

She **hit** me.

224- 女 /nǚ/ – Woman, girl, daughter

她有一个可爱的**女**儿。

tā yǒu yī gè kě ài de **nǚ** ér.

She has a sweet **daughter**.

225- 变 /biàn/ – Change; to transform

你**变**了。

nǐ **biàn** le.

You've **changed**.

226- 四 /sì/ – Four

我**四**天后要出差。

wǒ **sì** tiān hòu yào chū chāi.

I'll go for a business trip in **four** days.

227- 神 /shén/ – God

她是我的女**神**！

tā shì wǒ de nǚ **shén**!

She's my **God**dess!

228- 总 /zǒng/ – Always; total

她**总**是对我很好。

tā **zǒng** shì duì wǒ hěn hǎo.

She's **always** nice to me.

229- 何 /hé/ – *What, why, where, which, how*

我该如**何**帮助你？

wǒ gāi rú **hé** bāng zhù nǐ?

How can I help you?

230- 电 /diàn/ – *Electricity*

我们搬进了一栋通了**电**的小屋。

wǒ men bān jìn le yī dòng tōng le **diàn** de xiǎo wū.

We moved into a cabin with **electricity**.

231- 数 /shù/ – *Number*

你最喜欢哪个**数**？

nǐ zuì xǐ huān nǎ ge **shù**?

What is your favorite **number**?

232- 安 /ān/ – *Safe*

我把它放在了一个**安**全的地方。

wǒ bǎ tā fàng zài le yī gè **ān** quán de dì fāng

I put it in a **safe** place.

233- 少 /shǎo/ – *Less, few*

我挣钱比他**少**。

wǒ zhèng qián bǐ tā **shǎo**.

I earn **less** than him.

234- 报 /bào/ – *Report; newspaper*

你有什么需要上**报**吗？

nǐ yǒu shén me xū yào shàng **bào** ma?

Do you have anything to **report**?

235- 才 /cái/ – *Just now; talent*

你刚**才**去哪了？

nǐ gāng **cái** qù nǎ le?

Where have you been **just now**?

236- 结 /jié/ − Finish; result; over

游戏**结**束。

yóu xì **jié** shù.

Game **over**.

237- 反 /fǎn/ − Contrary, opposite

根本不费事，恰恰相**反**，非常荣幸能帮到你。

gēn běn bù fèi shì, qià qià xiāng **fǎn**, fēi cháng róng xìng néng bāng dào nǐ.

It's no trouble at all; on the **contrary**, it will be a great pleasure to help you.

238- 接受 /jiē shòu/ − Accept

我**接受**你的道歉。

wǒ **jiē shòu** nǐ de dào qiàn.

Apology **accepted**.

239- 目 /mù/ − Catalogue ; goal

你的人生**目**标是什么？

nǐ de rén shēng **mù** biāo shì shén me?

What is the **goal** of your life?

240- 太 /tài/ − Too, very, much

我**太**忙了。

wǒ **tài** máng le.

I'm **too** busy.

241- 量 /liáng/ − Measure

他们**量**了天花板的高度。

tā men **liáng** le tiān huā bǎn de gāo dù.

They **measured** the height of the ceiling.

242- 再 /zài/ − Again

请稍后**再**试。

qǐng shāo hòu **zài** shì.

Please try **again** later.

243- 感 /gǎn/ – Feel; emotion

我**感**到沮丧。

wǒ **gǎn** dào jǔ sàng.

I **feel** depressed.

244- 建 /jiàn/ – Build, establish

这栋大楼**建**于 2000 年。

zhè dòng dà lóu **jiàn** yú 2000 nián.

This building was **built** in 2000.

245- 务 /wù/ – Affair

孩子的抚养和教育是公共事**务**。

hái zi de fǔ yǎng hé jiào yù shì gōng gòng shì **wù**.

The care and education of the children is a public **affair**.

246- 做 /zuò/ – Do, make

你**做**了什么？

nǐ **zuò** le shén me?

What have you **done**?

247- 接 /jiē/ – Receive

他们会在仪式上**接**受颁奖。

tā men huì zài yí shì shàng **jiē** shòu bān jiǎng.

They will **receive** their awards at the ceremony.

248- 必 /bì/ – Must; surely

你**必**须离开。

nǐ **bì** xū lí kāi.

You **must** leave.

249- 场 /chǎng/ – Place

葬礼不是幽默的**场**合。

zàng lǐ bù shì yōu mò de **chǎng** hé.

A funeral is not the **place** for humor.

250- 件/jiàn/ – Measure word for clothes, tools, events, etc.

我刚买了**一件**新裙子。

wǒ gāng mǎi le **yī jiàn** xīn qún zi.

I just bought **a new dress**.

251- 计划/jì huà/ – Plan

你有什么**计划**?

nǐ yǒu shén me **jì huà**?

What's your **plan**?

252- 管/guǎn/ – Manage, control

他儿子现在**管**理着公司。

tā ér zǐ xiàn zài **guǎn** lǐ zhe gōng sī.

His son is **managing** the company now.

253- 日期/rì qī/ – Date

这个**日期**对你合适吗?

zhè gè **rì qī** duì nǐ hé shì ma?

Is this **date** suitable for you?

254- 市/shì/ – Market, city

他在集**市**上卖玩具。

tā zài jí **shì** shàng mài wán jù.

He sells toys on a **market**.

255- 直/zhí/ – Straight

沿这条路**直**走就到。

yán zhè tiáo lù **zhí** zǒu jiù dào.

Go **straight** along the road and you will be there.

256- 德/dé/ – Virtue

他品**德**高尚。

tā pǐn **dé** gāo shàng.

He excels in **virtue**.

257- 资/zī/ – *Property, fund*

这场音乐会将为那项研究筹**资**。

zhè chǎng yīn yuè huì jiāng wèi nà xiàng yán jiū chóu **zī**.

The concert will raise **fund** for that study.

258 – 命/mìng/ – *Life*

生**命**都是平等的。

shēng **mìng** dōu shì píng děng de.

Every single **life** is equal.

259- 山/shān/ – *Mountain*

世界上最高的**山**是哪座?

shì jiè shàng zuì gāo de **shān** shì nǎ zuò?

What is the highest **mountain** in the world?

260- 金/jīn/ – *Gold, metal*

黄**金**的价格在上涨。

huáng **jīn** de jià gé zài shàng zhǎng

The price of **gold** is going up.

261- 指/zhǐ/ – *Finger; point*

我在那场意外中失去了小手**指**。

wǒ zài nà chǎng yì wài zhōng shī qù le xiǎo shǒu **zhǐ**.

I lost my little **finger** in that accident.

262- 克/kè/ – *Gram; overcome*

萝丝已经**克**服了对蛇的恐惧。

luó sī yǐ jīng **kè** fú le duì shé de kǒng jù.

Rose had **overcome** her fear of snakes.

263- 许/xǔ/ – *Permit; permission*

未经**许**可不得入内。

wèi jīng **xǔ** kě bù dé rù nèi.

You are not allowed to enter without **permission**.

264- 统治 /tǒng zhì/ – Govern, to rule

谁**统治**这个国家？

shuí **tǒng zhì** zhè gè guó jiā?

Who **rules** this country?

265- 区 /qū/ – Area, district, region

我开车在商业**区**转了转。

wǒ kāi chē zài shāng yè **qū** zhuàn le zhuàn.

I drove around the business **district**.

266- 保 /bǎo/ – Protect

保护环境，人人有责。

bǎo hù huán jìng, rén rén yǒu zé.

It is everyone's responsibility to **protect** the environment.

267- 至 /zhì/ – To

请把这个包裹送**至**她家。

bǎ zhè gè bāo guǒ sòng **zhì** tā jiā.

Please send this package **to** her home.

268- 队 /duì/ – Team

我是这支**队**伍里的一员。

wǒ shì zhè zhī **duì** wǔ lǐ de yī yuán.

I'm a member of this **team**.

269- 形 /xíng/ – Form, shape

每面镜子都可以设计成任何**形**状。

měi miàn jìngzi dōu kěyǐ shèjì chéng rènhé **xíng** zhuàng.

Each mirror can be designed to any **shape**.

270- 社 /shè/ – Society

这反映了**社**会上盛行的价值观。

zhè fǎn yìng le **shè** huì shàng shèng xíng de jià zhí guān.

This reflects values prevailing in **society**.

271- 便/biàn/ – Convenient

请方**便**的时候再来。

qǐng fāng **biàn** de shí hòu zài lái.

Please come again when it is **convenient** for you.

272- 空/kōng/ – Empty

这个盒子是**空**的。

zhè gè hé zi shì **kōng** de.

This box is **empty**.

273- 决/jué/ – Decide; decision

现在是做出**决**定的时候了。

xiàn zài shì zuò chū **jué** dìng de shí hòu le.

It's time to make a **decision**.

274- 治/zhì/ – Govern, manage, to cure

青霉素**治**好了他的肺炎。

qīng méi sù **zhì** hǎo le tā de fèi yán.

Penicillin **cured** him of pneumonia.

275- 展/zhǎn/ – Unfold, extend; exhibition

欢迎参加**展**会。

huān yíng cān jiā **zhǎn** huì.

Welcome to the **exhibition**.

276- 马/mǎ/ – Horse

一个骑着**马**的男子出现了。

yī gè qí zhe **mǎ** de nán zǐ chū xiàn le.

A man on a **horse** had appeared.

277- 科学/kē xué/ – Science

伟大的**科学**发现都非常简单。

wěi dà de **kē xué** fā xiàn dōu fēi cháng jiǎn dān.

Great discoveries in **science** are very simple.

278- 司 /sī/ – *Take charge of; company*

这家公**司**是他的。

zhè jiā gōng **sī** shì tā de.

This **company** is owned by him.

279- 五 /wǔ/ – *Five*

飞机**五**分钟后起飞。

fēi jī **wǔ** fēn zhōng hòu qǐ fēi.

The plane will take off in **five** minutes.

280- 基 /jī/ – *Base, foundation*

诚实守信是企业合作的**基**础。

chéng shí shǒu xìn shì qǐ yè hé zuò de **jī** chǔ.

Honest and trustworthy is the **foundation** of business cooperation.

281- 眼 /yǎn/ – *Eye*

我眯了**眼**了。

wǒ mī le **yǎn** le.

Something got into my **eyes**.

282- 书 /shū/ – *Book*

桌子上有一本**书**。

zhuō zi shàng yǒu yī běn **shū**.

There is a **book** on the table.

283- 非 /fēi/ – *Not, no*

这件事**非**同小可。

zhè jiàn shì **fēi** tóng xiǎo kě.

This is **no** trivial matter.

284- 规则 /guī zé/ – *Rule, regulation*

这是游戏的**规则**。

zhè shì yóu xì de **guī zé**.

This is the **rule** of the game.

285- 听/tīng/ – Listen

仔细**听**我说。

zǐ xì **tīng** wǒ shuō.

Listen to me carefully.

286- 白/bái/ – White

我最喜欢的颜色是**白**色。

wǒ zuì xǐ huān de yán sè shì **bái** sè.

My favorite color is **white**.

287- 却/què/ – But, yet

他很爱她，**却**没有说出口。

tā hěn ài tā, **què** méi yǒu shuō chū kǒu.

He loved her, **yet** he didn't say anything.

288- 界/jiè/ – Boundary

科学无国**界**。

kē xué wú guó **jiè**.

Science is free from national **boundaries**.

289- 达/dá/ – Arrive at

飞机预计一小时后到**达**目的地。

fēi jī yù jì yī xiǎo shí hòu dào **dá** mù dì dì

The plane is expected to **arrive at** the destination in one hour.

290- 光/guāng/ – Light; only

光透过窗户照进来。

guāng tòu guò chuāng hù zhào jìn lái.

Light filtered through the windows.

291- 放/fàng/ – Put, release

他被从拘留所里**放**出来了。

tā bèi cóng jū liú suǒ lǐ **fàng** chū lái le.

He was **released** from custody.

292- 强 /qiáng/ – *Strong*

他们的目的是建立一个**强**大的经济体。

tā men de mù dì shì jiàn lì yī gè **qiáng** dà de jīng jì tǐ.

Their purpose is to build a **strong** economy.

293- 即使 /jí shǐ/ – *Even if*

即使你是对的，也不该那么说。

jí shǐ nǐ shì duì de, yě bù gāi nà me shuō.

Even if you are right, you should not say that.

294- 像 /xiàng/ – *Image; to be like*

我永远不会**像**那些人一样。

wǒ yǒng yuǎn bù huì **xiàng** nà xiē rén yī yàng.

I would never **be like** those people.

295- 难 /nán/ – *Difficult*

这是一个非常**难**的问题。

zhè shì yī gè fēi cháng **nán** de wèn tí.

This is a very **difficult** question.

296- 且 /qiě/ – *And, also*

他不但抽烟，而**且**喝酒。

tā bù dàn chōu yān, ér **qiě** hē jiǔ.

He not only smokes but **also** drinks.

297- 权 /quán/ – *Authority, power*

警方有**权**逮捕罪犯。

jǐng fāng yǒu **quán** dài bǔ zuì fàn.

The police have **authority** to arrest criminals.

298- 思 /sī/ – *Think; thinking*

三**思**而后行。

sān **sī** ér hòu xíng.

Think twice before you leap.

299- 王 /wáng/ – *King*

老虎是百兽之王。

lǎo hǔ shì bǎi shòu zhī **wáng**.

Tiger is the **king** of beasts.

300- 象 /xiàng/ – *Elephant*

我们去动物园看大象吧。

wǒ mén qù dòng wù yuán kàn dà **xiàng** ba.

Let's go to the zoo to see the **elephant**.

301- 完 /wán/ – *Complete, finish*

叛乱分子完全控制了局面。

pàn luàn fèn zi **wán** quán kòng zhì le jú miàn.

The rebels had taken **complete** control.

302- 设 /shè/ –*Design*

这是我设计的外套。

zhè shì wǒ **shè** jì de wài tào.

This is the coat **designed** by me.

303- 式 /shì/ – *Style*

你喜欢什么款式的鞋子？

nǐ xǐ huān shén me kuǎn **shì** de xié zi?

What **style** of shoes do you like?

304- 色 /sè/ – *Color*

我最喜欢的颜色是黑色。

wǒ zuì xǐ huān de yán sè shì hēi **sè**.

My favorite **color** is black.

305- 路 /lù/ – *Road*

路上没车。

lù shàng méi chē.

There is no car on the **road**.

306- 记/jì/ – Remember, record

你会**记**住我吗？

nǐ huì **jì** zhù wǒ ma?

Will you **remember** me?

307- 南/nán/ – South

小镇就在这边向**南**十公里的地方。

xiǎo zhèn jiù zài zhè biān xiàng **nán** shí gōng lǐ dì dì fāng.

The town lies ten kilometers to the **south** of here.

308- 品/pǐn/ – To taste

它**品**尝起来就像土豆泥。

tā **pǐn** cháng qǐ lái jiù xiàng tǔ dòu ní.

It **tastes** like mashed potatoes.

309- 住/zhù/ – To live

我喜欢**住**在乡下。

wǒ xǐ huān **zhù** zài xiāng xià.

I like to **live** in the countryside.

310- 告/gào/ – Tell, inform; accuse

我想**告**诉你一个秘密。

wǒ xiǎng **gào** sù nǐ yī gè mì mì.

I'd like to **tell** you a secret.

311- 类/lèi/ – Kind

我喜欢与各**类**人交朋友。

wǒ xǐ huān yǔ gè **lèi** rén jiāo péng yǒu.

I like to make friends with all **kinds** of people.

312- 求/qiú/ – Seek, request

这是我们曾寻**求**建议的原因之一。

zhè shì wǒ men céng xún **qiú** jiàn yì de yuán yīn zhī yī.

This is one of the reasons we **sought** advice.

313- 据/jù/ – Occupy; according to

用户须根据说明操作设备。

yòng hù xū gēn **jù** shuō míng cāo zuò shè bèi.

Users must operate the machine **according to** the instructions.

314- 程/chéng/ – Journey

行程少于 20 分钟。

xíng **chéng** shǎo yú 20 fēn zhōng.

The **journey** takes less than 20 minutes.

315- 北/běi/ – North

冷空气给北方带来了积雪。

lěng kōng qì gěi **běi** fāng dài lái le jī xuě.

The cold air brought snow to the **north**.

316- 边/biān/ – Side, border

他们穿越边界逃走了。

tā men chuān yuè **biān** jiè táo zǒu le.

They fled across the **border**.

317- 死/sǐ/ – Die; dead; death

我的狗早上死了。

wǒ de gǒu zǎo shang **sǐ** le.

My dog **died** in the morning.

318- 张/zhāng/ – Open, spread

请张开嘴。

qǐng **zhāng** kāi zuǐ.

Open your mouth, please.

319- 该/gāi/ – Should

我该做什么？

wǒ **gāi** zuò shén me?

What **should** I do?

320- 交/jiāo/ – *Hand over*

他还递**交**了一封道歉信。

tā hái dì **jiāo** le yī fēng dào qiàn xìn.

He also **handed over** a letter of apology.

321- 规/guī/ – *Rule, regulation*

很难理解为何需要新**规**。

hěn nán lǐ jiě wèi hé xū yào xīn **guī**.

It is difficult to understand why new **regulation** is necessary.

322- 万/wàn/ – *Ten thousand*

他花了一**万**美元买这辆车。

tā huā le yī **wàn** měi yuán mǎi zhè liàng chē.

He spent **ten thousand** dollars on buying this car.

323- 取/qǔ/ – *Take, get*

我去给你**取**。

wǒ qù gěi nǐ **qǔ**.

I'll **get** it for you.

324- 拉/lā/ – *Pull*

你怎么把它**拉**下来?

nǐ zěn me bǎ tā **lā** xià lái?

How will you **pull** it off?

325- 格式/gé shì/ – *Format*

求职信一般都有固定的**格式**。

qiú zhí xìn yī bān dōu yǒu gù dìng de **gé shì**.

Cover letters generally have a fixed **format**.

326- 望/wàng/ – *Expect, look forward to*

希**望**能收到你的回信。

xī **wàng** néng shōu dào nǐ de huí xìn.

Looking forward to hearing from you.

327- 觉/jué/ – Feel

我**觉**得不舒服。

wǒ **jué** dé bú shū fú.

I **feel** uncomfortable.

328- 术/shù/ – Technique, method

造纸**术**是古代中国最伟大的发明之一。

zào zhǐ **shù** shì gǔ dài zhōng guó zuì wěi dà de fā míng zhī yī.

The paper-making **technique** is one of the greatest inventions of Ancient China.

329- 领/lǐng/ – Guide, lead

他将**领**导我们走向胜利。

tā jiàng **lǐng** dǎo wǒ men zǒu xiàng shèng lì.

He will **lead** us to victory.

330- 共/gòng/ – Total

这些一**共**多少钱?

zhè xiē yī **gòng** duō shǎo qián?

How much are these in **total**?

331- 确/què/ – Sure

你**确**定吗?

nǐ **què** dìng ma?

Are you **sure**?

332- 传/chuán/ – Pass on

请把这本书**传**给他。

qǐng bǎ zhè běn shū **chuán** gěi tā.

Please **pass** this book **on** to him.

333- 师/shī/ – Teacher

她是我的中文老**师**。

tā shì wǒ de zhōng wén lǎo **shī**.

She's my Chinese **teacher**.

334- 观 /guān/ – *Observe, view*

该专家还研究及**观**察婴儿的行为。

gāi zhuān jiā hái yán jiū jí **guān** chá yīng ér de xíng wéi.

The expert also studies and **observes** the behavior of babies.

335- 清 /qīng/ – *Clear, clean*

我讲**清**楚了吗？

wǒ jiǎng **qīng** chǔle ma?

Have I made myself **clear**?

336- 今 /jīn/ – *Today*

你**今**天想做什么？

nǐ **jīn** tiān xiǎng zuò shén me?

What do you want to do **today**?

337- 切 /qiē/ – *Cut*

每根木材都被**切**成一定尺寸。

měi gēn mù cái dōu bèi **qiē** chéng yī dìng chǐ cùn.

Every piece of timber was **cut** to size.

338- 院 /yuàn/ – *Yard*

我看到他站在**院**子里。

wǒ kàn dào tā zhàn zài **yuàn** zi lǐ.

I saw him standing in the **yard**.

339- 让 /ràng/ – *Let*

我**让**她走了。

wǒ **ràng** tā zǒu le.

I **let** her go.

340- 识 /shí/ – *Recognize, know*

我认**识**你。

wǒ rèn **shí** nǐ.

I **know** you.

341- 候/hòu/ – Wait

抱歉让你等**候**多时。

bào qiàn ràng nǐ děng **hòu** duō shí.

Sorry to keep you **waiting** for a long time.

342- 带/dài/ – Bring

把他们**带**来见我。

bǎ tā men **dài** lái jiàn wǒ.

Bring them to me.

343- 导/dǎo/ – Guide

他引**导**她穿过马路。

tā yǐn **dǎo** tā chuān guò mǎ lù.

He **guided** her across the roads.

344- 争/zhēng/ – Fight

我没法跟他**争**。

wǒ méi fǎ gēn tā **zhēng**.

I can't **fight** him.

345- 运/yùn/ – Luck; transport

祝你好**运**。

zhù nǐ hǎo **yùn**.

Good **luck**.

346- 笑/xiào/ – Smile, laugh

她**笑**了。

tā **xiào** le.

She **smiled**.

347- 飞/fēi/ – To fly

我想**飞**。

wǒ xiǎng **fēi**.

I want to **fly**.

348- 风/fēng/ – Wind

风从东边吹来。

fēng cóng dōng bian chuī lái.

The **wind** blows easterly.

349- 步/bù/ – Step

我向他迈了一**步**。

wǒ xiàng tā mài le yī **bù**.

I took a **step** towards him.

350- 改/gǎi/ – Change

你还想**改**答案吗？.

nǐ hái xiǎng **gǎi** dá àn ma?

Do you still want to **change** the answer?

351- 收/shōu/ – Receive, collect

你**收**到样品了吗？

nǐ **shōu** dào yàng pǐn le ma?

Have you **received** the samples?

352- 根/gēn/ – Root

大多数植物会在七周左右生**根**。

dà duō shù zhí wù huì zài qī zhōu zuǒ yòu shēng **gēn**.

Most plants will **root** in about seven weeks.

353- 干/gàn/ – Do, to work

我**干**完了。

wǒ **gàn** wán le.

I've **done** it.

354- 造/zào/ – Make, manufacture

这家工厂**造**车。

zhè jiā gōng chǎng **zào** chē.

This factory **manufactures** vehicles.

355- 言/yán/ – Word

一言为定。

yī **yán** wéi dìng.

You have my **word**.

356- 联/lián/ – Unite

我们应该**联**合起来。

wǒ men yīng gāi **lián** hé qǐ lái.

We should **unite** as one.

357- 持/chí/ – Hold, support

坚**持**住！

jiān **chí** zhù!

Hold on to it!

358- 组/zǔ/ – Group; organize

我们被分成两**组**。

wǒ men bèi fēn chéng liǎng **zǔ**.

We are divided into two **groups**.

359- 每/měi/ – Every, each

我**每**天都玩电子游戏。

wǒ **měi** tiān dū wán diàn zǐ yóu xì.

I play video games **every**day.

360- 济/jì/ – To help, to relieve

这些钱都是用来救**济**贫民的。

zhè xiē qián dōu shì yòng lái jiù **jì** pín mín de.

The money is used to **help** the poor.

361- 车/chē/ – Vehicle

这是一家造**车**厂。

zhè shì yī jiā zào **chē** chǎng.

This is a factory manufacturing **vehicles**.

362- 亲/qīn/ – *Kiss*

她**亲**了我。

tā **qīn** le wǒ.

She **kissed** me.

363- 极/jí/ – *Extremely*

他**极**其聪明。

tā **jí** qí cōng míng.

He is **extremely** smart.

364- 林/lín/ – *Forest*

森**林**的一些部分仍很茂密。

sēn **lín** de yī xiē bù fèn réng hěn mào mì.

Parts of the **forest** are still dense.

365- 服/fú/ – *Clothes; obey, admire*

我需要换衣**服**。

wǒ xū yào huàn yī **fú**.

I need to change my **clothes**.

366- 快/kuài/ – *Quick*

你得**快**点了。

nǐ dé **kuài** diǎn le.

You'll have to be **quick**.

367- 办/bàn/ – *Do, handle, manage*

交给我来**办**吧。

jiāo gěi wǒ lái **bàn** ba.

I'll **handle** it.

368- 议/yì/ – *Suggest*

你有什么提**议**?

nǐ yǒu shé me tí **yì**?

What do you **suggest**?

369- 往/wǎng/ – *Go; previous*

他**往**北边去了。

tā **wǎng** běi biān qù le.

He **went** north.

370- 元/yuán/ – *Yuan (unit of money)*

一美**元**大概等于七**元**人民币。

yī měi **yuán** dà gài děng yú qī **yuán** rén mín bì.

One US dollar is roughly equal to seven Chinese **yuan**.

371- 英雄/yīng xióng/ – *Hero*

他是个**英雄**。

tā shì gè **yīng xióng**.

He's a **hero**.

372- 士/shì/ – *Scholar, bachelor, sergeant*

我们都有学**士**学位。

wǒ men dōu yǒu xué **shì** xué wèi.

We all have **bachelor's** degrees.

373- 证/zhèng/ – *Prove*

你怎么**证**明？

nǐ zěn me **zhèng** míng?

How do you **prove** it?

374- 近/jìn/ – *Near, close*

我家离学校很**近**。

wǒ jiā lí xué xiào hěn **jìn**.

My home is very **close** to the school.

375- 失/shī/ – *Lose*

我最后**失**去了她。

wǒ zuì hòu **shī** qù le tā.

I finally **lost** her.

376- 转 /zhuǎn/ – *Transfer, turn*

向右**转**。
xiàng yòu **zhuǎn**.
Turn right.

377- 夫 /fū/ – *Husband*

她的丈**夫**是工人。
tā de zhàng **fū** shì gōng rén.
Her **husband** is a worker.

378- 令 /lìng/ – *Order*

我不需要听你的命**令**。
wǒ bù xū yào tīng nǐ de mìng **lìng**.
I don't need to follow your **orders**.

379- 准 /zhǔn/ – *Standard; grant*

道德标**准**是否有所改进？
dào dé biāo **zhǔn** shì fǒu yǒu suǒ gǎi jìn?
Have **standards** of morality improved?

380- 布 /bù/ – *Cloth*

她用一块**布**清洗伤口。
tā yòng yī kuài **bù** qīng xǐ shāng kǒu.
She cleaned the wound with a piece of **cloth**.

381- 始 /shǐ/ – *Begin, start*

我们开**始**吧。
wǒ men kāi **shǐ** ba.
Let's **begin**.

382- 怎 /zěn/ – *How*

你**怎**么知道？
nǐ **zěn** me zhī dào?
How do you know?

383- 呢 /ne/ – *Interrogative or emphatic final*

你在干**什么呢**？

nǐ zài gàn **shén me ne**?

What are you doing?

384- 存 /cún/ – *Exist, save*

我想**存**点钱。

wǒ xiǎng **cún** diǎn qián.

I want to **save** some money.

385- 未 /wèi/ – *Not, have not*

这件事尚**未**解决。

zhè jiàn shì shàng **wèi** jiě jué.

This **has not** been solved yet.

386- 远 /yuǎn/ – *Far*

我家离学校很**远**。

wǒ jiā lí xué xiào hěn **yuǎn**.

My home is **far** from the school.

387- 叫 /jiào/ – *Shout*

谁在**叫**？

shuí zài **jiào**?

Who's **shouting**?

388- 台 /tái/ – *Platform, stage*

他从**台**上跳了下来。

tā cóng **tái** shàng tiào le xià lái.

He jumped down from the **platform**.

389- 单 /dān/ – *Bill; single, only*

他们无力支付账**单**。

tā men wú lì zhī fù zhàng **dān**.

They couldn't afford to pay the **bill**.

390- 影 /yǐng/ – Shadow, movie

你想去看电**影**吗？

nǐ xiǎng qù kàn diàn **yǐng** ma?

Do you want to go to a **movie?**

391- 工具 /gōng jù/ – Tool

我需要一些**工具**。

wǒ xū yào yī xiē **gōng jù.**

I need some **tools.**

392- 罗 /luó/ – Spread out

厂房**罗**列在山坡上。

chǎng fáng **luó** liè zài shān pō shàng.

Factory buildings **spread out** over the hillside.

393- 字 /zì/ – Character, letter

汉**字**很难写。

hàn **zì** hěn nán xiě.

Chinese **character** is hard to write.

394- 爱 /ài/ – Love

我**爱**你。

wǒ **ài** nǐ.

I **love** you.

395- 击 /jī/ – Hit, strike

那位球员最终**击**进了一球。

nà wèi qiú yuán zuì zhōng **jī** jìn le yī qiú.

The player was able to **hit** the ball in at last.

396- 流 /liú/ – Flow

一条小溪潺潺**流**进山谷。

yī tiáo xiǎo xī chán chán **liú** jìn shān gǔ.

A stream **flowed** gently down into the valley.

397- 备 /bèi/ – *Prepare; ready*

准**备**好了吗？

zhǔn **bèi** hǎo le ma?

Are you **ready**?

398- 兵 /bīng/ – *Soldier*

那个伤**兵**睁开了眼睛。

nà gè shāng **bīng** zhēng kāi le yǎn jīng.

The wounded **soldier** opened his eyes.

399- 连 /lián/ – *Connect*

你可以把设备**连**在手机上。

nǐ kě yǐ bǎ shè bèi **lián** zài shǒu jī shàng.

You can **connect** the equipment to your phone.

400- 调 /diào/ – *Investigate; tone, melody*

我们需要**调**查这件事。

xū yào **diào** chá zhè jiàn shì.

We need to **investigate** this matter.

401- 深 /shēn/ – *Deep*

这里水很**深**。

zhè lǐ shuǐ hěn **shēn**.

The water is **deep** here.

402- 商 /shāng/ – *Business*

我会说**商**务英语。

wǒ huì shuō **shāng** wù yīng yǔ.

I can speak **business** English properly.

403- 算 /suàn/ – *Calculate, count*

你是怎么**算**的？

nǐ shì zěn me **suàn** de?

How did you **calculate** it?

404- 质/zhì/ – Quality

每个人都可以改善生活**质**量。

měi gè rén dōu kě yǐ gǎi shàn shēng huó **zhì** liàng.

Everyone can improve the **quality** of life.

405- 团/tuán/ – Ball; gather

我讨厌吃饭**团**。

wǒ tǎo yàn chī fàn **tuán**.

I hate eating rice **balls**.

406- 集/jí/ – Collect

我喜欢**集**邮。

wǒ xǐ huān **jí** yóu.

I like **collecting** stamps.

407- 百/bǎi/ – Hundred

昨天有超过一**百**人被捕。

zuó tiān yǒu chāo guò yī **bǎi** rén bèi bǔ.

More than a **hundred** people were arrested yesterday.

408- 需/xū/ – Need

你**需**要什么？

nǐ **xū** yào shén me?

What do you **need**?

409- 价/jià/ – Price

价格比昨天高。

jià gé bǐ zuó tiān gāo.

The **price** is above yesterday's.

410- 花/huā/ – Flower

牡丹是艳丽的**花**。

mǔ dān shì yàn lì de **huā**.

A peony is a showy **flower**.

411- 党 /dǎng/ – *Party*

中国共产**党**是中国的执政**党**。

zhōng guó gòng chǎn **dǎng** shì zhōng guó de zhí zhèng **dǎng**.

The Communist **Party** of China is the ruling **party** of China.

412- 华 /huá/ – *Splendid*

这部电影里有大量**华**丽的场景。

zhè bù diàn yǐng lǐ yǒu dà liàng **huá** lì de chǎng jǐng.

The movie includes a wealth of **splendid** scenes.

413- 城 /chéng/ – *City*

我喜欢住在**城**里。

wǒ xǐ huān zhù zài **chéng** lǐ.

I like to live in the **city**.

414- 石 /shí/ – *Stone, rock*

山谷上方的小山全是**石**头。

shān gǔ shàng fāng de xiǎo shān quán shì **shí** tóu.

The hill above the valley is full of **rocks**.

415- 级 /jí/ – *Level, grade, rank*

防尘口罩根据防护效果分**级**。

fáng chén kǒu zhào gēn jù fáng hù xiào guǒ fēn **jí**.

Dust masks are **graded** according to the protection they offer.

416- 整 /zhěng/ – *Whole*

在电子表格中，单击就是选择**整**个单元格。

zài diàn zǐ biǎo gé zhōng, dān jī jiù shì xuǎn zé **zhěng** gè dān yuán gé.

A single-click will select exactly one **whole** cell in the spreadsheet.

417- 府 /fǔ/ – *Goverment*

政**府**提高了对烈性酒的赋税。

zhèng **fǔ** tí gāo le duì liè xìng jiǔ de fù shuì.

The **government** hiked the tax on hard liquor.

418- 离 /lí/ – Leave

他可能会被禁止**离**开该国。

tā kě néng huì bèi jìn zhǐ **lí** kāi gāi guó.

He would not be allowed to **leave** the country.

419- 况 /kuàng/ – Situation

现在是什么情**况**？

xiàn zài shì shén me qíng **kuàng**?

What's the **situation** now?

420- 亚 /yà/ – Second

他在本次比赛中获得**亚**军。

tā zài běn cì bǐ sài zhōng huò dé **yà** jūn.

He won the **second** place in this competition.

421- 请 /qǐng/ – Please

请跟我来。

qǐng gēn wǒ lái.

Please follow me.

422- 技 /jì/ – Skill

你能告诉我一些你的特殊**技**能吗？

nǐ néng gào sù wǒ yī xiē nǐ de tè shū **jì** néng ma?

Could you please tell me something about your special **skills**?

423- 际 /jì/ – Border; time; occasion

在此之**际**，我想说声抱歉。

zài cǐ zhī **jì**, wǒ xiǎng shuō shēng bào qiàn.

On this **occasion**, I want to say sorry.

424- 约 /yuē/ – Agreement

我们什么时候可以签**约**？

wǒ men shén me shí hòu kě yǐ qiān **yuē**?

When can we sign the **agreement**?

425- 示/shì/ – Show

图一所**示**为呼吸系统。

tú yī suǒ **shì** wéi hū xī xì tǒng.

Figure one **shows** the respiratory system.

426- 复/fù/ – Repeat

他反**复**说自己的话被断章取义了。

tā fǎn **fù** shuō zì jǐ de huà bèi duàn zhāng qǔ yì le.

He **repeated** that he had been misquoted.

427- 病/bìng/ – Illness

如果你的孩子出现任何患**病**症状，请带她去看医生。

rú guǒ nǐ de hái zǐ chū xiàn rèn hé huàn **bìng** zhèng zhuàng, qǐng dài tā qù kàn yī shēng.

If your child shows any signs of **illness**, take her to the doctor.

428- 息/xī/ – Rest

我得休**息**一下。

wǒ děi xiū **xī** yī xià.

I need to take a **rest**.

429- 究/jiū/ – Research

研究表明全国各地的口味大有不同。

yán **jiū** biǎo míng quán guó gè dì de kǒu wèi dà yǒu bù tóng.

Research shows a wide difference in tastes around the country.

430- 线/xiàn/ – Line, wire

沿那一页的中心画一条**线**。

yán nà yī yè de zhōng xīn huà yī tiáo **xiàn**.

Draw a **line** down that page's center.

431- 似/sì/ – Seem; similar

这计划看**似**可行。

zhè jì huà kàn **sì** kě xíng.

This plan **seems** to be feasible.

432- 官/guān/ – Official

一位**官**员称已有一百多人被捕。

yī wèi **guān** yuán chēng yǐ yǒu yī bǎi duō rén bèi bǔ.

According to an **official** more than a hundred people have been arrested.

433- 火/huǒ/ – Fire

房子着**火**了。

fáng zi zháo **huǒ** le.

The house is on **fire**.

434- 断/duàn/ – Break, cut off

他胳膊**断**了。

tā gē bó **duàn** le.

He **broke** his arm.

435- 精/jīng/ – Energy

我们必须集中**精**力治疗毒瘾。

wǒ men bì xū jí zhōng **jīng** lì zhì liáo dú yǐn.

We must concentrate our **energies** on treating addiction.

436- 满/mǎn/ – Full

容器**满**了。

róng qì **mǎn** le.

The container is **full**.

437- 支/zhī/ – Support

你**支**持我吗？

nǐ **zhī** chí wǒ ma?

Will you **support** me?

438- 视/shì/ – Look at, regard

我把创造力**视**为一种天赋。

wǒ bǎ chuàng zào lì **shì** wéi yī zhǒng tiān fù.

I **regard** creativity as a gift.

439- 消/xiāo/ – Eliminate, disappear

敌人已被**消**灭了。

dí rén yǐ bèi **xiāo** miè le.

The enemy has been **eliminated**.

440- 越/yuè/ – Exceed

你**越**权了！

nǐ **yuè** quán le!

You are **exceeding** your powers!

441- 器/qì/ - Device

该仪**器**几个月前曾投入运行。

gāi yí **qì** jǐ gè yuè qián céng tóu rù yùn xíng.

The **device** had been used operationally some months ago.

442- 容/róng/ – Contain, allow

这么做不被**容**许。

zhè me zuò bù bèi **róng** xǔ.

You're not **allowed** to do this.

443- 照/zhào/ – As; according to; to shine

照我说的做。

zhào wǒ shuō de zuò.

Do **as** I say.

444- 须/xū/ – Must

我必**须**走了。

wǒ bì **xū** zǒu le.

I **must** go.

445- 九/jiǔ/ – Nine

现在**九**点了。

xiàn zài **jiǔ** diǎn le.

It's **nine** o'clock now.

446- 增 /zēng/ – *Increase*

人口持续**增**长。

rén kǒu chí xù **zēng** zhǎng.

The population continues to **increase**.

447- 研 /yán/ – *Research*

我正在做一项**研**究。

wǒ zhèng zài zuò yī xiàng **yán** jiū.

I am doing a **research** paper.

448- 写 /xiě/ – *Write*

我想给她**写**封信。

wǒ xiǎng gěi tā **xiě** fēng xìn.

I want to **write** a letter to her.

449- 称 /chēng/ – *Name; to name, to weigh*

我们把它**称**为什么？

wǒ men bǎ tā **chēng** wéi shén me?

What do we **name** it?

450- 企 /qǐ/ – *Try, to plan a project*

他**企**图勒死那名警察。

tā **qǐ** tú lēi sǐ nà míng jǐng chá.

He **tried** to strangle that policeman.

451- 八 /bā/ – *Eight*

我们**八**点见。

wǒ men **bā** diǎn jiàn.

Let's meet at **eight** o'clock.

452- 功 /gōng/ – *Accomplishment*

这是你的**功**劳。

zhè shì nǐ de **gōng** láo.

This is your **accomplishment**.

453- 吗/ma/ – *Final interrogative particle*

你爱我**吗**?

nǐ ài wǒ **ma**?

Do you love me?

454- 包/bāo/ – *Bag; cover, wrap*

我喜欢这个红色的**包**。

wǒ xǐ huān zhè ge hóng sè de **bāo**.

I like this red **bag**.

455- 片/piàn/ – *Slice*

请给我一**片**面包。

qǐng gěi wǒ yī **piàn** miàn bāo.

Please give me a **slice** of bread.

456- 史/shǐ/ – *History*

他有酗酒**史**。

tā yǒu xù jiǔ **shǐ**.

He had a **history** of drinking problems.

457- 委/wěi/ – *Appoint, entrust*

我不能把孩子**委**托给陌生人。

wǒ bù néng bǎ hái zi **wěi** tuō gěi mò shēng rén.

I couldn't **entrust** my children to strangers.

458- 乎/hū/ – *Classical final particle expressing question, doubt, etc.*

天下事有难易**乎**?

tiān xià shì yǒu nán yì **hū**?

Is there a difference between hard things and easy things?

459- 查/chá/ – *Check, examine*

我想**查**一下账户余额。

wǒ xiǎng **chá** yī xià zhàng hù yú é.

I'd like to **check** the balance in my account please.

460- 轻/qīng/ – Light, gentle

那声音甜美**轻**柔。

nà shēng yīn tián měi **qīng** róu.

The voice was sweet and **light**.

461- 易/yì/ – Easy

那很容**易**。

nà hěn róng **yì**.

That's **easy**.

462- 早/zǎo/ – Early; morning

早安。

zǎo ān.

Good **morning**.

463- 曾/céng/ - Once, already

我**曾**和朋友露营。

wǒ **céng** hé péng yǒu lù yíng.

I **once** went camping with friends.

464- 除/chú/ – Exclude, remove

需要进一步检查以排**除**患病可能。

xū yào jìn yī bù jiǎn chá yǐ pái **chú** huàn bìng kě néng.

Further examination is needed to **exclude** the chance of disease.

465- 农/nóng/ – Farm, farmer, agriculture

我父亲是个**农**民。

wǒ fù qīn shì gè **nóng** mín.

My father is a **farmer**.

466- 找/zhǎo/ – Search, look for

你在**找**什么？

nǐ zài **zhǎo** shén me?

What are you **looking for**?

467- 装 /zhuāng/ – *Dress; install, wrap*

用箔纸把烤鸡**装**起来。

yòng bó zhǐ bǎ kǎo jī **zhuāng** qǐ lái.

Wrap the foil over the roast chicken.

468- 广 /guǎng/ – *Wide, vast; spread*

他为人文雅，结交**广**泛。

tā wéi rén wén yǎ, jié jiāo **guǎng** fàn.

He is a cultured man with a **wide** circle of friends.

469- 显 /xiǎn/ – *Conspicuous*

很明**显**,抽烟对健康有害。

hěn míng **xiǎn**, chōu yān duì jiàn kāng yǒu hài.

It is **conspicuous** that smoking is harmful to health.

470- 吧 /ba/ – *Modal particle indicating suggestion*

我们看电影去**吧**。

wǒ men kàn diàn yǐng qù **ba**.

Let's go to a movie.

471- 阿 /ā/ – *Prefix used to indicate familiarity*

这是我的朋友乔舒亚，我都叫他**阿乔**。

zhè shì wǒ de péng yǒu qiáo shū yà, wǒ dōu jiào tā **ā** qiáo.

This is my friend Joshua; I call him **Josh**.

472- 李子 /lǐ zi/ – *Plum*

快到吃**李子**的时节了。

kuài dào chī **lǐ zi** de shí jié le.

The **plum** season is about to begin.

473- 标 /biāo/ – *Sign, mark; to mark*

他用铅笔做了**标**记。

tā yòng qiān bǐ zuò le **biāo** jì.

He made **marks** with a pencil.

474- 谈/tán/ – Talk

你想**谈谈**吗？

nǐ xiǎng **tán tán** ma?

Do you want to **talk** about it?

475- 吃/chī/ – Eat

你想**吃**什么？

nǐ xiǎng **chī** shén me?

What would you like to **eat**?

476- 图/tú/ – Map, picture

我想买份地**图**。

wǒ xiǎng mǎi fèn dì **tú**.

I want to buy a **map**.

477- 念/niàn/ – Miss, read

你能帮我**念**下报纸吗？

nǐ néng bāng wǒ **niàn** xià bào zhǐ ma?

Can you **read** the newspaper for me?

478- 六/liù/ – Six

我来这里**六**年了。

wǒ lái zhè lǐ **liù** nián le.

I've been here for **six** years.

479- 引/yǐn/ – Lead, guide

过了一会儿，我把话题**引**到她的工作上。

guò le yī huǐ er, wǒ bǎ huà tí **yǐn** dào tā de gōng zuò shàng.

After a while I **led** the conversation around to her job.

480- 历/lì/ – Calendar, history; experience

墙上挂着日**历**。

qiáng shàng guà zhe rì **lì**.

There is a **calendar** on the wall.

481- 首 /shǒu/ – *First; leader*

我们**首**先应该做什么？

wǒ men **shǒu** xiān yīng gāi zuò shén me?

What should we do **first**?

482- 医 /yī/ – *Doctor; to cure*

我想当**医**生。

wǒ xiǎng dāng **yī** shēng.

I want to be a **doctor**.

483- 局 /jú/ – *Office*

邮**局**在哪里？

yóu **jú** zài nǎ lǐ?

Where is the post **office**?

484- 突 /tū/ – *Sudden; to break through*

银行**突**然破产了。

yín háng **tū** rán pò chǎn le.

The bank went bankrupt all of a **sudden**.

485- 专 /zhuān/ – *Expert; special; focus on*

专家马上就来。

zhuān jiā mǎ shàng jiù lái.

The **expert** is about to come.

486- 费 /fèi/ – *Expense; to cost*

他们希望削减公用事业**费**用。

tā men xī wàng xuē jiǎn gōng yòng shì yè **fèi** yòng.

They want to cut down their utility **expenses**.

487- 号 /hào/ – *Mark, sign*

他用钢笔做了记**号**。

tā yòng gāng bǐ zuò le jì **hào**.

He made **marks** with a pen.

488- 尽/jìn/ – Use up, to end

我们终于用尽了一切。

wǒ men zhōng yú yòng **jìn** le yī qiè.

We finally **used up** everything.

489- 另/lìng/ – Other, another

另一些人不这么认为。

lìng yī xiē **rén** bù zhè me rèn wéi.

Other people don't think so.

490- 周/zhōu/ – Week

你这周的计划是什么?

nǐ zhè **zhōu** de jì huà shì shén me?

What is your plan for this **week**?

491- 较/jiào/ – Compare, than

他较以前胖多了。

tā **jiào** yǐ qián pàng duō le.

He's much fatter **than** he used to be.

492- 注/zhù/ – Inject, concentrate, register

你来学校注册了吗?

nǐ lái xué xiào **zhù** cè le ma?

Have you come to **register** at the school?

493- 语/yǔ/ – Language

她会说多门语言。

tā huì shuō duō mén **yǔ** yán.

She can speak several **languages**.

494- 仅/jǐn/ – Only, barely

这仅是其中的一种可能。

zhè **jǐn** shì qí zhōng de yī zhǒng kě néng.

This is **only** one of the possibilities.

495- 考/kǎo/ – Test; take an exam

今天我们要考试。

jīn tiān wǒ men yào **kǎo** shì.

Today, we will have a **test**.

496- 落/luò/ – To fall

秋天，树叶纷纷从树上落下来。

qiū tiān, shù yè fēn fēn cóng shù shàng **luò** xià lái.

Leaves **fall** off the trees in the autumn.

497- 青/qīng/ – Blue, green, black

我喜欢青草的味道。

wǒ xǐ huān **qīng** cǎo de wèi dào.

I like the smell of **green** grass.

498- 随/suí/ – Follow, comply with

随我来。

suí wǒ lái.

Follow me.

499- 选/xuǎn/ – Choose, select

我选中了一个文件，按下了删除键。

wǒ **xuǎn** zhòng le yī gè wén jiàn, àn xià le shān chú jiàn.

I **selected** a file and pressed the Delete key.

500- 列/liè/ – Line up; list

请列出三种你喜欢的水果。

qǐng **liè** chū sān zhǒng nǐ xǐ huān de shuǐ guǒ.

Please **list** three kinds of fruits you like.

501- 武/wǔ/ – Military

双方的武装力量都有密集动作。

shuāng fāng de **wǔ** zhuāng lì liàng dōu yǒu mì jí dòng zuò.

The **military** on both sides are involved in intense activity.

502- 红 /hóng/ – *Red*

我喜欢这顶**红**色的帽子。

wǒ xǐ huān zhè dǐng **hóng** sè de mào zi.

I like this **red** cap.

503- 响 /xiǎng/ – *Sound, noise; make a sound; to ring*

你的手机**响**了。

nǐ de shǒu jī **xiǎng** le.

Your phone is **ringing**.

504- 虽 /suī/ – *Although*

虽价格昂贵，却经久耐用。

suī jià gé áng guì, què jīng jiǔ nài yòng.

Although they're expensive, they last forever.

505- 推 /tuī/ – *Push*

他们把她**推**进了车里。

tā men bǎ tā **tuī** jìn le chē lǐ.

They **pushed** her into the car.

506- 势 /shì/ – *Power, situation, gesture*

现在的形**势**十分严峻。

xiàn zài de xíng **shì** shí fēn yán jùn.

The current **situation** is very serious.

507- 参 /cān/ – *Take part in, join, attend*

欢迎你随时**参**加我们的活动。

huān yíng nǐ suí shí **cān** jiā wǒ men de huó dòng.

You are welcome to **attend** our events at any time.

508- 希 /xī/ – *To hope*

希望你过得好。

xī wàng nǐ guò dé hǎo.

Hope you are well.

509- 古/gǔ/ – Ancient

旅行的终点是那座**古**镇。

lǚ xíng de zhōng diǎn shì nà zuò **gǔ** zhèn.

The journey ends in that **ancient** town.

510- 众/zhòng/ – Public

我想将此事公之于**众**。

wǒ xiǎng jiāng cǐ shì gong zhī yú **zhòng**.

I'd like to make this matter known to the **public**.

511- 构/gòu/ – Make up, construct

他最终**构**筑了一个商业帝国。

tā zuì zhōng **gòu** zhù le yī gè shāng yè dì guó.

He eventually **constructed** a business empire.

512- 房/fáng/ – House

她搬进了一所小一些的**房**子。

tā bān jìn le yī suǒ xiǎo yī xiē de **fáng** zi.

She moved to a smaller **house**.

513- 半/bàn/ – Half

他**半**闭着眼。

tā **bàn** bì zhe yǎn.

His eyes were **half** closed.

514- 节/jié/ – Festival, joint; to save

离春**节**只有一周了。

lí chūn **jié** zhǐ yǒu yī zhōu le.

The Spring **Festival** is only a week away.

515- 土/tǔ/ – Soil

我们拥有该地区最肥沃的**土**地。

wǒ men yǒng yǒu gāi d ìqū zuì féi wò de **tǔ** dì.

We have the most fertile **soil** in this region.

516- 投/tóu/ – To cast

明亮的月光**投**射在院子里。

míng liàng de yuè guāng **tóu** shè zài yuan zi lǐ.

The moon **cast** a bright light over the yard.

517- 某/mǒu/ – Certain

他们不得不放弃**某**些研究。

tā men bù dé bù fàng qì **mǒu** xiē yán jiū.

They have to give up on **certain** of their studies.

518- 案/àn/ – File, (legal) case

他就这起**案**件向法官做了说明。

tā jiù zhè qǐ **àn** jiàn xiàng fǎ guān zuò le shuō míng.

He took the **case** to the judge.

519- 黑/hēi/ – Black

她喜欢穿**黑**裙子。

tā xǐ huān chuān **hēi** qún zi.

She likes to wear her **black** dress.

520- 维持/wéi chí/ – Maintain, preserve

水是**维持**生命的必需品。

shuǐ shì **wéi chí** shēng mìng de bì xū pǐn.

Water is necessary to **maintain** life.

521- 革/gé/ – Leather

他穿了一件皮**革**夹克。

tā chuān le yī jiàn pí **gé** jiá kè.

He wore a **leather** jacket.

522- 划/huá/ – Paddle, scratch

划水的时候穿上凉鞋。

huá shuǐ de shí hòu chuān shàng liáng xié.

Wear sandals when you **paddle**.

523- 敌 /dí/ – Enemy

海战的目标就是击沉**敌**舰。

hǎi zhàn de mù biāo jiù shì jí chén **dí** jiàn.

In a naval battle your aim is to sink the **enemy**'s fleet.

524- 致 /zhì/ – Send, cause

投资可能耗尽，而这会导**致**经济衰退。

tóu zī kě néng hào jìn, ér zhè huì dǎo **zhì** jīng jì shuāi tuì.

Investment could dry up and that could **cause** the economy to falter.

525- 陈 /chén/ – Explain, exhibit

他的作品**陈**列在最好的美术馆里。

tā de zuò pǐn **chén** liè zài zuì hǎo de měi shù guǎn lǐ.

His work was **exhibited** in the best galleries.

526- 律 /lǜ/ – Law

她有那所大学的法**律**学位。

tā yǒu nà suǒ dà xué de fǎ **lǜ** xué wèi.

She holds a **law** degree from that university.

527- 足 /zú/ – Foot

我喜欢踢**足**球。

wǒ xǐ huān tī **zú** qiú.

I like to play **foot**ball.

528- 态 /tài/ – Attitude

美是一种**态**度。

měi shì yī zhǒng **tài** dù.

Beauty is an **attitude**.

529- 护 /hù/ – Protect

它们怎么保**护**自己？

tā men zěn me bǎo **hù** zì jǐ?

How do they **protect** themselves?

530- 七 /qī/ – Seven

我们**七**分钟后见。

wǒ men **qī** fēn zhōng hòu jiàn.

We'll meet in **seven** minutes.

531- 兴 /xīng/ – Flourish, rise

一个建设的新高潮正在**兴**起。

yī gè jiàn shè de xīn gāo cháo zhèng zài **xīng** qǐ.

A new upsurge in construction is **rising**.

532- 派 /pài/ – Send, assign

我被**派**去执行任务。

wǒ bèi **pài** qù zhí xíng rèn wù.

I was **sent** to perform the task.

533- 孩 /hái/ – Child, children

他还是个**孩**子。

tā hái shì gè **hái** zi.

He's just a **child**.

534- 验 /yàn/ – Check, examine

我们需要做质量检**验**。

wǒ men xū yào zuò zhì liàng jiǎn **yàn**.

We need to perform a quality **check**.

535- 责 /zé/ – Responsibility

这是你的**责**任。

zhè shì nǐ de **zé** rèn.

This is your **responsibility**.

536- 营 /yíng/ – Camp

你记得去年的夏令**营**吗?

nǐ jì dé qù nián de xià lìng **yíng** ma?

Do you remember the summer **camp** last year?

537- 星 /xīng/ – Star

夜很黑，**星星**都躲在云的后面。

yè hěn hēi, **xīng xīng** dōu duǒ zài yún de hòu miàn.

The night was dark, the **stars** hidden behind cloud.

538- 够 /gòu/ – Enough

够了！

gòu le!

That's **enough**!

539- 章 /zhāng/ – Chapter, badge

我喜欢这一**章**。

wǒ xǐ huān zhè yī **zhāng**.

I like this **chapter**.

540- 音 /yīn/ – Sound, noise, tone

那是什么声**音**？

nà shì shén me sheng **yīn**?

What is that **noise**?

541- 跟 /gēn/ – Heel; with, from

我**跟**你不一样。

wǒ **gēn** nǐ bù yī yàng.

I'm different **from** you.

542- 志 /zhì/ – Ambition, sign, mark

他的**志**向是赢得金牌。

tā de **zhì** xiàng shì yíng dé jīn pái.

His **ambition** was to win the gold medal.

543- 底 /dǐ/ – Bottom

脚注附在每页**底**端。

jiǎo zhù fù zài měi yè **dǐ** duān.

Footnotes are given at the **bottom** of each page.

544- 站 /zhàn/ – Station; to stand

火车**站**在哪？

huǒ chē **zhàn** zài nǎ?

Where is the train **station**?

545- 严 /yán/ – Strict

我的父母非常**严**厉。

wǒ de fù mǔ fēi cháng **yán** lì.

My parents were very **strict**.

546- 巴不得 /bā bù dé/ – Wish (earnestly)

我**巴不得**这样。

wǒ **bā bù dé** zhè yàng.

I **wish** it were so.

547- 例 /lì/ – Example

这不过是你可做的试验中的一个**例**子。

zhè bù guò shì nǐ kě zuò de shì yàn zhōng de yī gè **lì** zi.

That's just one **example** of the experiments you can do.

548- 防 /fáng/ – Defend; defense

进攻是最好的**防**守。

jìn gōng shì zuì hǎo de **fáng** shǒu.

Offence is the best **defense**.

549- 族 /zú/ – Race

世界上有很多不同种**族**的人。

shì jiè shàng yǒu hěn duō bù tóng zhǒng **zú** de rén.

There are many people of different **races** in the world.

550- 供 /gōng/ – Supply

大脑需要持续**供**氧。

dà nǎo xū yào chí xù **gōng** yǎng.

The brain requires a constant **supply** of oxygen.

551- 效/xiào/ – *Effect; effectiveness*

整体**效**果很酷。

zhěng tǐ **xiào** guǒ hěn kù.

The whole **effect** is cool.

552- 续/xù/ – *Continue*

利率持**续**下调。

lì lǜ chí **xù** xià tiáo.

Interest rates **continue** to fall.

553- 施/shī/ – *Carry out*

他将实**施**这个计划。

tā jiāng shí **shī** zhè gè jì huà.

He will **carry out** this plan.

554- 留/liú/ – *Stay, leave (a message)*

你能**留**言吗?

nǐ néng **liú** yán ma?

Can you **leave** a message?

555- 讲/jiǎng/ – *Speak*

他**讲**话口齿不清。

tā **jiǎng** huà kǒu chǐ bù qīng.

He **speaks** with a lisp.

556- 型/xíng/ – *Model, type*

该疾病有各种类**型**。

gāi jí bìng yǒu gè zhǒng lèi **xíng**.

There are various **types** of the disease.

557- 料/liào/ – *Material, ingredient*

他对不同材**料**做了实验。

tā duì bù tóng cái **liào** zuò le shí yàn.

He did experiments on different **materials**.

558- 终/zhōng/ – End; finally

他**终**于出现了。

tā **zhōng** yú chū xiàn le.

He **finally** appeared.

559- 答/dá/ – Answer

问题的**答**案是什么？

wèn tí de **dá** àn shì shén me?

What's the **answer** to the question?

560- 紧/jǐn/ – Tight

他的牛仔裤太**紧**了。

tā de niú zǎi kù tài **jǐn** le.

His jeans were too **tight**.

561- 黄/huáng/ – Yellow

我喜欢这件**黄**色的毛衣。

wǒ xǐ huān zhè jiàn **huáng** sè de máo yī.

I like this **yellow** sweater.

562- 绝/jué/ – Extinct; absolutely

吉尔**绝**对正确。

jí ěr **jué** duì zhèng què.

Jill is **absolutely** right.

563- 奇/qí/ – Odd, weird

他很**奇**怪。

tā hěn **qí** guài.

He's **weird**.

564- 察/chá/ – Observe, inspect

经理每天到我们这里视**察**一次。

jīng lǐ měi tiān dào wǒ men zhè lǐ shì **chá** yī cì.

The manager **inspects** us once a day.

565- 母 /mǔ/ – *Mother*

这是我**母**亲。

zhè shì wǒ **mǔ** qīn.

This is my **mother**.

566- 京 /jīng/ – *The capital of China*

总统无人护卫的汽车在**京**畿重地遭到了伏击。

zǒng tǒng wú rén hù wèi de qì chē zài **jīng** jī zhòng dì zāo dào le fú jí.

The President's unescorted vehicle was ambushed just in the **capital**.

567- 段 /duàn/ – *Parapraph, section*

我们从第一**段**学到了什么？

wǒ men cóng dì yī **duàn** xué dào le shén me?

What do we learn from the first **paragraph**?

568- 依 /yī/ – *Depend on*

我只是讨厌不得不**依**赖他到处开车送我。

wǒ zhǐ shì tǎo yàn bù dé bù **yī** lài tā dào chù kāi chē sòng wǒ.

I just hate having to **depend on** him to drive me everywhere.

569- 批 /pī/ – *Criticize*

你**批**评他没错。

nǐ **pī** píng tā méi cuò.

You were right to **criticize** him.

570- 群 /qún/ – *Crowd, group*

这次骚乱涉及一**群**难民。

zhè cì sāo luàn shè jí yī **qún** nàn mín.

The trouble involved a **group** of refugees.

571- 项 /xiàng/ – *Neck, project*

她忙着完成她的**项**目。

tā máng zhe wán chéng tā de **xiàng** mù.

She was busy finishing her **project**.

572- 故 /gù/ – Old, former; reason

他是我的**故**交。

tā shì wǒ de **gù** jiāo.

He's an **old** friend of mine.

573- 按 /àn/ – Press; according to

不要**按**那个钮。

bù yào **àn** nà gè niǔ.

Don't **press** that button.

574- 河 /hé/ – River

我们学校就在**河**对岸。

wǒ men xué xiào jiù zài **hé** duì àn.

Our school is across the **river**.

575- 米 /mǐ/ – Rice, meter

我家离公园大概五百**米**。

wǒ jiā lí gong yuán dà gài wǔ bǎi **mǐ**.

My home is about 500 **meters** away from the park.

576- 围 /wéi/ – Surround

你们被包**围**了。

nǐ men bèi bāo **wéi** le.

You are **surrounded**.

577- 江 /jiāng/ – River

长**江**是中国最长的河。

cháng **jiāng** shì zhōng guó zuì zhǎng de hé.

The Yangtze **River** is the longest river in China.

578- 织 /zhī/ – Weave

人们把线**织**成布。

rén men bǎ xiàn **zhī** chéng bù.

People **weave** threads into cloth.

579- 害/hài/ – Harm

我不想伤**害**你。

wǒ bù xiǎng shāng **hài** nǐ.

I don't want to **harm** you.

580- 斗/dòu/ – Fight

在接下来的选举中我们将面临一场恶**斗**。

zài jiē xià lái de xuǎn jǔ zhōng wǒ men jiāng miàn lín yī chǎng è **dòu.**

We'll face a tough **fight** in the upcoming election.

581- 双/shuāng/ – Pair, double, two, both

我买了一**双**鞋。

wǒ mǎi le yī **shuāng** xié.

I bought a **pair** of shoes.

582- 境/jìng/ – Environment, place

我们必须保护环**境**。

wǒ men bì xū bǎo hù huán **jìng.**

We must protect the **environment**.

583- 客/kè/ – Guest, customer

她是参加婚礼的**客**人。

tā shì cān jiā hūn lǐ de **kè** rén.

She was a **guest** at the wedding.

584- 纪/jì/ – Discipline, age

那位老师无法维持课堂**纪**律。

nà wèi lǎo shī wú fǎ wéi chí kè táng **jì** lǜ.

The teacher can't keep **discipline** in her classroom.

585- 采/cǎi/ – Pick, pluck

我从树上**采**了一个苹果。

wǒ cóng shù shàng **cǎi** le yī gè píng guǒ.

I **plucked** an apple from the tree.

586- 举/jǔ/ – *Lift, raise*

学生们把他**举**到空中。

xué sheng men bǎ tā **jǔ** dào kōng zhōng.

The students **lifted** him into the air.

587- 杀/shā/ – *Kill*

很多人被武装部队**杀**死。

hěn duō rén bèi wǔ zhuāng bù duì **shā** sǐ.

Many people have been **killed** by the armed forces.

588- 攻/gōng/ – *Attack*

我们正遭受**攻**击。

wǒ men zhèng zāo shòu **gōng** jí.

We are under **attack**.

589- 父/fù/ – *Father*

他是三个孩子的**父**亲。

tā shì sān gè hái zi de **fù** qīn.

He is the **father** of three children.

590- 苏醒/sū xǐng/ – *Revive*

她试图让他**苏醒**过来。

tā shì tú ràng tā **sū xǐng** guò lái.

She tried to **revive** him.

591- 密/mì/ – *Secret; close, dense*

它的毛又短又**密**。

tā de máo yòu duǎn yòu **mì**.

Its fur is short and **dense**.

592- 低/dī/ – *Low*

他们要找**低**卡路里的食物。

tā men yào zhǎo **dī** kǎ lù lǐ de shí wù.

They look for foods that are **low** in calories.

593- 朝/cháo/ – Towards

她沿着走廊**朝**教室走去。

tā yán zhe zǒu láng **cháo** jiào shì zǒu qù.

She walked down the corridor **towards** the classroom.

594- 友/yǒu/ – Friend

我喜欢交**友**。

wǒ xǐ huān jiāo **yǒu**.

I like to make **friends**.

595- 诉/sù/ – Sue, tell

我需要告**诉**你些事。

wǒ xū yào gào **sù** nǐ xiē shì.

I need to **tell** you something.

596- 止/zhǐ/ – Prohibit

禁**止**钓鱼。

jìn **zhǐ** diào yú.

Fishing is **prohibited**.

597- 细/xì/ – Thin

一条**细**电缆将信号传送给电脑。

yī tiáo **xì** diàn lǎn jiāng xìn hào chuán sòng gěi diàn nǎo.

A **thin** cable carries the signal to a computer.

598- 愿/yuàn/ – Wish

许个**愿**吧。

xǔ gè **yuàn** ba.

Make a **wish**.

599- 千/qiān/ – Thousand

中国有超过五**千**年的历史。

zhōng guó yǒu chāo guò wǔ **qiān** nián de lì shǐ.

China has a history of more than five **thousand** years.

600- 值 /zhí/ – Value

这会破坏艺术的价**值**吗？

zhè huì pò huài yì shù de jià **zhí** ma?

Does this undermine the **value** of art?

601- 仍 /réng/ – Still

我**仍**爱你。

wǒ **réng** ài nǐ.

I **still** love you.

602- 男 /nán/ – Male

为了让我的**男**性读者受益，让我稍加解释。

wèi le ràng wǒ de **nán** xìng dú zhě shòu yì, ràng wǒ shāo jiā jiě shì.

For the benefit of any **male** readers, let me explain something.

603- 钱 /qián/ – Money

你能借我点**钱**吗？

nǐ néng jiè wǒ diǎn **qián** ma?

Can you lend me some **money**?

604- 破 /pò/ – Worn out, destroy

维生素 C 受热过度就会被**破**坏。

wéi sheng sù C shòu rè guò dù jiù huì bèi **pò** huài.

Vitamin C is **destroyed** when overheated.

605- 网 /wǎng/ – Net

他**网**了许多蝴蝶。

tā **wǎng** le xǔ duō hú dié.

He **netted** a lot of butterflies.

606- 热 /rè/ – Hot

天真**热**！

tiān zhēn **rè**!

What a **hot** day!

607- 助/zhù/ – Help, aid

出口产业有**助**于经济复苏。

chū kǒu chǎn yè yǒu **zhù** yú jīng jì fù sū.

The export sector may **aid** the economic recovery.

608- 倒/dǎo/ – To fall, collapse

公司**倒**闭后，他手头缺少现金。

gōng sī **dǎo** bì hòu, tā shǒu tóu quē shǎo xiàn jīn.

He was short of cash after the **collapse** of his business.

609- 育/yù/ – Educate

教**育**儿童需要耐心。

jiào **yù** ér tóng xū yào nài xīn.

It takes patience to **educate** children.

610- 属/shǔ/ – Belong

你不**属**于这里。

nǐ bù **shǔ** yú zhè lǐ.

You don't **belong** here.

611- 坐/zuò/ – Sit

请**坐**吧。

qǐng **zuò** ba.

Sit down, please.

612- 帝/dì/ – Emperor

皇**帝**必须意识到那些人都任由他处置。

huáng **dì** bì xū yì shí dào nà xiē rén dōu rèn yóu tā chǔ zhì.

The **Emperor** must realize that he has those people at his mercy.

613- 限/xiàn/ – Limit

抗议活动不只**限**于这座城市。

kàng yì huó dòng bù zhǐ **xiàn** yú zhè zuò chéng shì.

The protests were not **limited** to this city.

614- 船/chuán/ – Boat, ship

驾**船**和开车可不一样。

jià **chuán** hé kāi chē kě bù yī yàng.

Driving a **boat** is different from driving a car.

615- 脸/liǎn/ – Face

树枝刮破了我的**脸**。

shù zhī guā pò le wǒ de **liǎn**.

The branches scratched my **face**.

616- 职/zhí/ – Duty, profession

我的**职**责就是照看这些动物。

wǒ de **zhí** zé jiù shì zhào kàn zhè xiē dòng wù.

My **duty** is to look after these animals.

617- 速/sù/ – Fast; Speed

他承认自己超**速**了。

tā chéng rèn zì jǐ chāo **sù** le.

He admits he was exceeding the **speed** limit.

618- 刻/kè/ – Moment; to curve

此**刻**没人跟我说话。

cǐ **kè** méi rén gēn wǒ shuō huà.

No one is talking to me at the **moment**.

619- 乐/lè/ – Happy

你快**乐**吗？

nǐ kuài **lè** ma?

Are you **happy**?

620- 否/fǒu/ – Deny

她对两项指控均予以**否**认。

tā duì liǎng xiàng zhǐ kòng jūn yǔ yǐ **fǒu** rèn.

She **denied** both accusations.

621- 刚 /gāng/ – Just

我**刚**买了新房子。

wǒ **gāng** mǎi le xīn fáng zi.

I've **just** bought a new house.

622- 威 /wēi/ – Power; authority

他**威**信不足。

tā **wēi** xìn bù zú.

He lacks **authority**.

623- 毛 /máo/ – Feather

拔**毛**必须干净利落。

bá **máo** bì xū gān jìng lì luò.

The **feather** must be removed with a straight firm pull.

624- 状 /zhuàng/ – Shape, condition

政府鼓励人民改善生活**状**况。

zhèng fǔ gǔ lì rén mín gǎi shàn sheng huó **zhuàng** kuàng.

The government has encouraged its people to better their **condition**.

625- 率 /lǜ/ – Rate, frequency

通货膨胀**率**大约为 2.7%。

tōng huò péng zhàng **lǜ** dà yuē wéi 2.7%.

The **rate** of inflation is running at about 2.7%.

626- 甚 /shèn/ – Very, extremely; what

此处风景**甚**好。

cǐ chù fēng jǐng **shèn** hǎo.

The view is **very** beautiful.

627- 独 /dú/ – Alone; independent; only

他**独**自生活。

tā **dú** zì shēng huó.

He lives **alone**.

628- 球 /qiú/ – Ball

我喜欢打篮**球**。

wǒ xǐ huān dǎ lán **qiú**.

I like to play basket**ball**.

629- 般 /bān/ – Same as; in general

他和我一**般**高。

tā hé wǒ yī **bān** gāo.

He is the **same** height **as** me.

630- 普 /pǔ/ – Ordinary

我只是一个**普**通人。

wǒ zhǐ shì yī gè **pǔ** tōng rén.

I'm just an **ordinary** guy.

631- 怕 /pà/ – Afraid of, fear

我**怕**蜘蛛。

wǒ **pà** zhī zhū.

I'm **afraid of** spiders.

632- 弹 /tán/ – Play (an instrument)

她喜欢**弹**吉他。

tā xǐ huān **tán** jí tā.

She likes to **play** guitar.

633- 校 /xiào/ – School

学**校**在哪？

xué **xiào** zài nǎ?

Where is the **school**?

634- 苦 /kǔ/ – Bitter

这些叶子味道很**苦**。

zhè xiē yè zi wèi dào hěn **kǔ**.

The leaves taste **bitter**.

635- 创/chuàng/ – Create

是劳动**创**造了世界。

shì láo dòng **chuàng** zào le shì jiè.

It is labor that **creates** the world.

636- 假/jiǎ/ – Fake; suppose

这些是**假**钻石。

zhè xiē shì **jiǎ** zuàn shí.

These are **fake** diamonds.

637- 久/jiǔ/ – Long time

好**久**不见。

hǎo **jiǔ** bù jiàn.

Long time no see.

638- 错/cuò/ – Wrong; mistake

我**错**了。

wǒ **cuò** le.

I was **wrong**.

639- 承/chéng/ – To bear

冰太薄，**承**受不住你的重量。

bīng tài báo, **chéng** shòu bù zhù nǐ de zhòng liàng.

The ice is too thin to **bear** your weight.

640- 印/yìn/ – Print, seal

我想**印**些东西。

wǒ xiǎng **yìn** xiē dōng xī.

I want to **print** something.

641- 晚/wǎn/ – Night; late

你来**晚**了。

nǐ lái **wǎn** le.

You are **late**.

642- 兰/lán/ – Orchid

我从没种过兰花。

wǒ cóng méi zhòng guò **lán** huā.

I have never planted **orchids**.

643- 试/shì/ – Try; text, experiment

我**试试**吧。

wǒ **shì shì** ba.

I'll **try**.

644- 股/gǔ/ – Share

股价一直非常稳定。

gǔ jià yī zhí fēi cháng wěn dìng.

The **share** price remained fairly static.

645- 拿/ná/ – Take

我帮你**拿**外套。

wǒ bāng nǐ **ná** wài tào.

Let me **take** your coat.

646- 脑/nǎo/ – Brain

丧尸喜欢吃**脑**子。

sāng shī xǐ huān chī **nǎo** zi.

Zombies like to eat **brains**.

647- 预/yù/ – Beforehand

她怎么会**预**先知道我要出去？

tā zěn me huì **yù** xiān zhī dào wǒ yào chū qù?

How could she tell **beforehand** that I was going to go out?

648- 谁/shuí/ – Who

你是**谁**？

nǐ shì **shuí**?

Who are you?

649- 益 /yì/ – *Benefit*

双方都从谈判中获**益**。

shuāng fāng dōu cóng tán pàn zhōng huò **yì**.

Both sides have **benefited** from the negotiations.

650- 阳 /yáng/ – *Sun*

远处夕**阳**西下。

yuǎn chù xī **yáng** xī xià.

Far off to the west the **sun** was sinking.

651- 若 /ruò/ – *As, if*

若你热爱生活，生活就会厚爱你。

ruò nǐ rè ài shēng huó, shēng huó jiù huì hòu ài nǐ.

If you love life, life will love you back.

652- 哪 /nǎ/ – *Where*

你在**哪**？

nǐ zài **nǎ**?

Where are you?

653- 微 /wēi/ – *Tiny, trivial*

她有一个**微**小的手机。

tā yǒu yī gè **wēi** xiǎo de shǒu jī.

She has a **tiny** phone.

654- 尼 /ní/ – *(Buddhist) nun*

她最终还是做了**尼**姑。

tā zuì zhōng hái shì zuò le **ní** gū.

She eventually became a **nun**.

655- 继 /jì/ – *Inherit, continue*

他没有儿子**继**承田产。

tā méi yǒu ér zi **jì** chéng tián chǎn.

He has no son to **inherit** his land.

656- 送 /sòng/ – Send

我给经理**送**了一份副本。

wǒ gěi jīng lǐ **sòng** le yī fèn fù běn.

I **sent** a copy to the manager.

657- 急 /jí/ – Urgent, critical

情况紧**急**。

qíng kuàng jǐn **jí**.

The situation is **urgent**.

658- 血 /xiě/ – Blood

他用纸巾将**血**擦去。

tā yòng zhǐ jīn jiāng **xiě** cā qù.

He wiped away the **blood** with a napkin.

659- 惊 /jīng/ – Surprise

我很**惊**讶。

wǒ hěn **jīng** yà.

I'm **surprised**.

660- 伤 /shāng/ – Wound, injury

伤口正在愈合。

shāng kǒu zhèng zài yù hé.

The **wound** is healing.

661- 素 /sù/ – Element, vegetarian

健康已成为我们生活中的一个要**素**。

jiàn kāng yǐ chéng wéi wǒ men shēng huó zhōng de yī gè yào **sù**.

Fitness has become an important **element** in our lives.

662- 药 /yào/ – Medicine, drug

你现在该吃**药**了。

nǐ xiàn zài gāi chī **yào** le.

You should take the **medicine** now.

663- 适 /shì/ – *Suitable, proper*

她没有**适**合这种场合穿的裙装。

tā méi yǒu **shì** hé zhè zhǒng chǎng hé chuān de qún zhuāng.

She had no dress **suitable** for the occasion.

664- 波 /bō/ – *Wave*

地震的冲击**波**在这里都能感觉到。

dì zhèn de chōng jí **bō** zài zhè lǐ dōu néng gǎn jué dào.

The shocking **waves** of the earthquake were felt here.

665- 夜 /yè/ – *Night*

他一**夜**没合眼。

tā yī **yè** méi hé yǎn.

He didn't sleep a wink all **night**.

666- 省 /shěng/ – *Province; save*

中国有 32 个**省**。

zhōng guó yǒu 32 gè **shěng**.

China has 32 **provinces**.

667- 初 /chū/ – *Initial*

最**初**的反应非常好。

zuì **chū** de fǎn yìng fēi cháng hǎo.

The **initial** reaction was excellent.

668- 喜 /xǐ/ – *Like*

她**喜**欢唱歌。

tā **xǐ** huān chàng gē.

She **likes** singing.

669- 卫 /wèi/ – *Defend*

我们要保**卫**城市。

wǒ men yào bǎo **wèi** chéng shì.

We must **defend** the city.

670- 源 /yuán/ –Origin

我们应该追查谣言的**源**头。

wǒ men yīng gāi zhuī chá yáo yán de **yuán** tóu.

We should track the rumor back to its **origin**.

671- 食 /shí/ – Eat; food

中国有很多美**食**。

zhōng guó yǒu hěn duō měi **shí**.

There are many delicious **foods** in China.

672- 险 /xiǎn/ – Danger

他的生命可能有危**险**。

tā de shēng mìng kě néng yǒu wēi **xiǎn**.

His life could be in **danger**.

673- 待 /dài/ – Wait, treat

他们不应这样无礼地对**待**老师。

tā men bù yīng zhè yàng wú lǐ dì duì **dài** lǎo shī.

They shouldn't **treat** their teacher in this disrespectful way.

674- 述 /shù/ – Narrate

他们从三个视角讲**述**了同样的事。

tā men cóng sān gè shì jiǎo jiǎng **shù** le tóng yàng de shì.

They **narrate** the same events from three perspectives.

675- 陆 /lù/ – Continent

她热爱美洲大**陆**。

tā rè ài měi zhōu dà **lù**.

She loved the America **continent**.

676- 习 /xí/ – Pratice, study

他在练**习**英语口语。

tā zài liàn **xí** yīng yǔ kǒu yǔ.

He is **practicing** oral English.

677- 置/zhì/ – *Put, to place*

他将自己**置**于危险之地。

tā jiāng zì jǐ **zhì** yú wēi xiǎn zhī dì.

He was **putting** himself at risk.

678- 居/jū/ – *Reside*

玛丽**居**住在郊区。

mǎ lì **jū** zhù zài jiāo qū.

Mary **resides** in a suburb.

679- 劳/láo/ – *Labor*

他的**劳**动不需要很多技能。

tā de **láo** dòng bù xū yào hěn duō jì néng.

His **labor** did not require a great deal of skill.

680- 财/cái/ – *Wealth*

他的个人**财**富增长了。

tā de gè rén **cái** fù zēng zhǎng le.

His own **wealth** grew.

681- 环/huán/ – *Loop*

把绳子**环**绕在柱子上。

bǎ sheng zi **huán** rào zài zhù zi shàng.

Loop the rope around the pole.

682- 排/pái/ – *Row; set in order, line up*

她坐在前**排**。

tā zuò zài qián **pái**.

She was sitting in the front **row**.

683- 福/fú/ – *Happiness*

大家都羡慕他们的幸**福**。

dà jiā dōu xiàn mù tā men de xìng **fú**.

Everyone envies their **happiness**.

684- 纳/nà/ – Bring into, accept

他最终被他们接**纳**了。

tā zuì zhōng bèi tā men jiē **nà** le.

He was finally **accepted** by them.

685- 欢/huān/ – Joyous

她使他们的童年充满**欢**乐。

tā shǐ tā men de tóng nián chōng mǎn **huān** lè.

She made their childhood so **joyous**.

686- 雷/léi/ – Thunder

雷电交加，大雨倾盆。

léi diàn jiāo jiā, dà yǔ qīng pén.

There was frequent **thunder** and lightning, and torrential rain.

687- 警/jǐng/ – Alert, warn; police

他是一名**警**察。

tā shì yī míng **jǐng** chá.

He's a **police**man.

688- 获/huò/ – Obtain

让我们帮他**获**得政府的财政支持。

ràng wǒ men bāng tā **huò** dé zhèng fǔ de cái zhèng zhī chí.

Let's help him to **obtain** financial support from the government.

689- 模/mó/ – Model

她是个**模**范的专业人士。

tā shì gè **mó** fàn de zhuān yè rén shì.

She's a **model** professional.

690- 充/chōng/ – Fill, charge

他给汽车的电池**充**了电。

tā gěi qì chē de diàn chí **chōng** le diàn.

He **charged** the battery of his car.

691- 负 /fù/ – Defeat; to bear, carry (on the back)

该队以三胜一**负**的成绩排名小组第二。

gāi duì yǐ sān shèng yī **fù** de chéng jī pái míng xiǎo zǔ dì èr.

The team finished second in its group with three wins and one **defeat**.

692- 云 /yún/ – Cloud

天空被**云**遮蔽。

tiān kōng bèi **yún** zhē bì.

The sky was obscured by **cloud**.

693- 停 /tíng/ – Stop

停车！

tíng chē!

Stop the car!

694- 木 /mù/ – Wood

他们的盘子是**木**制的。

tā men de pán zi shì **mù** zhì de.

Their dishes were made of **wood**.

695- 游 /yóu/ – Swim

她喜欢**游**泳。

tā xǐ huān **yóu** yǒng.

She likes **swimming**.

696- 龙 /lóng/ – Dragon

他是屠**龙**者。

tā shì tú **lóng** zhě.

He is the **dragon** slayer.

697- 树 /shù/ – Tree

这些苹果**树**是我栽的。

zhè xiē píng guǒ **shù** shì wǒ zāi de.

I planted these apple **trees**.

698- 疑 /yí/ – Doubt

他们怀**疑**自己的人气。

tā men huái **yí** zì jǐ de rén qì.

They **doubt** their own popularity.

699- 层 /céng/ – Layer

街上覆盖了一**层**雪。

jiē shàng fù gài le yī **céng** xuě.

A **layer** of snow covered the street.

700- 冷 /lěng/ – Cold

我感觉好**冷**。

wǒ gǎn jué hǎo **lěng**.

I feel so **cold**.

701- 洲 /zhōu/ – Continent

他去过非**洲**大陆。

tā qù guò fēi **zhōu** dà lù.

He has been to the African **continent**.

702- 冲 /chōng/ – Flush, infuse

他总是忘记**冲**马桶。

tā zǒng shì wàng jì **chōng** mǎ tǒng.

He always forgets to **flush** the toilet.

703- 射 /shè/ – Shoot

他们开始向我们**射**击。

tā men kāi shǐ xiàng wǒ men **shè** jī.

They started **shooting** at us.

704- 略 /luè/ – Strategy; roughly

让人出丑不是我的策**略**。

ràng rén chū chǒu bù shì wǒ de cè **lüè**.

Making people feel foolish is not my **strategy**.

705- 范/fàn/ – Model

还是个小女孩时，她就是模**范**学生。

hái shì gè xiǎo nǔ hái shí, tā jiù shì mó **fàn** xué shēng.

As a girl, she had been a **model** pupil.

706- 竟/jìng/ – Unexpectedly, actually

你**竟**然做到了。

nǐ **jìng** rán zuò dào le.

You **actually** did it.

707- 句/jù/ – Sentence

这一**句**怎么翻译？

zhè yī **jù** zěn me fān yì?

How to translate this **sentence**?

708- 室/shì/ - Room

室内很安静。

shì nèi hěn ān jìng.

The **room** was quiet.

709- 异/yì/ – Different, unusual

她来自**异**国。

tā lái zì **yì** guó.

She came from a **different** country.

710- 激/jī/ – Excite, fierce

我很**激**动。

wǒ hěn **jī** dòng.

I'm so **excited**.

711- 汉/hàn/– Man

他是个勇敢的**汉**子。

tā shì gè yǒng gǎn de **hàn** zi.

He's a brave **man**.

712- 村 /cūn/ – *Village*

他来自一个小乡**村**。

tā lái zì yī gè xiǎo xiāng **cūn**.

He comes from a small **village**.

713- 哈 /hā/ – *Ha (sound of laughter)*

太有趣了，**哈哈**。

tài yǒu qù le, **hā hā**.

That's so funny, **haha**.

714- 策 /cè/ – *Policy*

计划生育曾是中国的国**策**。

jì huà shēng yù céng shì zhōng guó de guó **cè**.

Birth control used to be a national **policy** in China.

715- 演 /yǎn/ – *Act*

她向父母坦言了自己想**演**戏的愿望。

tā xiàng fù mǔ tǎn yán le zì jǐ xiǎng **yǎn** xì de yuan wàng.

She confessed to her parents her desire to **act**.

716- 简 /jiǎn/ – *Simple*

那很**简**单。

nà hěn **jiǎn** dān.

That's **simple**.

717- 卡 /kǎ/ – *Card*

我过生日时她寄来一张贺**卡**。

wǒ guò shēng rì shí tā jì lái yī zhāng hè **kǎ**.

She sends me a **card** on my birthday.

718- 罪 /zuì/ – *Sin, crime*

堕胎是种**罪**孽。

duò tāi shì zhǒng **zuì** niè.

Abortion is a **sin**.

719- 判/pàn/ – *To sentence*

他被**判**死刑。

tā bèi **pàn** sǐ xíng.

He was **sentenced** to death.

720- 担/dān/ – *Undertake*

她承**担**了监督选举的任务。

tā chéng **dān** le jiān dū xuǎn jǔ de rèn wù.

She **undertook** the task of monitoring the elections.

721- 州/zhōu/ – *State*

美国有多少个**州**？

měi guó yǒu duō shǎo gè **zhōu**?

How many **states** are there in the U.S.?

722- 静/jìng/ – *Quiet, calm*

保持安**静**。

bǎo chí ān **jìng**.

Keep **quiet**.

723- 退/tuì/ – *Retreat, move back*

我们需要撤**退**。

wǒ men xū yào chè **tuì**.

We need to **retreat**.

724- 既/jì/ – *Now that, since*

你**既**然来了，最好还是留下。

nǐ **jì** rán lái le, zuì hào hái shì liú xià.

Now that you are here, you'd better stay.

725- 衣/yī/ – *Clothes*

她回房间换**衣**服。

tā huí fáng jiān huàn **yī** fú.

She went back to the room to change **clothes**.

726- 您/nín/ – You (formal)

您贵姓?

nín guì xìng?

May I have **your** surname please?

727- 宗/zōng/ – Ancestor

人类和猿类有相同的祖**宗**。

rén lèi hé yuán lèi yǒu xiāng tóng de zǔ **zōng**.

Human and apes have the same **ancestor**.

728- 积/jī/ – Accumulate

铅会在体内**积**聚。

qiān huì zài tǐ nèi **jī** jù.

Lead can **accumulate** in the body.

729- 余/yú/ – Remaining

我们需要再次会面解决**余**下的分歧。

wǒ men xū yào zài cì huì miàn jiě jué **yú** xià de fēn qí.

We need to meet again to work out **remaining** differences.

730- 痛/tòng/ – Ache, pain

我头**痛**。

wǒ tóu **tòng**.

I have a head**ache**.

731- 检/jiǎn/ – Check

你的行李需要**检**查。

nǐ de xíng lǐ xū yào **jiǎn** chá.

Your baggage needs to be **checked**.

732- 差/chā/ – Difference; differ

两件样品**差**别不大。

liǎng jiàn yang pǐn **chā** bié bù dà.

There is little **difference** between the two samples.

733- 富 /fù/ – Rich

他是个**富**人。

tā shì gè **fù** rén.

He's a **rich** guy.

734- 灵 /líng/ – Soul

她是我的**灵**魂伴侣。

tā shì wǒ de **líng** hún bàn lǚ.

She's my **soul** mate.

735- 协 /xié/ – Assist

我们来这里**协**助你。

wǒ men lái zhè lǐ **xié** zhù nǐ.

We are here to **assist** you.

736- 角 /jiǎo/ – Angle, corner, horn

船正以 30 度**角**倾斜。

chuán zhèng yǐ 30 dù **jiǎo** qīng xié.

The boat is now leaning at a 30-degree **angle**.

737- 占 /zhàn/ – Occupy

哪怕很小的飞机也要**占**很大的空间。

nǎ pà hěn xiǎo de fēi jī yě yào **zhàn** hěn dà de kōng jiān.

Even quite small aircraft **occupies** a lot of space.

738- 配 /pèi/ – Match, deserve

她和我简直是绝**配**。

tā hé wǒ jiǎn zhí shì jué **pèi**.

She was a perfect **match** for me.

739- 征 /zhēng/ – Expedition; to conquer, recruit

英格兰曾被维京人**征**服。

yīng gé lán céng bèi wéi jīng rén **zhēng** fú.

England was once **conquered** by the Vikings.

740- 修 /xiū/ – *Repair*

许多建筑需要整**修**。

xǔ duō jiàn zhú xū yào zhěng **xiū**.

Many buildings are in need of **repair**.

741- 皮 /pí/ – *Skin*

她的**皮**肤十分光滑。

tā de **pí** fū shí fēn guāng huá.

Her **skin** is very smooth.

742- 挥 /huī/ – *To wave*

她向我**挥**手告别。

tā xiàng wǒ **huī** shǒu gào bié.

She **waved** goodbye to me.

743- 胜 /shèng/ – *Victory*

你**胜**利了。

nǐ **shèng** lì le.

Victory is yours.

744- 降 /xiáng/ – *Surrender*

我投**降**。

wǒ tóu **xiáng**.

I **surrender**.

745- 阶 /jiē/ – *Stairs, rank*

南希开始爬台**阶**。

nán xī kāi shǐ pá tái **jiē**.

Nancy began to climb the **stairs**.

746- 审 /shěn/ – *Investigate*

他觉得有必要作进一步**审**查。

tā jué dé yǒu bì yào zuò jìn yī bù **shěn** chá.

He felt impelled to **investigate** further.

747- 沉 /chén/ – *Sink, submerge; heavy*

船开始快速下**沉**。

chuán kāi shǐ kuài sù xià **chén**.

The boat was beginning to **sink** fast.

748- 坚 /jiān/ – *Strong*

你要**坚**强。

nǐ yào **jiān** qiáng.

You need to be **strong**.

749- 善 /shàn/ – *Good*

她是个**善**良的女孩。

tā shì gè **shàn** liáng de nǚ hái.

She's a **good** girl.

750- 妈 /mā/ – *Mom*

妈，我饿了。

mā, wǒ è le.

Mom, I'm hungry.

751- 刘 /liú/ – *Liu (surname)*

他姓**刘**。

tā xìng **liú**.

His surname is **Liu**.

752- 读 /dú/ – *Read*

你**读**过这本书吗？

nǐ **dú** guò zhè běn shū ma?

Have you **read** this book?

753- 啊 /ā/ – *Ah (interjection)*

啊！在那。

ā! zài nà.

Ah! That's it.

754- 超/chāo/ – Surpass

她才学**超**群。

tā cái xué **chāo** qún.

Her ability and learning **surpass** the average.

755- 免/miǎn/ – Exempt

大学在校生**免**服兵役。

dà xué zài xiào shēng **miǎn** fú bīng yì.

Students in college were **exempt** from military service.

756- 压/yā/ – Press; pressure

你能在**压**力下工作吗?

nǐ néng zài **yā** lì xià gōng zuò ma?

Can you work under **pressure**?

757- 银/yín/ – Silver

这对夫妻去年庆祝了他们的**银**婚。

zhè duì fū qī qù nián qìng zhù le tā men de **yín** hūn.

The couple celebrated their **silver** wedding last year.

758- 买/mǎi/ – Buy

我想**买**本书。

wǒ xiǎng **mǎi** běn shū.

I want to **buy** a book.

759- 皇/huáng/ – Royal

他在**皇**家海军服役。

tā zài **huáng** jiā hǎi jūn fú yì.

He spent his national service in the **Royal** Navy.

760- 养/yǎng/ – Raise, bring up

她**养**大了四个孩子。

tā **yǎng** dà le sì gè hái zi.

She **brought up** four children.

761- 伊/yī/ – *That person*

所谓**伊**人，在水一方。

suǒ wèi **yī** rén, zài shuǐ yī fāng.

That person of whom I think, is on the water somewhere.

762- 怀/huái/ – *Bosom, in arms*

他把一本小册子抱在**怀**里。

tā bǎ yī běn xiǎo cè zi bào zài **huái** lǐ.

He kept a little book in his **arms**.

763- 执/zhí/ – *Execute*

我们将**执**行该计划。

wǒ men jiāng **zhí** xíng gāi jì huà.

We're going to **execute** the plan.

764- 副/fù/ – *Deputy*

她是这家公司的**副**经理。

tā shì zhè jiā gōng sī de **fù** jīng lǐ.

She is the **deputy** manager of this company.

765- 乱/luàn/ – *Riot; disorder*

两名犯人在一场监狱暴**乱**中被杀害。

liǎng míng fàn rén zài yī chǎng jiān yù bào **luàn** zhōng bèi shā hài.

Two inmates were killed during a **riot** at the prison.

766- 抗/kàng/ – *Resist*

我无法**抗**拒。

wǒ wú fǎ **kàng** jù.

I can't **resist** it.

767- 犯/fàn/ – *Criminal, inmate*

囚**犯**骗过警卫逃跑了。

qiú **fàn** piàn guò jǐng wèi táo pǎo le.

The **inmate** outwitted his guards and escaped.

768- 追/zhuī/ – Chase

她**追**了窃贼 100 码远。

tā **zhuī** le qiè zéi 100 mǎ yuǎn.

She **chased** the thief for 100 yards.

769- 帮/bāng/ – Help

需要**帮**助吗？

xū yào **bāng** zhù ma?

Can I **help** you?

770- 宣/xuān/ – Declare, announce

政府已向邻国**宣**战。

zhèng fǔ yǐ xiàng lín guó **xuān** zhàn.

The government has **declared** war on the neighboring country.

771- 佛/fó/ – Buddha

他向**佛**叩拜。

tā xiàng **fó** kòu bài.

He kowtowed to **Buddha**.

772- 岁/suì/ – Year, age

我儿子八**岁**了。

wǒ ér zi bā **suì** le.

My son is eight **years** old.

773- 航/háng/ – Sail, navigate

这种船可以在尼罗河上**航**行。

zhè zhǒng chuán kě yǐ zài ní luó hé shàng **háng** xíng.

Such boats can **navigate** on the Nile.

774- 优/yōu/ – Excellent

我不是一个**优**秀的作家。

wǒ bù shì yī gè **yōu** xiù de zuò jiā.

I'm not an **excellent** writer.

775- 怪 /guài/ – Odd; blame

真奇**怪**。

zhēn qí **guài**.

That's **odd**.

776- 香 /xiāng/ – Fragrant

空气里弥漫着花**香**。

kōng qì lǐ mí màn zhe huā **xiāng**.

The air was **fragrant** with the smell of blossoms.

777- 著 /zhù/ – Writings; write

这本书是他的**著**作之一。

zhè běn shū shì tā de **zhù** zuò zhī yī.

This book is one of his **writings**.

778- 田 /tián/ – Field

他们一起在**田**野里漫步。

tā men yī qǐ zài **tián** yě lǐ màn bù.

They went for walks together in the **fields**.

779- 铁 /tiě/ – Iron

铁门紧锁着。

tiě mén jǐn suǒ zhe.

The **iron** gate was locked.

780- 控 /kòng/ – Control, accuse

他的车失**控**了。

tā de chē shī **kòng** le.

He lost **control** of his car.

781- 税 /shuì/ – Tax

没人喜欢交**税**。

méi rén xǐ huān jiāo **shuì**.

No one enjoys paying **tax**.

782- 左/zuǒ/ – *Left*

向**左**转。

xiàng **zuǒ** zhuǎn.

Turn **left**.

783- 右/yòu/ – *Right*

向**右**转。

xiàng **yòu** zhuǎn.

Turn **right**.

784- 份/fèn/ – *Portion*

甜点可以用一**份**新鲜水果代替。

tián diǎn kě yǐ yòng yī **fèn** xīn xiān shuǐ guǒ dài tì.

Desserts can be substituted by a **portion** of fresh fruit.

785- 穿/chuān/ – *Wear*

我每天都**穿**那双旧鞋。

wǒ měi tiān dōu **chuān** nà shuāng jiù xié.

I **wear** my old shoes every day.

786- 艺/yì/ – *Art*

他是个**艺**术家。

tā shì gè **yì** shù jiā.

He's an **art**ist.

787- 背/bèi/ – *Back*

她转过身**背**对观众。

tā zhuǎn guò shēn **bèi** duì guān zhòng.

She turned her **back** to the audience.

788- 阵/zhèn/ – *Array*

我们的部队已严**阵**以待。

wǒ men de bù duì yǐ yán **zhèn** yǐ dài.

Our troops were drawn up in battle **array**.

118

789- 草 /cǎo/ – Grass

我要去修剪**草**坪。

wǒ yào qù xiū jiǎn **cǎo** píng.

I'm going to cut the **grass**.

790- 脚 /jiǎo/ – Foot

他被火车撞上失去了一只**脚**。

tā bèi huǒ chē zhuàng shàng shī qù le yī zhǐ **jiǎo**.

He lost a **foot** when he was struck by a train.

791- 概 /gài/ – General, approximate

他大**概**下个月出发。

tā dà **gài** xià gè yuè chū fā.

The **approximate** date of his departure is next month.

792- 恶 /è/ – Evil

她是个邪**恶**的女人。

tā shì gè xié **è** de nǚ rén.

She's an **evil** woman.

793- 块 /kuài/ – Piece

你能给我一**块**蛋糕吗？

nǐ néng gěi wǒ yī **kuài** dàn gāo ma?

Can you give me a **piece** of cake?

794- 顿 /dùn/ – Pause

他稍稍**顿**了一下。

tā shāo shāo **dùn** le yī xià.

He **paused** ever so slightly.

795- 敢 /gǎn/ – Dare

他们怎么**敢**做出这样的事？

tā men zěn me **gǎn** zuò chū zhè yàng de shì?

How **dare** they do something like this?

796- 守/shǒu/ – Defend

他决心**守**卫山谷。

tā jué xīn **shǒu** wèi shān gǔ.

He was committed to **defend** the valley.

797- 酒/jiǔ/ – Liquor

房间里堆满了整箱的**酒**。

fáng jiān lǐ duī mǎn le zhěng xiāng de **jiǔ**.

The room was filled with cases of **liquor**.

798- 岛/dǎo/ – Island

日本是个**岛**国。

rì běn shì gè **dǎo** guó.

Japan is an **island** country.

799- 托/tuō/ – Hold, entrust, support

我愿把终身**托**付给他。

wǒ yuàn bǎ zhōng shēn **tuō** fù gěi tā.

I'd **entrust** my life to him.

800- 央/yāng/ – Center; to beg, plead

他跪在地上**央**求宽恕。

tā guì zài dì shàng **yāng** qiú kuān shù.

He was kneeling on the floor **pleading** for mercy.

801- 户/hù/ – Household

全村共三十**户**。

quán cūn gòng sān shí **hù**.

There are thirty **households** in the village.

802- 烈/liè/ – Fierce

他的话遭到激**烈**反对。

tā de huà zāo dào jī **liè** fǎn duì.

What he said met with **fierce** opposition.

803- 洋 /yáng/ – Ocean

他们在太平洋航行了很多天。

tā men zài tài píng **yáng** háng xíng le hěn duō tiān.

They spent many days cruising the Pacific **Ocean**.

804- 哥 /gē/ – Elder brother

他是我哥。

tā shì wǒ **gē**.

He's my **elder brother**.

805-索 /suǒ/ – Ask for

他向我索取钱财。

tā xiàng wǒ **suǒ** qǔ qián cái.

He **asked** me **for** money.

806- 胡 /hú/ – Beard

比尔精心修剪了胡子。

bǐ ěr jīng xīn xiū jiǎn le **hú** zi.

Bill preened his **beard**.

807- 款 /kuǎn/ – Fund

我需要这笔款。

wǒ xū yào zhè bǐ **kuǎn**.

I need the **fund**.

808- 靠 /kào/ – Depend on, lean on

全靠你了。

quán **kào** nǐ le.

I'm **depending on** you.

809- 评 /píng/ – Comment

他没有对我们的提议作评论。

tā méi yǒu duì wǒ men de tí yì zuò **píng** lùn.

He made no **comments** on our proposal.

810- 版 /bǎn/ – *Edition, version*

他有这本书的新**版**。

tā yǒu zhè běn shū de xīn **bǎn**.

He has an updated **version** of this book.

811- 宝 /bǎo/ – *Treasure, precious*

他们到山洞寻找**宝**藏。

tā men dào shān dòng xún zhǎo **bǎo** zàng.

They went to the cave in quest of hidden **treasure**.

812- 座 /zuò/ – *Seat*

这是我的**座**位。

zhè shì wǒ de **zuò** wèi.

This is my **seat**.

813- 释 /shì/ – *Release*

他们**释放**了俘虏。

tā men **shì fàng** le fú lǔ.

They **released** the prisoners.

814- 景 /jǐng/ – *Scenery*

那里的风**景**美得无法形容。

nà lǐ de fēng **jǐng** měi dé wú fǎ xíng róng.

The **scenery** is beautiful beyond description.

815- 顾 /gù/ – *Look after*

我喜欢照**顾**小孩。

wǒ xǐ huān zhào **gù** xiǎo hái.

I love **looking after** the children.

816- 弟 /dì/ – *Young brother*

他是我**弟**。

tā shì wǒ **dì**.

He is my **young brother**.

817- 登 /dēng/ – Ascend

我们**登**上了那座山。

wǒ men **dēng** shàng le nà zuò shān.

We **ascended** that mountain.

818- 货 /huò/ – Goods

货已由铁路托运到你处。

huò yǐ yóu tiě lù tuō yùn dào nǐ chù.

The **goods** were consigned to you by railway.

819- 互 /hù/ – Mutual

让我们相**互**支持。

ràng wǒ men xiāng **hù** zhī chí.

Let's give **mutual** support to each other.

820- 付 /fù/ – Pay

我想用信用卡**付**钱。

wǒ xiǎng yòng xìn yòng kǎ **fù** qián.

I'd like to **pay** with my credit card.

821- 伯 /bó/ – Uncle (father's elder brother)

这是我大**伯**。

zhè shì wǒ dà **bó.**

This is my **uncle**.

822- 慢 /màn/ – Slow

慢点！

màn diǎn!

Slow down!

823- 欧洲 /ōu zhōu / – Europe

她来自**欧洲**。

tā lái zì **ōu zhōu**.

She's from **Europe**.

824- 换 /huàn/ – *Change*

你**换**水了吗？

nǐ **huàn** shuǐ le ma?

Have you **changed** the water?

825- 闻 /wén/ – *To smell*

我**闻**得出牛奶不新鲜。

wǒ **wén** dé chū niú nǎi bù xīn xiān.

I could **smell** that the milk was not fresh.

826- 危 /wēi/ – *Endanger; danger*

该地的开发将**危**及野生生物。

gāi dì de kāi fā jiāng **wēi** jí yě shēng shēng wù.

Development of the area would **endanger** wildlife.

827- 忙 /máng/ – *Busy*

我很**忙**。

wǒ hěn **máng**.

I'm **busy**.

828- 核 /hé/ – *Nuclear; verify*

他们决定建一所**核**电站。

tā men jué dìng jiàn yī suǒ **hé** diàn zhàn.

They decided to establish a **nuclear** power station.

829- 暗 /àn/ – *Dark*

在**暗**处阅读对眼睛不好。

zài **àn** chù yuè dú duì yǎn jīng bù hǎo.

Reading in the **dark** is bad for the eyes.

830- 姐 /jiě/ – *Elder sister*

这是我**姐**。

zhè shì wǒ **jiě**.

This is my **elder sister**.

831- 介/jiè/ – Introduce; between

你能把我**介**绍给她吗？

nǐ néng bǎ wǒ **jiè** shào gěi tā ma?

Can you **introduce** me to her?

832- 坏/huài/ – Bad, broken

他是个**坏**人。

tā shì gè **huài** rén.

He's a **bad** guy.

833- 讨论/tǎo lùn/ – Discuss

我需要和父母**讨论**一下。

wǒ xū yào hé fù mǔ **tǎo lùn** yī xià.

I need to **discuss** with my parents.

834- 丽/lì/ – Beautiful

她美**丽**动人。

tā měi **lì** dòng rén.

She's **beautiful** and attractive.

835- 良/liáng/ – Good

机器状态**良**好。

jī qì zhuàng tài **liáng** hǎo.

The machine is in **good** condition.

836- 序/xù/ – Order, sequence

请有**序**排队。

qǐng yǒu **xù** pái duì.

Please line up in **order**.

837- 升/shēng/ – Liter; rise

这个瓶子装一**升**。

zhè ge píng zi zhuāng yī **shēng**.

This bottle holds one **liter**.

838- 监 /jiān/ – *Supervise*

我**监**督工人把货物装上卡车。

wǒ **jiān** dū gōng rén bǎ huò wù zhuāng shàng kǎ chē.

I **supervised** the workers loading the lorry.

839- 临 /lín/ – *Adjacent; to face*

中国东**临**太平洋。

zhōng guó dōng **lín** tài píng yáng.

China **faces** the Pacific on the east.

840- 亮 /liàng/ – *Bright*

这座宫殿在明**亮**的月光下显得光彩夺目。

zhè zuò gōng diàn zài míng **liàng** de yuè guāng xià xiǎn dé guāng cǎi duó mù.

The **bright** moonlight showed the palace in all its glory.

841- 露 /lù/ – *Dew*

露水在叶子上凝结。

lù shuǐ zài yè zi shàng níng jié.

The **dew** gathered on the leaves.

842- 永 /yǒng/ – *Always*

我**永**远爱你。

wǒ **yǒng** yuǎn ài nǐ.

I have **always** loved you.

843- 呼 /hū/ – *Shout, call*

他大声**呼**叫他的妻子。

tā dà shēng **hū** jiào tā de qī zi.

He **called** out for his wife.

844- 味 /wèi/ – *Taste, smell*

那是什么**味**道？

nà shì shén me **wèi** dào?

What's that **smell**?

845- 野 /yě/ – Field, wild

许多农民在田**野**里干活。

xǔ duō nóng mín zài tián **yě** lǐ gàn huó.

Many farmers are working in the **fields**.

846- 架 /jià/ – Frame, rack, shelf

他把鞋放在**架**子上。

tā bǎ xié fàng zài **jià** zi shàng.

He put his shoes on the **rack**.

847- 域 /yù/ – Area

我们将在该区**域**建一所学校。

wǒ men jiāng zài gāi qū **yù** jiàn yī suǒ xué xiào.

We are going to build a school in this **area**.

848- 沙 /shā/ – Sand

干**沙**吸收水分。

gān **shā** xī shōu shuǐ fèn.

Dry **sand** absorbs water.

849- 掉 /diào/ – To drop, lose

我钱包**掉**了。

wǒ qián bāo **diào** le.

I **lost** my wallet.

850- 括 /kuò/ – Include

他的作品包**括**诗和散文。

tā de zuò pǐn bāo **kuò** shī hé sǎn wén.

His writings **include** poetry and prose.

851- 舰 /jiàn/ – Warship

海军上将命令所有战**舰**开火。

hǎi jūn shàng jiàng mìng lìng suǒ yǒu zhàn **jiàn** kāi huǒ.

The admiral ordered all the **warships** to fire.

852- 钓鱼 /diào yú/ – Fish

我们去**钓鱼**吧。
wǒ men qù **diào yú** ba.
Let's go **fish**ing.

853- 杂 /zá/ – Mix

你不能把油和水混**杂**在一起。
nǐ bù néng bǎ yóu hé shuǐ hùn **zá** zài yī qǐ.
You can't **mix** oil with water.

854- 误 /wù/ – Mistake, error

我犯了个错**误**。
wǒ fàn le gè cuò **wù**.
I made a **mistake**.

855- 湾 /wān/ – Bay

阳光在海**湾**的水面上闪烁。
yang guāng zài hǎi **wān** de shuǐ miàn shàng shǎn shuò.
Sunlight shimmers on the waters of the **bay**.

856- 吉 /jí/ – Luck

为了图**吉**利，他一直保存着这尊佛像。
wèi le tú **jí** lì, tā yī zhí bǎo cún zhe zhè zūn fó xiàng.
He kept the figure of Buddha for **luck**.

857- 减 /jiǎn/ – Subtract, decrease

他们设法**减**少成本。
tā men shè fǎ **jiǎn** shǎo chéng běn.
They tried to **decrease** the costs.

858- 编 /biān/ – Edit, weave, compile

我试着把所有想法**编**织在一起。
wǒ shì zhe bǎ suǒ yǒu xiǎng fǎ **biān** zhī zài yī qǐ.
I try to **weave** all of the concepts together.

859- 楚/chǔ/ – Clear

我清**楚**地告诉他，我拒绝了他的提议。

wǒ qīng **chǔ** de gào sù tā, wǒ jù jué le tā de tí yì.

I made it **clear** to him that I rejected his proposal.

860- 肯/kěn/ – Willing

你**肯**帮忙吗？

nǐ **kěn** bang máng ma?

Are you **willing** to help?

861- 测/cè/ – To measure

他们**测**量了天花板的高度。

tā men **cè** liáng le tiān huā bǎn de gāo dù.

They **measured** the height of the ceiling.

862- 败/bài/ – Defeat, fail

失**败**让他沮丧。

shī **bài** ràng tā jǔ sàng.

He was depressed by his **defeat**.

863- 屋/wū/ – House, room

我喜欢这间**屋**子。

wǒ xǐ huān zhè jiān **wū** zi.

I like this **room**.

864- 跑/pǎo/ – Run

她**跑**了。

tā **pǎo** le.

She **ran** away.

865- 梦/mèng/ – Dream

他**梦**到了克莱尔。

tā **mèng** dào le kè lái ěr.

He had a **dream** about Claire.

866- 散 /sàn/ – *Scatter, disperse*

油好像在扩**散**。

yóu hǎo xiàng zài kuò **sàn**.

The oil appeared to be **dispersing**.

867- 温 /wēn/ – *Warm*

室内很**温**暖。

shì nèi hěn **wēn** nuǎn.

It's **warm** in the room.

868- 困 /kùn/ – *Sleepy; to trap*

我**困**了。

wǒ **kùn** le.

I'm **sleepy**.

869- 剑 /jiàn/ – *Sword*

我喜欢这把**剑**。

wǒ xǐ huān zhè bǎ **jiàn**.

I like this **sword**.

870- 渐 /jiàn/ – *Gradually*

海水逐**渐**侵蚀了陆地。

hǎi shuǐ zhú **jiàn** qīn shí le lù dì.

The sea is **gradually** encroaching on the land.

871- 封 /fēng/ – *Seal*

这个瓶子上的**封**条破了。

zhè ge píng zi shàng de **fēng** tiáo pò le.

The **seal** on this bottle is broken.

872- 救 /jiù/ – *Save*

你**救**了我的命！

nǐ **jiù** le wǒ de mìng!

You **saved** my life!

873- 贵/guì/ – *Expensive*

太**贵**了！

tài **guì** le!

That's too **expensive**!

874- 枪/qiāng/ – *Gun*

中国禁**枪**。

zhōng guó jìn **qiāng**.

Guns are forbidden in China.

875- 缺/quē/ – *Lack*

我们**缺**少食物。

wǒ men **quē** shǎo shí wù.

We **lacked** food.

876- 楼/lóu/ – *(A storied) building*

这栋**楼**朝北。

zhè dòng **lóu** cháo běi.

The **building** faces north.

877- 县/xiàn/ – *County*

他被选为**县**里的警长。

tā bèi xuǎn wèi **xiàn** lǐ de jǐng zhǎng.

He was elected sheriff of the **county**.

878- 尚/shàng/ – *Still, yet; advocate*

这项政策**尚**未成为法律。

zhè xiàng zhèng cè **shàng** wèi chéng wéi fǎ lǜ.

This policy has not **yet** become law.

879- 毫/háo/ – *Hair of animal; milli-*

我们以**毫**米测量雨量。

wǒ men yǐ **háo** mǐ cè liáng yǔ liàng.

We measure rainfall by the **milli**meter.

880- 移 /yí/ – To move, to shift

会议从巴黎**移**到伦敦。

huì yì cóng bā lí **yí** dào lún dūn.

The meeting has been **moved** from Paris to London.

881- 姑娘 /gū niáng/ – Personal pronoun for female

她还是个**小姑娘**。

tā hái shì gè **xiǎo gū niáng.**

She's still **a little girl.**

882- 朋 /péng/ – Friend

我有很多**朋**友。

wǒ yǒu hěn duō **péng** yǒu.

I have lots of **friends.**

883- 画 /huà/ - Picture, painting; paint

我喜欢这幅**画**。

wǒ xǐ huān zhè fú **huà.**

I like this **painting.**

884- 班 /bān/ – Shift, squad

他们轮流值夜**班**。

tā men lún liú zhí yè **bān.**

They were taking turns to be on the night **shift.**

885- 智 /zhì/ – Wisdom

他认为他的**智**慧来自书本。

tā rèn wéi tā de **zhì** huì lái zì shū běn.

He attributes his **wisdom** to books.

886- 亦 /yì/ – Also

有朋自远方来，不**亦**乐乎？

yǒu péng zì yuǎn fāng lái, bù **yì** lè hū?

Meeting a friend coming from afar is **also** a joyful thing, isn't it?

887- 耳 /ěr/ – Ear

他在她**耳**边低声说了些什么。

tā zài tā **ěr** biān dī shēng shuō le xiē shén me.

He whispered something in her **ear**.

888- 恩 /ēn/ – Kindness

你的**恩**情我无以言表。

nǐ de **ēn** qíng wǒ wú yǐ yán biǎo.

Your **kindness** quite overwhelmed me.

889- 短 /duǎn/ – Short

夏天留**短**发很凉快。

xià tiān liú **duǎn** fǎ hěn liáng kuài.

Short hair is cool in summer.

890- 掌 /zhǎng/ – Palm of the hand

他把电话号码写在手**掌**上。

tā bǎ diàn huà hào mǎ xiě zài shǒu **zhǎng** shàng.

He wrote the phone number on his **palm**.

891- 恐 /kǒng/ – Afraid, frightened

恐怕不成。

kǒng pà bù chéng.

I'm **afraid** it won't do.

892- 遗 /yí/ – Bequeath, leave

他**遗**下一妻二子。

tā **yí** xià yī qī èr zi.

He **left** a wife and two sons.

893- 固 /gù/ – Solid

冰是水的**固**体状态。

bīng shì shuǐ de **gù** tǐ zhuàng tài.

Ice is water in **solid** state.

894- 席 /xí/ – Seat, banquet, woven mat

经理应邀在宴**席**上讲了话。

jīng lǐ yìng yāo zài yàn **xí** shàng jiǎng le huà.

The manager was called on to speak at the **banquet**.

895- 松 /sōng/ – Pine; Loose

松树不畏严寒。

sōng shù bù wèi yán hán.

The **pine** trees defy severe cold.

896- 秘 /mì/ – Secret

我会告诉你一个**秘**密。

wǒ huì gào sù nǐ yī gè **mì** mì.

I'll tell you a **secret**.

897- 谢 /xiè/ – Thank

多**谢**。

duō **xiè**.

Thanks a lot.

898- 鲁 /lǔ/ – Rude

他是个粗**鲁**的人。

tā shì gè cū **lǔ** de rén.

He's a **rude** guy.

899- 遇 /yù/ – Meet, encounter

我在罗马**遇**到一个老朋友。

wǒ zài luó mǎ **yù** dào yī gè lǎo péng yǒu.

I **encountered** an old friend at Rome.

900- 康 /kāng/ – Healthy

他是个很健**康**的男孩。

tā shì gè hěn jiàn **kāng** de nán hái.

He's a very **healthy** boy.

901- 虑/lǜ/ – Anxiety

他的焦**虑**难以掩饰。

tā de jiāo **lǜ** nán yǐ yǎn shì.

It proved difficult to disguise his **anxiety**.

902- 幸/xìng/ – Lucky

你是个**幸**运的家伙。

nǐ shì gè **xìng** yùn de jiā huo.

You are a **lucky** guy.

903- 均/jūn/ – Even, average

4、6、8 的平**均**数是 6.

4,6,8 de píng **jūn** shù shì 6.

The **average** of 4, 6 and 8 is 6.

904- 销/xiāo/ – Sell, cancel

我们的产品在世界各地的多个国家**销**售。

wǒ men de chǎn pǐn zài shì jiè gè dì de duō gè guó jiā **xiāo** shòu.

Our products **sell** in many countries in the world.

905- 钟/zhōng/ – Clock

时**钟**的针指着两点半。

shí **zhōng** de zhēn zhǐ zhe liǎng diǎn bàn.

The **clock** shows half past two.

906- 诗/shī/ – Poem

这首**诗**由三部分组成。

zhè shǒu **shī** yóu sān bù fèn zǔ chéng.

The **poem** is composed of three sections.

907- 藏/cáng/ – Hide

他**藏**在哪儿？

tā **cáng** zài nǎ er?

Where is he **hiding**?

908- 赶 /gǎn/ – *Catch up*

我会**赶**上你，先走吧。

wǒ huì **gǎn** shàng nǐ, xiān zǒu ba.

You go on, I will **catch** you **up**.

909- 剧 /jù/ – *Drama*

我对戏**剧**不感兴趣。

wǒ duì xì **jù** bù gǎn xìng qù.

I have no interest in **drama**.

910- 票 /piào/ – *Ticket*

你拿到火车**票**了吗？

nǐ ná dào huǒ chē **piào** le ma?

Have you got your train **ticket**?

911- 损 /sǔn/ – *Damage, harm*

暴风雨并未造成严重**损**失。

bào fēng yǔ bìng wèi zào chéng yán zhòng **sǔn** shī.

The storm didn't do much **damage**.

912- 忽 /hū/ – *Suddenly; ignore*

他**忽**然开始大喊。

tā **hū** rán kāi shǐ dà hǎn.

He **suddenly** began to shout.

913- 巨 /jù/ – *Huge*

鲸是**巨**大的动物。

jīng shì **jù** dà de dòng wù.

A whale is a **huge** animal.

914- 炮 /pào/ – *Cannon*

士兵们开**炮**。

shì bīng men kāi **pào.**

The soldier fired the **cannon**.

915- 旧/jiù/ – Old

我非常喜欢这个旧包。

wǒ fēi cháng xǐ huān zhè ge **jiù** bāo.

I like this **old** bag very much.

916- 端/duān/ – Hold; end

请帮我**端**一下。

qǐng bāng wǒ **duān** yī xià.

Please help me to **hold** it.

917- 探/tàn/ – Explore

我们必须**探**讨所有的可能性。

wǒ men bì xū **tàn** tǎo suǒ yǒu de kě néng xìng.

We must **explore** all the possibilities.

918- 湖/hú/ – Lake

他掉进了**湖**里。

tā diào jìn le **hú** lǐ.

He fell into the **lake**.

919- 录/lù/ – Record

我**录**了他的演讲。

wǒ **lù** le tā de yǎn jiǎng.

I **recorded** his lecture.

920- 叶/yè/ – Leaf

叶子落了。

yè zi luò le.

Leaves fell off.

921- 春/chūn/ – Spring

春天来了。

chūn tiān lái le.

Spring is here.

922- 乡 /xiāng/ – *Village*

她来自一个小**乡**村。

tā lái zì yī gè xiǎo **xiāng** cūn.

She comes from a small **village**.

923- 附 /fù/ – *Attach*

我**附**上笔记一份以供参考。

wǒ **fù** shàng bǐ jì yī fèn yǐ gōng cān kǎo.

I **attached** a copy of notes for your information.

924- 吸 /xī/ – *Suck, inhale*

他深深**吸**了口气。

tā shēn shēn **xī** le kǒu qì.

He **inhaled** deeply.

925- 予 /yǔ/ – *Give*

这是他给**予**我的。

zhè shì tā jǐ **yǔ** wǒ de.

This is what he **gave** me.

926- 礼 /lǐ/ – *Gift*

这是送你的**礼**物。

zhè shì sòng nǐ de **lǐ** wù.

This is a **gift** for you.

927- 港 /gǎng/ – *Port, harbor*

我们的船今晚出**港**。

wǒ men de chuán jīn wǎn chū **gǎng**.

Our ship leaves **port** tonight.

928- 雨 /yǔ/ – *Rain*

要下**雨**了。

yào xià **yǔ** le.

It is going to **rain**.

929- 呀 /ya/ – Particle expressing surprise or doubt

是你呀！

shì nǐ **ya**!

It's you!

930- 板 /bǎn/ – Plate, board

木匠在刨一块木板。

mù jiàng zài páo yī kuài mù **bǎn**.

The carpenter was shaving a **board**.

931- 庭 /tíng/ – Courtyard

他们进入了庭院。

tā men jìn rù le **tíng** yuàn.

They entered the **courtyard**.

932- 妇 /fù/ – Woman

她是职业妇女而不是家庭主妇。

tā shì zhí yè **fù** nǚ ér bù shì jiā tíng zhǔ **fù**.

She's a career **woman** rather than a housewife.

933- 归 /guī/ – Return

请把它归还给我。

qǐng bǎ tā **guī** huán gěi wǒ.

Please **return** it to me.

934- 睛 /jīng/ – Eye

他在战争中失去了一只眼睛。

tā zài zhàn zhēng zhōng shī qù le yī zhī yǎn **jīng**.

He lost an **eye** in the war.

935- 饭 /fàn/ – Meal

我们吃了一顿便饭。

wǒ men chī le yī dùn biàn **fàn**.

We had a plain **meal**.

936- 额 /é/ – Forehead

他**额**头很宽。

tā **é** tóu hěn kuān.

He has a broad **forehead**.

937- 含 /hán/ – Contain

海水**含**有盐分。

hǎi shuǐ **hán** yǒu yán fèn.

Sea water **contains** salt.

938- 顺 /shùn/ – Obey, follow

狗**顺**从它的主人。

gǒu **shùn** cóng tā de zhǔ rén.

The dog **obeyed** his master.

939- 输 /shū/ – Lose

你要**输**了。

nǐ yào **shū** le.

You are **losing**.

940- 摇 /yáo/ – Shake

他**摇**头表示反对。

tā **yáo** tóu biǎo shì fǎn duì.

He **shook** his head in disapproval.

941- 招 /zhāo/ – Beckon, recruit, confess

他**招**呼服务员过来。

tā **zhāo** hū fú wù yuán guò lái.

He **beckoned** to the waitress.

942- 婚 /hūn/ – Marriage

婚姻是终身大事。

hūn yīn shì zhōng shēn dà shì.

Marriage is for life.

943- 脱 /tuō/ – *Take off*

你最好别**脱**衣服。

nǐ zuì hǎo bié **tuō** yī fú.

You'd better not **take off** your clothes.

944- 补 /bǔ/ – *Patch, mend*

他**补**了几条车胎。

tā **bǔ** le jǐ tiáo chē tāi.

He **patched** up a couple of tires.

945- 谓 /wèi/ – *To call, designate*

此之**谓**形式主义。

cǐ zhī **wèi** xíng shì zhǔ yì.

This is **called** formalism.

946- 督 /dū/ – *Supervise*

市场需要国家监**督**。

shì chǎng xū yào guó jiā jiān **dū**.

The market needs to be **supervised** by the nation.

947- 毒 /dú/ – *Poison*

他曾试图服**毒**自杀。

tā céng shì tú fú **dú** zì shā.

He tried to kill himself by taking **poison**.

948- 油 /yóu/ – *Oil*

油和水无法相溶。

yóu hé shuǐ wú fǎ xiāng róng.

Oil and water do not mix.

949- 疗 /liáo/ – *Treat; therapy*

该**疗**法不会立即见效。

gāi **liáo** fǎ bù huì lì jí jiàn xiào.

The **therapy** does not cure at once.

950- 旅/lǚ/ – *Trip, travel*

她喜欢**旅**行。

tā xǐ huān **lǚ** xíng.

She likes **travel**.

951- 泽/zé/ – *Swamp*

我们在沼**泽**地受到蚊子的围攻。

wǒ men zài zhǎo **zé** dì shòu dào wén zi de wéi gōng.

In the **swamp**, we were beset by mosquitoes.

952- 材/cái/ – *Material*

这种**材**质质地均匀。

zhè zhǒng **cái** zhì zhì dì jūn yún.

This **material** is homogeneous.

953- 灭/miè/ – *Wipe out, extinguish*

只有这样我们才能消**灭**敌人。

zhǐ yǒu zhè yàng wǒ men cái néng xiāo **miè** dí rén.

Only in this way can we **wipe out** the enemy.

954- 逐/zhú/ – *Pursue; one by one*

他们**逐**个走了出去。

tā men **zhú** gè zǒu le chū qù.

They went out **one by one**.

955- 莫/mò/ – *Not, nothing, no*

莫之能御。

mò zhī néng yù.

Nothing can resist it.

956- 笔/bǐ/ – *Pen*

我买了一只新**笔**。

wǒ mǎi le yī zhǐ xīn **bǐ**.

I bought a new **pen**.

957- 亡 /wáng/ – Deceased, dead; die

宁可自**亡**，不可行凶。

nìng kě zì **wáng**, bù kě xíng xiōng.

It is better to **die** oneself than to kill.

958- 鲜 /xiān/ – Fresh

这肉不新**鲜**。

zhè ròu bù xīn **xiān**.

The meat is not **fresh**.

959- 词 /cí/ – Word

这个**词**啥意思？

zhè ge **cí** shá yì si?

What does this **word** mean?

960- 圣 /shèng/ – Holy

他们过着**圣**洁的生活。

tā men guò zhe **shèng** jié de shēng huó.

They led a **holy** life.

961- 择 /zé/ – Select, choose

请从左边选**择**一个频道。

qǐng cóng zuǒ biān xuǎn **zé** yī gè pín dào.

Please **select** a channel from the left side.

962- 寻 /xún/ – Search, seek

人们热切**寻**求和平。

rén men rè qiè **xún** qiú hé píng.

People are eager to **seek** peace.

963- 厂 /chǎng/ – Factory

我在一家纺织**厂**找到工作。

wǒ zài yī jiā fǎng zhī **chǎng** zhǎo dào gōng zuò.

I got a job in a textile **factory**.

964- 睡 /shuì/ – Sleep

昨晚我没**睡**安稳。

zuó wǎn wǒ méi **shuì** ān wěn.

I didn't **sleep** well last night.

965- 博 /bó/ – Extensive; to gain

我必须**博**得他们的信任。

wǒ bì xū **bó** dé tā men de xìn rèn.

I have to **gain** their trust.

966- 勒 /lēi/ – Rein in

她**勒**住缰绳在十字路口停了下来。

tā **lēi** zhù jiāng shéng zài shí zì lù kǒu tíng le xià lái.

She **reined in** the horse and stopped at the crossroads.

967- 烟 /yān/ – Smoke

炉子里冒出一股**烟**。

lú zi lǐ mào chū yī gǔ **yān**.

The stove let out a puff of **smoke**.

968- 授 /shòu/ – Teach, give

他在那所学校**授**课。

tā zài nà suǒ xué xiào **shòu** kè.

He **teaches** in that school.

969- 诺 /nuò/ – Promise

一旦许下**诺**言，他就会坚守。

yī dàn xǔ xià **nuò** yán, tā jiù huì jiān shǒu.

Once he made a **promise**, he would stick to it.

970- 伦 /lún/ – Relations

他们听了她关于人**伦**的演讲。

tā men tīng le tā guān yú rén **lún** de yǎn jiǎng.

They listened to her lecture on human **relations**.

971- 岸 /àn/ – *Shore*

咱们沿**岸**边散个步吧。

zán men yán **àn** biān sàn gè bù ba.

Let's go for a walk along the **shore**.

972- 奥 /ào/ –*Mystery*

这个**奥**秘始终无解。

zhè ge **ào** mì shǐ zhōng wú jiě.

The **mystery** was never solved.

973- 唐 /táng / – *Tang (a dynasty in history; surname)*

唐朝是中国古诗的极盛时期。

táng cháo shì zhōng guó gǔ shī de jí shèng shí qí.

The **Tang** Dynasty was the golden age of classical Chinese poetry.

974- 卖 /mài / – *Sell*

商人买进**卖**出。

shāng rén mǎi jìn **mài** chū.

Merchants buy and **sell**.

975- 俄 /é/ – *Abbreviation for 俄罗斯 (Russia)*

俄国是全世界最大的国家。

é guó shì quán shì jiè zuì dà de guó jiā.

The biggest country in the world is **Russia**.

976- 炸 /zhá/ – *Fry*

晚饭要不要我**炸**鱼？

wǎn fàn yào bù yào wǒ **zhá** yú?

Shall I **fry** the fish for dinner?

977- 载 /zài/ – *Load*

我们得用起重机装**载**货物。

wǒ men děi yòng qǐ zhòng jī zhuāng **zài** huò wù.

We must use mechanical hoisting to **load** the goods.

978- 洛 /luò/ – Luo (Used to name places, rivers, etc.)

洛阳是一座大城市。

luò yáng shì yī zuò dà chéng shì.

Luoyang is a big city.

979- 健 /jiàn/ – Healthy

他身体健壮。

tā shēn tǐ **jiàn** zhuàng.

He's a **healthy** man.

980- 堂 /táng/ – Hall

演讲会在大堂进行。

yǎn jiǎng huì zài dà **táng** jìn xíng.

The lecture is to be delivered at the **hall**.

981- 旁 /páng/ – Beside; one side

小女孩正坐在妈妈旁边。

xiǎo nǚ hái zhèng zuò zài mā mā **páng** biān.

The little girl is sitting **beside** her mother.

982- 宫 /gōng/ – Palace

宫殿里有好几群游客。

gōng diàn lǐ yǒu hǎo jǐ qún yóu kè.

There are many flocks of tourists in the **palace**.

983- 喝 /hē/ – To drink

空腹喝酒不好。

kōng fù **hē** jiǔ bù hǎo.

It is not good to **drink** on an empty stomach.

984- 借 /jiè/ – Borrow, lend

我可以借你的课本吗?

wǒ kě yǐ **jiè** nǐ de kè běn ma?

May I **borrow** your textbooks?

985- 君 /jūn/ – Monarch

君主享有对罪犯的赦免权。

jūn zhǔ xiǎng yǒu duì zuì fàn de shè miǎn quán.

A **monarch** has the prerogative of pardoning criminals.

986- 禁 /jìn/ – Forbid

此处**禁**止吸烟。

cǐ chù **jìn** zhǐ xī yān.

Smoking is **forbidden** in this place.

987- 阴 /yīn/ – Cloudy

今天**阴**天。

jīn tiān **yīn** tiān.

It's **cloudy** today.

988- 园 /yuán/ – Park

她喜欢在公**园**散步。

tā xǐ huān zài gōng **yuán** sàn bù.

She likes walking in the **park**.

989- 谋 /móu/ – Scheme

他们的阴**谋**暴露了。

tā men de yīn **móu** bào lù le.

Their **scheme** was exposed.

990- 宋 /sòng/ – Song (a dynasty in history; surname)

他姓**宋**。

tā xìng **sòng**.

His surname is **Song**.

991- 避 /bì/ – Avoid

我尽可能**避**开他。

wǒ jìn kě néng **bì** kāi tā.

I **avoided** him as much as possible.

992- 抓 /zhuā/ – *Grab, catch*

杰克**抓**住他的衣领。

jié kè **zhuā** zhù tā de yī lǐng.

Jack **grabbed** him by the collar.

993- 荣 /róng/ – *Glory, honor*

他玷污了家族的**荣**誉。

tā diàn wū le jiā zú de **róng** yù.

He stained the family **honor**.

994- 姑 /gū/ – *Aunt (father's sister)*

她是我**姑姑**。

tā shì wǒ **gū gū**.

She's my **aunt**.

995- 孙 /sūn/ – *Grandchild, grandson, granddaughter*

我还没有**孙**子。

wǒ hái méi yǒu **sūn** zi.

I don't have a **grandson**.

996- 逃 /táo/ – *Escape*

犯人**逃**走了。

fàn rén **táo** zǒu le.

The prisoner has **escaped**.

997- 牙 /yá/ – *Tooth*

我**牙**疼。

wǒ **yá** téng.

I have a **tooth**ache.

998- 束 /shù/ – *Bundle*

桌上有一**束**花。

zhuō shàng yǒu yī **shù** huā.

On the table, there is a **bundle** of flowers.

999- 跳 /tiào/ – Jump

我**跳**过了栅栏。

wǒ **tiào** guò le zhà lán.

I **jumped** over the fence.

1000- 顶 /dǐng/ – Top, peak

山**顶**终年积雪。

shān **dǐng** zhōng nián jī xuě.

The mountain **peaks** are covered with snow all year.

1001- 玉 /yù/ – Jade

他送给我们一对**玉**狮子。

tā sòng gěi wǒ men yī duì **yù** shī zi.

He presented us with a couple of **jade** lions.

1002- 镇 /zhèn/ – Town

他住在一个靠海的**镇**上。

tā zhù zài yī gè kào hǎi de **zhèn** shàng.

He lived in a **town** beside the sea.

1003- 雪 /xuě/ – Snow

天正在下大**雪**。

tiān zhèng zài xià dà **xuě**.

It was **snowing** heavily.

1004- 午 /wǔ/ – Noon

正**午**，烈日当空。

zhèng **wǔ**, liè rì dāng kōng.

At **noon**, the sun is high in the sky.

1005- 练 /liàn/ – Pratice

你需要更多**练**习。

nǐ xū yào gèng duō **liàn** xí.

You need more **practice**.

1006- 迫/pò/ – *Compel; urgent*

除非强**迫**我，否则我不去。

chú fēi qiáng **pò** wǒ, fǒu zé wǒ bù qù.

I will not go unless you **compel** me.

1007- 爷/yé/ – *Grandfather*

他是我**爷爷**。

tā shì wǒ **yé yé**.

He's my **grandfather**.

1008- 篇/piān/ – *Measure word for written items*

我读了一**篇报道**。

wǒ dú le **yī piān bào dào**.

I read **a report**.

1009- 肉/ròu/ – *Meat*

肉如果不冷藏就会腐败。

ròu rú guǒ bù lěng cáng jiù huì fǔ bài.

The **meat** will rot if it isn't kept cool.

1010- 嘴/zuǐ/ – *Mouth*

请把**嘴**张开。

qǐng bǎ **zuǐ** zhāng kāi.

Open your **mouth**, please.

1011- 馆/guǎn/ – *Shop*

我喜欢那家咖啡**馆**。

wǒ xǐ huān nà jiā kā fēi **guǎn**.

I like that coffee **shop**.

1012- 遍/biàn/ – *All over, everywhere*

遍地都在兴建工厂。

biàn dì dōu zài xīng jiàn gōng chǎng.

New factories are going up **everywhere**.

1013- 凡/fán/ – *Ordinary*

他只是个平**凡**的人。

tā zhǐ shì gè píng **fán** de rén.

He's just an **ordinary** man.

1014- 础/chǔ/ – *Basis*

他的研究成果是这本新书的基**础**。

tā de yán jiū chéng guǒ shì zhè běn xīn shū de jī **chǔ**.

His research formed the **basis** of his new book.

1015- 洞/dòng/ – *Cave, hole*

我袜子上有个**洞**。

wǒ wà zi shàng yǒu gè **dòng**.

There's a **hole** in my sock.

1016- 卷/juǎn/ – *To roll*

请帮我**卷**支烟。

qǐng bāng wǒ **juǎn** zhī yān.

Please **roll** me a cigarette.

1017- 坦/tǎn/ – *Flat*

我们县大部分地方很平**坦**。

wǒ men xiàn dà bù fèn dì fāng hěn píng **tǎn**.

Most of our county is **flat**.

1018- 牛/niú/ – *Bull*

这是一头**牛**。

zhè shì yī tóu **niú**.

This is a **bull**.

1019- 安宁/ān níng/ – *Peaceful*

今天的世界仍很不**安宁**。

jīn tiān de shì jiè réng hěn bù **ān níng**.

The world today is far from **peaceful**.

1020- 纸/zhǐ/ – Paper

我需要个**纸**盒。

wǒ xū yào gè **zhǐ** hé.

I need a **paper** box.

1021- 诸/zhū/ – Every, all

诸位有什么意见，欢迎提出来。

zhū wèi yǒu shé me yì jiàn, huān yíng tí chū lái.

All of you are welcome to put forward views.

1022- 训/xùn/ – To train

他们正在**训**练。

tā men zhèng zài **xùn** liàn.

They are **training**.

1023- 私/sī/ – Private

这是一辆**私**家车。

zhè shì yī liàng **sī** jiā chē.

It is a **private** car.

1024- 庄/zhuāng/ – Manor

小偷晚上闯进了**庄**园。

xiǎo tōu wǎn shàng chuǎng jìn le **zhuāng** yuán.

Thieves broke into the **manor** at night.

1025- 祖/zǔ/ – Ancestor

她已经拜过了**祖**先。

tā yǐ jīng bài guò le **zǔ** xiān.

She has worshipped her **ancestor**.

1026- 丝/sī/ – Silk

我们进口生**丝**。

wǒ men jìn kǒu shēng **sī**.

We import raw **silk**.

1027- 翻/fān/ – Flip over, turn over

应该用耙子**翻**土。

yīng gāi yòng pá zǐ **fān** tǔ.

The soil should be **turned over** with a fork.

1028- 暴/bào/ – Violent

她**暴**跳如雷。

tā **bào** tiào rú léi.

She was in a **violent** temper.

1029- 森/sēn/ – Forest

森林里是如此宁静。

sēn lín lǐ shì rú cǐ níng jìng.

It is peaceful in the **forest**.

1030- 塔/tǎ/ – Tower

伦敦**塔**很高。

lún dūn **tǎ** hěn gāo.

The **Tower** of London is very tall.

1031- 默/mò/ – Silent

那是一部**默**片。

nà shì yī bù **mò** piàn.

It is a **silent** film.

1032- 握/wò/ – Hold

握住我的手。

wò zhù wǒ de shǒu.

Hold my hand.

1033- 戏/xì/ – Drama

他是**戏**剧系的学生。

tā shì **xì** jù xì de xué shēng.

He is a student of **drama**.

1034- 隐/yǐn/ – *Concealed*

机枪从**隐**蔽阵地开始射击。

jī qiāng cóng **yǐn** bì zhèn dì kāi shǐ shè jí.

Machine guns fired from a **concealed** position.

1035- 熟/shú/ – *Cooked*

你要**熟**的菜还是生的？

nǐ yào **shú** de cài hái shì shēng de?

Do you want your vegetable **cooked** or raw?

1036- 骨/gǔ/ – *Bone*

狗在啃**骨**头。

gǒu zài kěn **gǔ** tóu.

The dog was chewing a **bone**.

1037- 访/fǎng/ – *Visit*

我们的**访**问取得了成效。

wǒ men de **fǎng** wèn qǔ dé le chéng xiào.

Our **visit** accomplished something.

1038- 弱/ruò/ – *Weak*

你太软**弱**了。

nǐ tài ruǎn **ruò** le.

You are so **weak**.

1039-蒙/mēng/ – *Deceive*

你**蒙**不了我。

nǐ **mēng** bù liǎo wǒ.

You can't **deceive** me.

1040- 歌/gē/ – *Song*

给我们唱首**歌**吧。

gěi wǒ men chàng shǒu **gē** ba.

Sing us a **song**.

1041- 店 /diàn/ – Store

我要去书**店**。

wǒ yào qù shū **diàn**.

I'm going to the book**store**.

1042- 鬼 /guǐ/ – Ghost

你相信有**鬼**吗？

nǐ xiāng xìn yǒu **guǐ** ma?

Do you believe in **ghosts**?

1043- 软 /ruǎn/ – Soft

这是张**软**床。

zhè shì zhāng **ruǎn** chuáng.

It's a **soft** bed.

1044- 典礼 /diǎn lǐ/ – Ceremony

典礼在教堂举行。

diǎn lǐ zài jiào táng jǔ xíng.

The **ceremony** took place in the church.

1045- 欲 /yù/ – Desire

求知**欲**使我买了这本书。

qiú zhī **yù** shǐ wǒ mǎi le zhè běn shū.

My **desire** for knowledge prompted me to buy the book.

1046- 菩萨 /pú sà/ – Bodhisattva

第三世虚空藏**菩萨**正在诵经。

dì sān shì xū kōng zàng **pú sà** zhèng zài sòng jīng.

The 3rd Akasagarbha **Bodhisattva** was chanting sutras.

1047- 伙 /huǒ/ – Companion

他被坏**伙**伴引入歧途。

tā bèi huài **huǒ** bàn yǐn rù qí tú.

He was perverted by his evil **companions**.

1048- 遭 /zāo/ – *Come across, suffer*

他们在经济危机时**遭**受了巨大损失。

tā men zài jīng jì wéi jī shí **zāo** shòu le jù dà sǔn shī.

They **suffered** huge losses in the financial crisis.

1049- 盘 /pán/ – *Tray, plate*

把**盘**子放那边。

bǎ **pán** zi fàng nà biān.

Put the **tray** over there.

1050- 爸 /bà/ – *Dad*

早上好，**爸**。

zǎo shàng hǎo, **bà**.

Good morning, **dad**.

1051- 扩 /kuò/ – *Expand, enlarge*

码头已被**扩**建。

mǎ tóu yǐ bèi **kuò** jiàn.

The dock has been **expanded**.

1052- 盖 /gài/ – *Cover*

水开时，拿下锅**盖**。

shuǐ kāi shí, ná xià guō **gài**.

When the water boils, take the **cover** from the pan.

1053- 弄 /nòng/ – *Mess with, handle*

我来**弄**吧。

wǒ lái **nòng** ba.

I'll **handle** it.

1054- 雄 /xióng/ – *Male*

这朵花是**雄**花。

zhè duǒ huā shì **xióng** huā.

This flower is a **male** flower.

1055- 稳 /wěn/ – *Steady*

这个凳子很**稳**。

zhè ge dèng zǐ hěn **wěn**.

The stool is **steady** enough.

1056- 忘 /wàng/ – *Forget*

我**忘**了关窗户。

wǒ **wàng** le guān chuāng hù.

I **forgot** to close the windows.

1057- 亿 /yì/ – *One hundred million*

他资产过**亿**。

tā zī chǎn guò **yì**.

He has assets of over **one hundred million**.

1058- 刺 /cì/ – *Stab*

她用刀子**刺**伤了他。

tā yòng dāo zi **cì** shāng le tā.

She **stabbed** him with a knife.

1059- 拥 /yōng/ – *Embrace*

我们彼此相**拥**。

wǒ men bǐ cǐ xiāng **yōng**.

We **embraced** each other.

1060- 徒 /tú/ – *Disciple*

他是宗教**徒**。

tā shì zōng jiào **tú**.

He's a **disciple** of religion.

1061- 姆 /mǔ/ – *Nurse, nanny*

保**姆**逗得孩子一笑。

bǎo **mǔ** dòu dé hái zi yī xiào.

The **nurse** coaxed a smile from the baby.

1062- 杨 /yáng/ – *Poplar*

庭院里有几棵**杨**树。

tíng yuàn lǐ yǒu jǐ kē **yáng** shù.

There are some **poplars** in the garden.

1063- 齐 /qí/ – *Level with*

河水上涨到与堤岸**齐**平。

hé shuǐ shàng zhǎng dào yǔ dī àn **qí** píng.

The water rose until it was on a **level with** the riverbanks.

1064- 赛 /sài/ – *Competition*

下星期有场国际象棋**赛**。

xià xīng qī yǒu chǎng guó jì xiàng qí **sài**.

There will be a chess **competition** next week.

1065- 趣 /qù/ – *Interesting*

听起来很有**趣**。

tīng qǐ lái hěn yǒu **qù**.

That sounds **interesting**.

1066- 曲 /qǔ/ – *Tune*

她自己哼着小**曲**。

tā zì jǐ hēng zhe xiǎo **qǔ**.

She was humming a **tune** to herself.

1067- 刀 /dāo/ – *Knife*

那把**刀**很钝。

nà bǎ **dāo** hěn dùn.

The **knife** is dull.

1068- 床 /chuáng/ – *Bed*

这张**床**可当椅子用。

zhè zhāng **chuáng** kě dāng yǐ zi yòng.

This **bed** can function as a chair.

1069- 欢迎/huān yíng/ – Welcome

欢迎来我家。

huān yíng lái wǒ jiā.

Welcome to my house.

1070- 冰/bīng/ – Ice

我一踩**冰**就裂了。

wǒ yī cǎi **bīng** jiù liè le.

The **ice** cracked as I stepped onto it.

1071- 虚/xū/ – Weak, false

她并不像看上去的那么**虚**弱。

tā bìng bù xiàng kàn shàng qù de nà me **xū** ruò.

She is not as **weak** as she looks.

1072- 玩/wán/ – Play

孩子们喜欢**玩**。

hái zi men xǐ huān **wán**.

Children like to **play**.

1073- 析/xī/ – Analyze

你应该剖**析**问题的实质。

nǐ yīng gāi pōu **xī** wèn tí de shí zhì.

You should **analyze** the essence of the problem.

1074- 窗/chuāng/ – Window

请关上**窗**户。

qǐng guān shàng **chuāng** hù.

Please close the **windows**.

1075- 醒/xǐng/ – Wake up

我通常**醒**得很早。

wǒ tōng cháng **xǐng** dé hěn zǎo.

I usually **wake up** early.

1076- 妻/qī/ – Wife

我爱我的**妻**子。

wǒ ài wǒ de **qī** zi.

I love my **wife**.

1077- 透/tòu/ – Transparent; pass through

普通的玻璃是**透**明的。

pǔ tōng de bō lí shì **tòu** míng de.

Plain glass is **transparent**.

1078- 购/gòu/ – Purchase

这是采**购**单。

zhè shì cǎi **gòu** dān.

This is the **purchase** order.

1079- 替/tì/ – Replace

母爱无可**替**代。

mǔ ài wú kě **tì** dài.

Nothing can **replace** a mother's love.

1080- 塞/sāi/ – Squeeze in, plug up

有什么东西**塞**住了水池。

yǒu shén me dōng xī **sāi** zhù le shuǐ chí.

Something has **plugged up** the sink.

1081- 努/nǔ/ – Strive

我们共同**努**力以实现祖国统一。

wǒ men gòng tóng **nǔ** lì yǐ shí xiàn zǔ guó tǒng yī.

We should all **strive** to reunify the motherland.

1082- 休/xiū/ – Rest

我得**休**息下。

wǒ děi **xiū** xī xià.

I need a **rest**.

1083- 虎/hǔ/ – Tiger

老虎咆哮。

lǎo **hǔ** páo xiāo.

The **tiger** roared.

1084- 扬/yáng/ – Raise

她扬了扬眉。

tā **yáng** le **yáng** méi.

She **raised** her brows.

1085- 途/tú/ – Journey

她要作一次长途旅行。

tā yào zuò yī cì cháng **tú** lǚ xíng.

She is going to make a long **journey**.

1086- 侵/qīn/ – Invade

这些国家遭到了入侵。

zhè xiē guó jiā zāo dào le rù **qīn**.

These countries have been **invaded**.

1087- 刑/xíng/ – Punishment

他已受到应有的刑罚。

tā yǐ shòu dào yīng yǒu de **xíng** fá.

He has received a just **punishment**.

1088- 绿/ lǜ/ – Green

中国人不喜欢绿色的帽子。

zhōng guó rén bù xǐ huān **lǜ** sè de mào zi.

Chinese people don't like **green** hats.

1089- 兄/xiōng/ – Elder brother

他是我兄长。

tā shì wǒ **xiōng** zhǎng.

He's an **elder brother** of mine.

1090- 迅/xùn/ – *Rapid*

改进极为**迅**速。

gǎi jìn jí wéi **xùn** sù.

The improvement was very **rapid**.

1091- 套/tào/ – *Sheath, cover*

椅子上罩了**套**子。

yǐ zi shàng zhào le **tào** zi.

The chairs are fitted with **covers**.

1092- 贸/mào/ – *Trade*

中国和许多国家进行**贸**易。

zhōng guó hé xǔ duō guó jiā jìn xíng **mào** yì.

China **trades** with many countries.

1093- 毕/bì/ – *Complete, graduate*

我去年大学**毕**业。

wǒ qù nián dà xué **bì** yè.

I **graduated** from college last year.

1094- 唯/wéi/ – *Only*

他是那次空难**唯**一的幸存者。

tā shì nà cì kōng nàn **wéi** yī de xìng cún zhě.

He's the **only** survivor of the plane crash.

1095- 谷/gǔ/ – *Valley, grain*

他们步行穿过山**谷**。

tā men bù xíng chuān guò shān **gǔ**.

They traversed the **valley** on foot.

1096- 轮/lún/ – *Wheel ; turn*

轮到我了。

lún dào wǒ le.

It's my **turn**.

1097- 库/kù/ – *Warehouse*

他们把货存在仓**库**里。

tā men bǎ huò cún zài cāng **kù** lǐ.

They stored the goods in a **warehouse**.

1098- 迹/jì/ – *Trace*

在浴室里发现了一点血**迹**。

zài yù shì lǐ fā xiàn le yī diǎn xiě **jì**.

Traces of blood were found in the bathroom.

1099- 尤/yóu/ – *Especially*

我喜欢这乡村，**尤**其是在春天。

wǒ xǐ huān zhè xiāng cūn, **yóu** qí shì zài chūn tiān.

I love the country, **especially** in spring.

1100- 竞/jìng/ – *Compete*

我们能与最好的队伍**竞**争。

wǒ men néng yǔ zuì hǎo de duì wǔ **jìng** zhēng.

We can **compete** with the best team.

1101- 街/jiē/ – *Street*

我在**街**上遇到他。

wǒ zài **jiē** shàng yù dào tā.

I met him in the **street**.

1102- 促/cù/ – *Promote, urge*

他敦**促**妹妹学习。

tā dūn **cù** mèi mei xué xí.

He **urges** his sister to study.

1103- 延/yán/ – *Extend, prolong*

签证到期后怎样**延**长？

qiān zhèng dào qī hòu zěn yàng **yán** cháng?

How to **extend** a visa if it expires?

1104- 震/zhèn/ – *Vibrate*

当重型卡车经过时，这座桥就会**震**动。

dāng zhòng xíng kǎ chē jīng guò shí, zhè zuò qiáo jiù huì **zhèn** dòng.

The bridge **vibrated** when a heavy truck passed.

1105- 弃/qì/ – *Abandon*

敌人**弃**城而逃。

dí rén **qì** chéng ér táo.

The enemy **abandoned** the city and fled.

1106- 甲/jiǎ/ – *Armor*

过去的骑士在战斗中身着盔**甲**。

guò qù de qí shì zài zhàn dòu zhōng shēn zhuó kuī **jiǎ**.

Knights used to wear **armor** in battle in the past.

1107- 伟/wěi/ – *Great*

这是个**伟**大的国家。

zhè shì gè **wěi** dà de guó jiā.

This is a **great** country.

1108- 麻/má/ – *Numb*

他已**麻**木不仁。

tā yǐ **má** mù bù rén.

His mind has been **numbed**.

1109- 川/chuān/ – *River, stream*

汽车**川**流不息。

qì chē **chuān** liú bù xī.

Automobiles speed in an endless **stream**.

1110- 申/shēn/ – *State, apply*

他**申**请入党。

tā **shēn** qǐng rù dǎng.

He **applied** to join the party.

1111- 缓/huǎn/ – Postpone; slow

人欲**缓**而时不待。

rén yù **huǎn** ér shí bù dài.

One wants to **slow** but time does not await him.

1112- 潜/qián/ – Dive, hide

你会**潜**水吗？

nǐ huì **qián** shuǐ ma?

Can you **dive**?

1113- 闪/shǎn/ – Flash

灯塔在远处**闪**光。

dēng tǎ zài yuǎn chù **shǎn** guāng.

A lighthouse was **flashing** afar.

1114- 售/shòu/ – Sell

你们出**售**邮票吗？

nǐ men chū **shòu** yóu piào ma?

Do you **sell** stamps?

1115- 灯/dēng/ – Lamp, lantern

那盏**灯**悬挂在桌子上方。

nà zhǎn **dēng** xuán guà zài zhuō zi shàng fāng.

The **lamp** hung over the table.

1116- 针/zhēn/ – Pin, needle

针刺进了她的手指。

zhēn cì jìn le tā de shǒu zhǐ.

The **needle** pierced her finger.

1117- 哲/zhé/ – Philosophy

他信奉罗素的**哲**学。

tā xìn fèng luō sù de **zhé** xué.

He believed in the **philosophy** of Russell.

1118- 网络/wǎng luò/ – Network

他们建成了全国性的**网络**。

tā men jiàn chéng le quán guó xìng de **wǎng luò**.

They have built the national **network**.

1119- 抵/dǐ/ – Resist

他们无力**抵**抗。

tā men wú lì **dǐ** kàng.

They were powerless to **resist**.

1120- 朱/zhū/ – Zhu (surname); red

她姓**朱**。

tā xìng **zhū**.

Her surname is **Zhu**.

1121- 埃/āi/ – Dust, dirt

他的衣服上落满了尘**埃**。

tā de yī fú shàng luò mǎn le chén **āi**.

His clothes were covered with **dust**.

1122- 抱/bào/ – Hug

他抱住了我。

tā **bào** zhù le wǒ.

He gave me a **hug**.

1123- 鼓/gǔ/ – Drum

鼓声很平稳。

gǔ shēng hěn píng wěn.

The beats of the **drum** were steady.

1124- 植/zhí/ – Plant

四月是**植**树的时节。

sì yuè shì **zhí** shù de shí jié.

April is the time to **plant** trees.

1125- 纯 /chún/ – *Pure*

你吸过**纯**氧吗？

nǐ xī guò **chún** yǎng ma?

Have you ever breathed **pure** oxygen?

1126- 夏 /xià/ – *Summer*

我最喜欢**夏**季。

wǒ zuì xǐ huān **xià** jì.

Summer is my favorite season.

1127- 忍 /rěn/ – *Endure*

他**忍**受着寒冷与饥饿。

tā **rěn** shòu zhe hán lěng yǔ jī è.

He **endured** cold and hunger.

1128- 页 /yè/ – *Page*

把这份报告改短五**页**。

bǎ zhè fèn bào gào gǎi duǎn wǔ **yè**.

Shorten the report by five **pages**.

1129- 杰 /jié/ – *Distinguished*

她是一位**杰**出的小说家。

tā shì yī wèi **jié** chū de xiǎo shuō jiā.

She is a **distinguished** novelist.

1130- 筑 /zhù/ – *Construct*

他们修**筑**了 15 公里长的堤坝。

tā men xiū **zhù** le 15 gōng lǐ cháng de dī bà.

They **constructed** fifteen kilometers of dikes.

1131- 折 /zhé/ – *To bend, twist, break*

他**折**断了胳膊。

tā **zhé** duàn le gē bó.

He **broke** his arm.

1132- 郑 /zhèng/ – Zheng (surname)

他姓**郑**。

tā xìng **zhèng**.

His surname is **Zheng**.

1133- 贝 /bèi/ – Shell

有些**贝**壳可以用来装水。

yǒu xiē **bèi** ké kě yǐ yòng lái zhuāng shuǐ.

Some **shells** can be used to hold water.

1134- 尊 /zūn/ – Respect

他们很**尊重**我。

tā men hěn **zūn zhòng** wǒ.

They treated me with **respect**.

1135- 吴 /wú/ –Wu (surname)

我姓**吴**。

wǒ xìng **wú**.

My surname is **Wu**.

1136- 秀 /xiù/ – Elegant

她的字体很**秀**气。

tā de zì tǐ hěn **xiù** qì.

Her handwriting is **elegant**.

1137- 混 /hùn/ – Mix

有些化学品不相**混**合。

yǒu xiē huà xué pǐn bù xiāng **hùn** hé.

Some chemicals do not **mix**.

1138- 臣 /chén/ – Personal pronoun for a ruler's advisor

他是晚清重**臣**。

tā shì wǎn qīng zhòng **chén**.

He was an important **advisor** in the late Qing Dynasty.

1139- 雅/yǎ/ – Elegant

他是个文雅的人。

tā shì gè wén yǎ de rén.

He is an **elegant** man.

1140- 振/zhèn/ – Vibrate

它们将引起扬声器薄膜振动。

tā men jiāng yǐn qǐ yáng shēng qì bó mó zhèn dòng.

They will cause the speaker's diaphragm to **vibrate**.

1141- 染/rǎn/ – Dye

这料子染不好。

zhè liào zi rǎn bù hǎo.

The material does not **dye** well.

1142- 盛/shèng/ – Flourish

作物在肥沃的土壤中长得茂盛。

zuò wù zài féi wò de tǔ rǎng zhōng zhǎng dé mào shèng.

Crops **flourish** in rich soil.

1143- 怒/nù/ – Anger

他勃然大怒。

tā bó rán dà nù.

His **anger** blazed forth.

1144- 舞/wǔ/ – Dance

你能和我跳舞吗？

nǐ néng hé wǒ tiào wǔ ma?

Can you **dance** with me?

1145- 圆/yuán/ – Circle, round

他在板上画了个圆。

tā zài bǎn shàng huà le gè yuán.

He drew a **circle** on the board.

1146- 搞/gǎo/ – *Set up*

我们**搞**个公司吧。

wǒ men **gǎo** gè gōng sī ba.

Let's **set up** a company.

1147- 狂/kuáng/ – *Mad*

他们对足球很**狂**热。

tā men duì zú qiú hěn **kuáng** rè.

They are **mad** about football.

1148- 措/cuò/ – *Arrangment*

我希望这些举**措**会得到你的同意。

wǒ xī wàng zhè xiē jǔ **cuò** huì dé dào nǐ de tóng yì.

I hope that the **arrangements** meet with your approval.

1149- 姓/xìng/ – *Surname*

你**姓**什么？

nǐ **xìng** shén me?

What is your **surname**?

1150- 残/cán/ – *Remnant; cruel; disabled*

狮子生性**残**暴。

shī zǐ shēng xìng **cán** bào.

Lions are **cruel** by nature.

1151- 秋/qiū/ – *Autumn*

我最喜欢**秋**季。

wǒ zuì xǐ huān **qiū** jì.

My favorite season is **autumn**.

1152- 培/péi/ – *Cultivate*

父亲试图**培**养我对艺术的爱好。

fù qīn shì tú **péi** yǎng wǒ duì yì shù de ài hào.

Father tries to **cultivate** my love for art.

1153- 迷 /mí/ – *Confuse, puzzle*

我对这种情况感到**迷**惑。

wǒ duì zhè zhǒng qíng kuàng gǎn dào **mí** huò.

I'm **puzzled** about this situation.

1154- 诚 /chéng/ – *Honest*

他是个**诚**实的人。

tā shì gè **chéng** shí de rén.

He's an **honest** man.

1155- 宽 /kuān/ – *Wide*

这个花园有十码**宽**。

zhè ge huā yuán yǒu shí mǎ **kuān**.

The garden is ten yards **wide**.

1156- 宇 /yǔ/ – *Universe*

宇宙存在于太空。

yǔ zhòu cún zài yú tài kōng.

The **universe** exists in space.

1157- 猛 /měng/ – *Ferocious*

那只凶**猛**的猎豹正追赶一只兔子。

nà zhī xiōng **měng** de liè bào zhèng zhuī gǎn yī zhǐ tù zi.

The **ferocious** panther is chasing a rabbit.

1158- 摆 /bǎi/ – *Arrange, swing*

柳枝迎风摇**摆**。

liǔ zhī yíng fēng yáo **bǎi**.

The willow branches **swing** in the breeze.

1159- 梅 /méi/ – *Plum*

我喜欢**梅**花。

wǒ xǐ huān **méi** huā.

I like the **plum** flower.

1160- 毁/huǐ/ – *Destroy*

他似乎正在自**毁**。

tā sì hū zhèng zài zì **huǐ**.

It seems he's **destroying** himself.

1161- 伸/shēn/ – *Stretch*

草场向东**伸**展。

cǎo chǎng xiàng dōng **shēn** zhǎn.

Meadows **stretch** to the east.

1162- 摩/mó/ – *Rub*

摩擦鼻子以示问候是爱斯基摩人的习俗。

mó cā bí zǐ yǐ shì wèn hòu shì ài sī jī mó rén de xí sú.

It is an Eskimo custom to **rub** noses as a greeting.

1163- 盟/méng/ – *Ally*

该国已与另一国结**盟**。

gāi guó yǐ yǔ lìng yī guó jié **méng**.

This country **allied** with another country.

1164- 末/mò/ – *Final*

我期**末**考得不错。

wǒ qī **mò** kǎo dé bù cuò.

I did well at the **final** exam.

1165- 乃/nǎi/ – *Be*

汝**乃**何人？

rǔ **nǎi** hé rén?

Who **are** you?

1166- 悲/bēi/ – *Sad*

我很**悲**伤。

wǒ hěn **bēi** shāng.

I'm **sad**.

1167- 拍/pāi/ – Pat, slap

他**拍**了**拍**狗。

tā **pāi** le **pāi** gǒu.

He **patted** the dog.

1168- 丁/dīng/ – Ding (surname) ; man

他姓**丁**。

tā xìng **dīng**.

His surname is **Ding**.

1169- 赵/zhào/ – Zhao (surname)

他姓**赵**。

tā xìng **zhào**.

His surname is **Zhao**.

1170- 硬/yìng/ – Hard

这罐子里有**硬**糖。

zhè guàn zi lǐ yǒu **yìng** táng.

The jar contained **hard** candies.

1171- 麦/mài/ – Wheat

今年小**麦**的收成很好。

jīn nián xiǎo **mài** de shōu chéng hěn hǎo.

The **wheat** has cropped well this year.

1172- 蒋/jiǎng/ – Jiang (surname)

他姓**蒋**。

tā xìng **jiǎng**.

His surname is **Jiang**.

1173- 操/cāo/ – Operate

你知道这机器怎么**操**作吗？

nǐ zhī dào zhè jī qì zěn me **cāo** zuò ma?

Do you know how to **operate** the machine?

1174- 耶/yé/ – Final particle indicating enthusiasm

这里好有趣**耶**！

zhè lǐ hǎo yǒu qù **yé**!

What an interesting place!

1175- 阻/zǔ/ – To block

树**阻**挡了阳光。

shù **zǔ** dǎng le yáng guāng.

The trees **block** the sun.

1176- 订/dìng/ – Subscribe, conclude

请**订**阅我们的频道。

qǐng **dìng** yuè wǒ men de pín dào.

Please **subscribe** to our channel.

1177- 彩/cǎi/ – Color

我喜欢明亮的色**彩**。

wǒ xǐ huān míng liàng de sè **cǎi**.

I like bright **colors**.

1178- 抽/chōu/ – Draw

第一次**抽**牌他拿了两张红桃。

dì yī cì **chōu** pái tā ná le liǎng zhāng hóng táo.

He got two hearts on the first **draw**.

1179- 赞/zàn/ – Praise

老师称**赞**了她的勇气。

lǎo shī chēng **zàn** le tā de yǒng qì.

The teacher **praised** her for her courage.

1180- 魔/mó/ – Demon; magic power

恶**魔**用咒语控制了这个女人。

è **mó** yòng zhòu yǔ kòng zhì le zhè ge nǚ rén.

The **demon** charmed the woman with his spell.

1181- 纷/fēn/ – *Disorderly*

文件**纷**乱地堆放在一起。

wén jiàn **fēn** luàn de duī fàng zài yī qǐ.

The papers lay in a **disorderly** pile.

1182- 沿/yán/ – *Go along*

沿这条路走你就到了。

yán zhè tiáo lù zǒu nǐ jiù dào le.

Go along the road and you will be there.

1183- 喊/hǎn/ – *Yell*

别朝我**喊**。

bié cháo wǒ **hǎn**.

Don't **yell** at me.

1184- 违/wéi/ – *Disobey, violate*

该国**违**背了国际协议。

gāi guó **wéi** bèi le guó jì xié yì.

The country **violates** the international agreements.

1185- 妹/mèi/ – *Younger sister*

她是我**妹**。

tā shì wǒ **mèi**.

She's my **younger sister**.

1186- 浪/làng/ – *Wave*

暴风雨掀起了巨**浪**。

bào fēng yǔ xiān qǐ le jù **làng**.

The storm whipped up huge **waves**.

1187- 汇/huì/ – *Remit*

他给母亲**汇**了些钱。

tā gěi mǔ qīn **huì** le xiē qián.

He **remitted** some money to his mother.

1188- 币/bì/ – Coin

金**币**在他手里作响。

jīn **bì** zài tā shǒu lǐ zuò xiǎng.

Gold **coins** clinked in his hand.

1189- 丰/fēng/ – Abundant

明年将是个**丰**年。

míng nián jiāng shì gè **fēng** nián.

Next year will be an **abundant** year.

1190- 蓝/lán/ – Blue

我喜欢这条**蓝**裤子。

wǒ xǐ huān zhè tiáo **lán** kù zi.

I like this pair of **blue** pants.

1191- 殊/shū/ – Special, different

如果需要，告诉我们你的特**殊**要求。

rú guǒ xū yào, gào sù wǒ men nǐ de tè **shū** yāo qiú.

Give us your **special** requirements if needed.

1192- 献/xiàn/ – Donate, present

你最好给她**献**束花。

nǐ zuì hǎo gěi tā **xiàn** shù huā.

You'd better **present** a bunch of flowers to her.

1193- 桌/zhuō/ – Table

我想买这张**桌**子。

wǒ xiǎng mǎi zhè zhāng **zhuō** zi.

I want to buy this **table**.

1194- 啦/lā/ – Final partical indicating exclamation

这儿太美**啦**！

zhè er tài měi **la**!

What a beautiful place!

1195- 瓦 /wǎ/ – *Roof tile*

我喜欢西班牙式房屋的**瓦**。

wǒ xǐ huān xī bān yá shì fáng wū de **wǎ**.

I love the **roof tiles** on a Spanish-style house.

1196- 莱 /lái/ – *Lai (used to name places)*

这座城市叫**莱**芜。

zhè zuò chéng shì jiào **lái** wú.

This city is called **Lai**wu.

1197- 援 /yuán/ – *To aid*

我们**援**助他们抗击敌人。

wǒ men **yuán** zhù tā men kàng jí dí rén.

We **aid** them to fight against their enemy.

1198- 译 /yì/ – *Translate*

这怎么**译**？

zhè zěn me **yì**?

How to **translate** this?

1199- 夺 /duó/ – *Take (by force)*

你不能从我这**夺**走它。

nǐ bù néng cóng wǒ zhè **duó** zǒu tā.

You can't **take** this from me.

1200- 汽 /qì/ – *Steam*

蒸**汽**可以推动机器。

zhēng **qì** kě yǐ tuī dòng jī qì.

Steam drives machinery.

1201- 烧 /shāo/ – *Burn*

蜡烛已**烧**去一半。

là zhú yǐ **shāo** qù yī bàn.

Half the candle had **burnt** away.

1202- 距/jù/ – *Distance*

他判断**距**离很准。

tā pàn duàn **jù** lí hěn zhǔn.

He judged the **distance** to a nicety.

1203- 裁/cái/ – *Cut*

我们用剪刀**裁**纸和布。

wǒ men yòng jiǎn dāo **cái** zhǐ hé bù.

We **cut** paper and cloth with scissors.

1204- 偏见/piān jiàn/ – *Prejudice*

他对现代音乐有**偏见**。

tā duì xiàn dài yīn yuè yǒu **piān jiàn**.

He has a **prejudice** against modern music.

1205- 符/fú/ – *Symbol*

铜的化学**符**号是 Cu。

tóng de huà xué **fú** hào shì Cu.

The chemical **symbol** for copper is "Cu".

1206- 勇/yǒng/ – *Brave*

我想成为一个**勇**敢的人。

wǒ xiǎng chéng wéi yī gè **yǒng** gǎn de rén.

I want to be a **brave** man.

1207- 触/chù/ – *Touch*

油漆未干，请勿**触**摸。

yóu qī wèi gān, qǐng wù **chù** mō.

Don't **touch** the paint until it's dry.

1208- 课/kè/ – *Class, lesson*

他教美术**课**。

tā jiāo měi shù **kè**.

He gives **lessons** in drawing.

1209- 敬/jìng/ – *Respect*

我们十分尊**敬**他。

wǒ men shí fēn zūn **jìng** tā.

We deeply **respect** him.

1210- 哭/kū/ – *Cry*

别**哭**。

bié **kū**.

Don't **cry**.

1211- 懂/dǒng/ – *Understand*

你**懂**了吗？

nǐ **dǒng** le ma?

Do you **understand**?

1212- 墙/qiáng/ – *Wall*

墙很厚。

qiáng hěn hòu.

The **walls** are very thick.

1213- 袭/xí/ – *Attack*

我们受到**袭**击。

wǒ men shòu dào **xí** jí.

We are under **attack**.

1214- 召/zhào/ – *Summon*

将军**召**集了所有军官。

jiāng jūn **zhào** jí le suǒ yǒu jūn guān.

The general **summoned** all his officers.

1215- 罚/fá/ – *Punish*

她将受到惩**罚**。

tā jiāng shòu dào chéng **fá**.

She will be **punished**.

1216- 侠 /xiá/ – *Hero*

他是一位真正的大**侠**。

tā shì yī wèi zhēn zhèng de dà **xiá**.

He's a true **hero**.

1217- 厅 /tīng/ – *Hall*

厅里可以容纳 200 人。

tīng lǐ kě yǐ róng nà 200 rén.

The **hall** can contain 200 people.

1218- 拜 /bài/ – *Worship, visit*

你在哪里做礼**拜**?

nǐ zài nǎ lǐ zuò lǐ **bài**?

Where do you **worship**?

1219- 巧 /qiǎo/ – *Coincidence; skillful*

真是太**巧**了！

zhēn shì tài **qiǎo** le!

What a **coincidence**!

1220- 侧 /cè/ – *Side*

公园在路的左**侧**。

gōng yuán zài lù de zuǒ **cè**.

The park is on the left **side** of the street.

1221- 韩 /hán/ – *Han (surname); Korea*

我姓**韩**。

wǒ xìng **hán**.

My surname is **Han**.

1222- 冒 /mào/ – *Take (risks), send out*

不要**冒**险。

bù yào **mào** xiǎn.

Don't **take** risks.

1223- 债/zhài/ – Debt

他保证在 1 个月内偿**债**。

tā bǎo zhèng zài 1 gè yuè nèi cháng **zhài**.

He promised to pay his **debt** within a month.

1224- 曼/màn/ – Beautiful

我喜欢她**曼妙**的舞姿。

wǒ xǐ huān tā **màn** miào de wǔ zī.

I like her **beautiful** dance.

1225- 融/róng/ – Melt, blend

太阳使雪**融**化。

tài yáng shǐ xuě **róng** huà.

The sun **melted** the snow.

1226- 惯/guàn/ – Accustomed to, to spoil

他被**惯**坏了。

tā bèi **guàn** huài le.

He was **spoiled**.

1227- 享/xiǎng/ – Enjoy

他们**享**受自己辛勤努力的成果。

tā men **xiǎng** shòu zì jǐ xīn qín nǔ lì de chéng guǒ.

They **enjoy** the fruits of their hard work.

1228- 戴/dài/ – Put on, wear

我不喜欢**戴**眼镜。

wǒ bù xǐ huān **dài** yǎn jìng.

I don't like to **wear** glasses.

1229- 童/tóng/ – Child

儿**童**喜欢去游乐园。

ér **tóng** xǐ huān qù yóu lè yuán.

Children like to go to the amusement park.

1230- 犹/yóu/ – *Still, just as, just like*

流星划过天空，而我却意**犹**未尽。

liú xīng huá guò tiān kōng, ér wǒ què yì **yóu** wèi jìn.

A meteor streaked across the sky, but I am **still** lost in the scene.

1231- 乘/chéng/ – *Ride, multiply*

他五岁学会做**乘**法。

tā wǔ suì xué huì zuò **chéng** fǎ.

He learned to **multiply** at the age of 5.

1232- 挂/guà/ – *Hang*

我的外套**挂**在门厅里。

wǒ de wài tào **guà** zài mén tīng lǐ.

My coat is **hanging** in the hall.

1233- 奖/jiǎng/ – *Prize*

他终于赢得诺贝尔**奖**。

tā zhōng yú yíng dé nuò bèi ěr **jiǎng**.

He finally won the Nobel **Prize**.

1234- 绍/shào/ – *Introduce*

她把我介**绍**给她的朋友。

tā bǎ wǒ jiè **shào** gěi tā de péng yǒu.

She **introduced** me to her friends.

1235- 厚/hòu/ – *Thick*

她还穿着那件**厚**外套。

tā hái chuān zhe nà jiàn **hòu** wài tào.

She was still wearing her **thick** coat.

1236- 纵/zòng/ – *Vertical; to indulge*

他太**纵**容他的孩子了。

tā tài **zòng** róng tā de hái zi le.

He **indulged** his children too much.

1237- 障/zhàng/ – *Obstruct; obstacle*

缺少教育是成功的**障**碍。

quē shǎo jiào yù shì chéng gōng de **zhàng** ài.

Lack of education is an **obstacle** of success.

1238- 讯/xùn/ – *Information; interrogate*

法官可以**讯**问被告人。

fǎ guān kě yǐ **xùn** wèn bèi gào rén.

The judges may **interrogate** the defendant.

1239- 涉/shè/ – *To wade, to be involved*

我们将在溪流最浅的地方**涉**水过去。

wǒ men jiāng zài xī liú zuì qiǎn de dì fāng **shè** shuǐ guò qù.

We'll **wade** the stream at its shallowest point.

1240- 彻/chè/ – *Thorough*

把房间**彻**底打扫一下。

bǎ fáng jiān **chè** dǐ dǎ sǎo yī xià.

Give the room a **thorough** clean.

1241- 刊/kān/ – *Publication; publish*

他去世的消息**刊**登在了报纸上。

tā qù shì de xiāo xī **kān** dēng zài le bào zhǐ shàng.

The news of his death was **published** in the newspaper.

1242- 丈/zhàng/ – *To measure; old man; male relatives by marriage*

请仔细**丈**量这块土地。

qǐng zǐ xì **zhàng** liáng zhè kuài tǔ dì.

Please **measure** this land carefully.

1243- 爆/bào/ – *Explode, burst*

炸弹**爆**炸了。

zhà dàn **bào** zhà le.

The bomb **exploded**.

1244- 乌/wū/ – Black

她有一头**乌**黑浓密的秀发。

tā yǒu yī tóu **wū** hēi nóng mì de xiù fà.

She has thick and **black** hair.

1245- 役/yì/ –Service, campaign

他服过一年兵**役**。

tā fú guò yī nián bīng **yì**.

He did a year's military **service**.

1246- 描/miáo/ – Depict

他的小说**描**述的是伦敦现代的生活。

tā de xiǎo shuō **miáo** shù de shì lún dūn xiàn dài de shēng huó.

His novel **depicts** life in modern London.

1247- 洗/xǐ/ – Wash

饭前必须**洗**手。

fàn qián bì xū **xǐ** shǒu.

You must **wash** your hands before dinner.

1248- 玛/mǎ/ – Agate

他看到前面有一段**玛**瑙做的台阶。

tā kàn dào qián miàn yǒu yī duàn **mǎ** nǎo zuò de tái jiē.

He saw before him a flight of **agate** steps.

1249- 患/huàn/ – Suffer

他**患**了肝病。

tā **huàn** le gān bìng.

He **suffered** from a liver ailment.

1250- 妙/miào/ – Wonderful

太**妙**了。

tài **miào** le.

That's **wonderful**.

1251- 镜/jìng/ – *Mirror*

她正在照**镜**子。

tā zhèng zài zhào **jìng** zi.

She was looking at herself in the **mirror**.

1252- 唱/chàng/ – *Sing*

我想**唱**首歌。

wǒ xiǎng **chàng** shǒu gē.

I want to **sing** a song.

1253- 烦/fán/ – *Bother*

别**烦**我。

bié **fán** wǒ.

Don't **bother** me.

1254- 签/qiān/ – *To sign*

他在账单上**签**了名。

tā zài zhàng dān shàng **qiān** le míng.

He **signed** his name on the bill.

1255- 仙/xiān/ – *Immortal*

谁也不相信人能成**仙**的神话。

shuí yě bù xiāng xìn rén néng chéng **xiān** de shén huà.

Nobody believes in the myth about humans becoming **immortals**.

1256- 彼/bǐ/ – *Other*

我们**彼**此熟悉。

wǒ men **bǐ** cǐ shú xī.

We know each **other** well.

1257- 弗/fú/ – *Not*

瞒人之事**弗**为。

mán rén zhī shì **fú** wèi.

Do **not** do something deceptive.

1258- 症/zhèng/ – Symptom

发烧是很多疾病的病**症**。

fā shāo shì hěn duō jí bìng de bìng **zhèng**.

Fever is a **symptom** of many illnesses.

1259- 仿/fǎng/ – Imitate

他的笔迹很难模**仿**。

tā de bǐ jì hěn nán mó **fǎng**.

His handwriting is difficult to **imitate**.

1260- 倾/qīng/ – Incline, lean

我**倾**向于持反对观点。

wǒ **qīng** xiàng yú chí fǎn duì guān diǎn.

I **incline** to take the opposite point of view.

1261- 牌/pái/ – Signboard, medal, brand

这枚奖**牌**是银制的。

zhè méi jiǎng **pái** shì yín zhì de.

This **medal** is in silver.

1262- 陷/xiàn/ – Trap

这是个**陷**阱。

zhè shì gè **xiàn** jǐng.

It's a **trap**.

1263- 鸟/niǎo/ – Bird

鸟都下蛋。

niǎo dōu xià dàn.

All **birds** lay eggs.

1264- 轰/hōng/ – Boom, rumble

炮声**轰轰**。

pào shēng **hōng hōng**.

The guns **boomed**.

1265- 咱/zán/ – *We, us*

他邀请**咱**们参加晚会。

tā yāo qǐng **zán** men cān jiā wǎn huì.

He invited **us** to the party.

1266- 菜/cài/ – *Vegetable*

新鲜的**菜**在夏季很便宜。

xīn xiān de **cài** zài xià jì hěn pián yí.

Fresh **vegetables** are very cheap in summer.

1267- 闭/bì/ – *Close, shut*

闭嘴！

bì zuǐ!

Shut up!

1268- 奋/fèn/ – *Strive*

那些年，他只是为成名而**奋**斗。

nà xiē nián, tā zhǐ shì wèi chéng míng ér **fèn** dòu.

In those years, he just **strove** for fame.

1269- 庆/qìng/ – *Celebrate*

让我们**庆**祝吧！

ràng wǒ men **qìng** zhù ba!

Let's **celebrate**!

1270- 撤/chè/ – *Withdraw, fall back*

莉莉**撤**回了评论。

lì lì **chè** huí le píng lùn.

Lily **withdrew** the remark.

1271- 泪/lèi/ – *Tear*

她很难忍住不流**泪**。

tā hěn nán rěn zhù bù liú **lèi**.

It was difficult for her to fight back her **tears**.

1272- 茶/chá/ – Tea

他正在沏**茶**。

tā zhèng zài qī **chá**.

He's making **tea**.

1273- 疾/jí/ – Disease, sickness

该**疾**病仍在初发阶段。

gāi **jí** bìng réng zài chū fā jiē duàn.

The **disease** is still in its primary stage.

1274- 缘/yuán/ – Fate

咱俩又在一起了，真是有**缘**。

zán liǎ yòu zài yī qǐ le, zhēn shì yǒu **yuán**.

We're together again. It must be **fate**.

1275- 播/bō/ – Broadcast

你听广**播**吗？

nǐ tīng guǎng **bō** ma?

Do you listen to the **broadcast**?

1276- 朗/lǎng/ – Bright, clear

早晨的天气非常晴**朗**。

zǎo chén de tiān qì fēi cháng qíng **lǎng**.

In the morning, it was **bright**.

1277- 杜/dù/ – Du (surname)

我姓**杜**。

wǒ xìng **dù**.

My surname is **Du**.

1278- 奶/nǎi/ – Grandmother; milk

她是我**奶奶**。

tā shì wǒ **nǎi** nai.

She's my **grandmother**.

1279- 季/jì/ – Season

一年中有四**季**。

yī nián zhōng yǒu sì **jì**.

There are four **seasons** in a year.

1280- 丹/dān/ – Red, pellet

天边的**丹**霞好美。

tiān biān de **dān** xiá hǎo měi.

The **red** glow in the sky is beautiful.

1281- 狗/gǒu/ – Dog

狗是忠诚的动物。

gǒu shì zhōng chéng de dòng wù.

Dogs are faithful animals.

1282- 尾/wěi/ – Tail

这狗摇着**尾**巴。

zhè gǒu yáo zhe **wěi** bā.

The dog wags its **tail**.

1283- 仪/yí/ – Rite, appearance

这个**仪**式不仅象征转变为成年人。

zhè ge **yí** shì bù jǐn xiàng zhēng zhuǎn biàn wéi chéng nián rén.

The **rite** is more than a transition into adulthood.

1284- 偷/tōu/ – Steal

他因**偷**窃被送入监狱。

tā yīn **tōu** qiè bèi sòng rù jiān yù.

He was sent into prison for **stealing**.

1285- 奔/bēn/ – Run

我长长地松了一口气，停止了**奔**跑。

wǒ cháng cháng de sōng le yī kǒu qì, tíng zhǐ le **bēn** pǎo.

With immense relief, I stopped **running**.

1286- 珠/zhū/ – Pearl, bead

他满脸都是汗**珠**。

tā mǎn liǎn dōu shì hàn **zhū**.

His face was covered with **beads** of sweat.

1287- 虫/chóng/ – Bug, worm

我们要杀**虫**剂干啥？

wǒ men yào shā **chóng** jì gàn shá?

Why do we need **bug** spray?

1288- 驻/zhù/ – Halt, be stationed

部队**驻**扎在山上。

bù duì **zhù** zhā zài shān shàng.

The troops were **stationed** on a hill.

1289- 孔/kǒng/ – Hole

我裤子上有个**孔**。

wǒ kù zi shàng yǒu gè **kǒng**.

There is a **hole** in my pants.

1290- 宜/yí/ – Suitable, appropriate

这些衣服适**宜**周末穿。

zhè xiē yī fú shì **yí** zhōu mò chuān.

These clothes are **suitable** for weekends.

1291- 艾/ài/ – Moxa

你不一定要服用苦的药或用热的**艾**炙来治疗。

nǐ bù yī dìng yào fú yòng kǔ de yào huò yòng rè de **ài** jiū lái zhì liáo.

You don't have to take bitter medicine or stand for hot **moxa** treatment.

1292- 桥/qiáo/ – Bridge

这**桥**很危险。

zhè **qiáo** hěn wēi xiǎn.

This **bridge** is very dangerous.

1293- 淡/dàn/ – *Tasteless, dilute*

水能使酒变**淡**。

shuǐ néng shǐ jiǔ biàn **dàn**.

The water will **dilute** the wine.

1294- 翼/yì/ – *Wing*

这只鸟的左**翼**受伤了。

zhè zhī niǎo de zuǒ **yì** shòu shāng le.

The bird's left **wing** was hurt.

1295- 恨/hèn/ – *Hate; hatred*

他们彼此憎**恨**。

tā men bǐ cǐ zēng **hèn**.

They **hate** each other.

1296- 繁/fán/ – *Complicate*

向公司索取退款手续**繁**琐。

xiàng gōng sī suǒ qǔ tuì kuǎn shǒu xù **fán** suǒ.

Obtaining a refund from the company is a **complicated** procedure.

1297- 寒/hán/ – *Cold*

天气**寒**冷。

tiān qì **hán** lěng.

The weather is **cold**.

1298- 伴/bàn/ – *Companion*

他是个好旅**伴**。

tā shì gè hǎo lǚ **bàn**.

He is a good **companion** on the journey.

1299- 叹/tàn/ – *Sigh*

他绝望地**叹**了口气。

tā jué wàng de **tàn** le kǒu qì.

He **sighed** with despair.

1300- 且/dàn/ – *Dawn, morning*

他经常通宵达**且**地工作。

tā jīng cháng tōng xiāo dá **dàn** de gōng zuò.

He often works all night till **dawn**.

1301- 愈/yù/ – *Heal*

伤口尚未**愈**合。

shāng kǒu shàng wèi **yù** hé.

The wound has not yet **healed**.

1302- 潮/cháo/ – *Humid, damp*

那**潮**湿的气候对他不合适。

nà **cháo** shī de qì hòu duì tā bù hé shì.

The **humid** climate didn't agree with him.

1303- 粮/liáng/ – *Grain*

我们把**粮**食运往非洲。

wǒ men bǎ **liáng** shí yùn wǎng fēi zhōu.

We ship **grain** to Africa.

1304- 缩/suō/ – *Shrink*

它**缩**小了。

tā **suō** xiǎo le.

It **shrunk**.

1305- 罢/bà/ – *Dismiss, suspend*

他被**罢**免了。

tā bèi **bà** miǎn le.

He was **dismissed**.

1306- 聚/jù/ – *Gather*

人群正在**聚**集。

rén qún zhèng zài **jù** jí.

The crowd is **gathering**.

1307- 径/jìng/ – *Path*

公路的尽头是一条狭窄的小**径**。

gōng lù de jìn tóu shì yī tiáo xiá zhǎi de xiǎo **jìng**.

The road finished in a narrow **path**.

1308- 恰/qià/ – *Exactly, just*

事实**恰恰**相反。

shì shí **qià qià** xiāng fǎn.

The truth is **exactly** the opposite.

1309- 挑/tiāo/ – *To pick, choose*

挑最好的吧。

tiāo zuì hǎo de ba.

Pick the best one.

1310- 袋/dài/ – *Bag, pocket*

桌子上有两**袋**猫食。

zhuō zi shàng yǒu liǎng **dài** māo shí.

There are two **bags** of cat food on the table.

1311- 灰/huī/ – *Grey*

有些人喜欢**灰**色。

yǒu xiē rén xǐ huān **huī** sè.

Some people like **gray**.

1312- 捕/bǔ/ – *Capture, arrest*

我们**捕**获了那个罪犯。

wǒ men **bǔ** huò le nà gè zuì fàn.

We **captured** the criminal.

1313- 徐/xú/ – *Slowly, gently*

清风**徐**来。

qīng fēng **xú** lái.

A refreshing breeze is blowing **gently**.

1314- 珍/zhēn/ – *Rare, valuable*

这是一种**珍**贵的金属。

zhè shì yī zhǒng **zhēn** guì de jīn shǔ.

This is a **rare** metal.

1315- 幕/mù/ – *Curtain, screen*

幕拉开，剧就开演了。

mù lā kāi, jù jiù kāi yǎn le.

The **curtain** divided and the play began.

1316- 映/yìng/ – *Reflect, shine*

镜子能**映**像。

jìng zi néng **yìng** xiàng.

A mirror **reflects**.

1317- 裂/liè/ – *Crack*

盘子掉地上摔**裂**了。

pán zi diào dì shàng shuāi **liè** le.

The plate **cracked** when it dropped.

1318- 泰/tài/ – *Good, peaceful; Thailand*

国**泰**民安。

guó **tài** mín ān.

Peaceful and prosperous times.

1319- 隔/gé/ – *Separate, partition*

我们的办公室用一个**隔**板分开了。

wǒ men de bàn gōng shì yòng yī gè **gé** bǎn fēn kāi le.

Our office is separated by a **partition** board.

1320- 启/qǐ/ – *Start, initiate*

车**启**动不了。

chē **qǐ** dòng bù liǎo.

The car will not **start**.

1321- 尖/jiān/ – *Sharp, pointy*

不要用**尖**头戳我。

bù yào yòng **jiān** tóu chuō wǒ.

Don't use the **pointy** head to poke me.

1322- 忠/zhōng/ – *Loyal*

我们**忠**于祖国。

wǒ men **zhōng** yú zǔ guó.

We are **loyal** to our motherland.

1323- 累/lèi/ – *Tired*

我**累**了。

wǒ **lèi** le.

I'm **tired**.

1324- 炎/yán/ – *Flame, inflammation*

他有**炎**症。

tā yǒu **yán** zhèng.

He has **inflammation**.

1325- 暂/zàn/ – *Temporary*

这种安排只是**暂**时的。

zhè zhǒng ān pái zhǐ shì **zàn** shí de.

The arrangement is only **temporary**.

1326- 估/gū/ – *Estimate*

这是最高的**估**价。

zhè shì zuì gāo de **gū** jià.

This is an outside **estimate** of the price.

1327- 泛/fàn/ – *Flood; general; float*

河水**泛**滥。

hé shuǐ **fàn** làn.

The river was in **flood**.

1328- 荒/huāng/ –Desolate

战争期间，这个火车站变得**荒**凉了。

zhàn zhēng qī jiān, zhè ge huǒ chē zhàn biàn dé **huāng** liáng le.

The railway station became **desolate** in the war.

1329- 偿/cháng/ – Repay, compensate

你必须赔**偿**我们的损失。

nǐ bì xū péi **cháng** wǒ men de sǔn shī.

You will have to **compensate** us for the loss.

1330- 横/héng/ – Horizontal; across

请在这一页画条**横**线。

qǐng zài zhè yī yè huà tiáo **héng** xiàn.

Please draw a **horizontal** line on the page.

1331- 拒/jù/ – Resist, repel, refuse

她**拒**绝了我。

tā **jù** jué le wǒ.

She **refused** me.

1332- 瑞/ruì/ – Auspicious, lucky

瑞雪兆丰年。

ruì xuě zhào fēng nián.

A timely snow gives **auspicious** promise of a good harvest.

1333- 忆/yì/ – Memory

和你的记**忆**告别吧。

hé nǐ de jì **yì** gào bié ba.

Say goodbye to your **memory**.

1334- 孤/gū/ – Lonely

他感到**孤**独。

tā gǎn dào **gū** dú.

He feels **lonely**.

1335- 鼻 /bí/ – Nose

我**鼻**子痒。

wǒ **bí** zi yǎng.

My **nose** is itching.

1336- 闹 /nào/ – Noisy; disturb

这屋里太**闹**。

zhè wū lǐ tài **nào**.

This room is too **noisy**.

1337- 羊 /yáng/ – Sheep, goat

那是一只迷途的羔**羊**。

nà shì yī zhǐ mí tú de gāo **yáng**.

It is a stray **sheep**.

1338- 呆 /dāi/ – Stupid, foolish

他是一个很**呆**的人。

tā shì yī gè hěn **dāi** de rén.

He is a very **stupid** person.

1339- 厉 /lì/ – Strict

她是位严**厉**的教师。

tā shì wèi yán **lì** de jiào shī.

She is a **strict** teacher.

1340- 衡 /héng/ – To weigh; balance

他在脑中权**衡**这些想法。

tā zài nǎo zhōng quán **héng** zhè xiē xiǎng fǎ.

He **weighed** the ideas in his mind.

1341- 胞 /bāo/ – Compatriot

亲爱的同**胞**们，为国效劳的时候到了。

qīn ài de tóng **bāo** men, wèi guó xiào láo de shí hòu dào le.

My dear **compatriot**, it is time that we did something for our country.

1342- 零 /líng/ – Zero

气温将在**零**度以上。

qì wēn jiāng zài **líng** dù yǐ shàng.

The temperature will be above **zero**.

1343- 穷 /qióng/ – Poor

他**穷**得买不起新外套。

tā **qióng** dé mǎi bù qǐ xīn wài tào.

He was too **poor** to buy a new coat.

1344- 舍 /shě/ – Abandon, give alms

杰克**舍**弃了那辆旧车。

jié kè **shě** qì le nà liàng jiù chē.

Jack has **abandoned** his old car.

1345- 码 /mǎ/ – Code, yard

三英尺是一**码**。

sān yīng chǐ shì yī **mǎ**.

Three feet make one **yard**.

1346- 赫 /hè/ – Famous

他是位**赫赫**有名的将军。

tā shì wèi **hè hè** yǒu míng de jiāng jūn.

He's a **famous** general.

1347- 婆 /pó/ – Personal pronoun for female

她是我老**婆**。

tā shì wǒ lǎo **pó**.

She's my **wife**.

1348- 魂 /hún/ – Soul

创新是一个民族的灵**魂**。

chuàng xīn shì yī gè mín zú de líng **hún**.

Creativity is the **soul** of a nation.

1349- 灾/zāi/ – *Disaster*

灾难发生时，她就在那里。

zāi nàn fā shēng shí, tā jiù zài nà lǐ.

She was there when the **disaster** happened.

1350- 洪/hóng/ – *Flood*

洪水把我们挡住，回不了家。

hóng shuǐ bǎ wǒ men dǎng zhù, huí bù liǎo jiā.

The **floods** cut us off from our homes.

1351- 腿/tuǐ/ – *Leg*

他在战争中失去了左**腿**。

tā zài zhàn zhēng zhōng shī qù le zuǒ **tuǐ**.

He lost his left **leg** in the war.

1352- 胆/dǎn/ – *Gall, courage*

他是个有**胆**量的人。

tā shì gè yǒu **dǎn** liàng de rén.

He's a man of **courage**.

1353- 津/jīn/ – *Abbreviation for 天津 (Tian Jin)*

我们常把天津市称为**津**。

wǒ men cháng bǎ tiān **jīn** shì chēng wéi **jīn**.

We often refer to Tianjin City as **Jin**.

1354- 俗/sú/ – *Convention, coarse, vulgar*

我觉得这座房子很**俗**气。

wǒ jué dé zhè zuò fáng zi hěn **sú** qì.

I think it's a very **vulgar** house.

1355- 辩/biàn/ – *Debate, argue*

我不想就我的看法同你**辩**论。

wǒ bù xiǎng jiù wǒ de kàn fǎ tóng nǐ **biàn** lùn.

I don't want to **debate** my opinions with you.

1356- 胸/xiōng/ – Chest

那头熊的**胸**前毛茸茸的。

nà tóu xióng de **xiōng** qián máo róng róng de.

The bear's **chest** is hairy.

1357- 晓/xiǎo/ – Dawn; to know

我已经**晓**得了。

wǒ yǐ jīng **xiǎo** dé le.

I've **known** already.

1358- 劲/jìn/ – Strength, energy

他没**劲**了。

tā méi **jìn** le.

His **strength** ran out.

1359- 贫/pín/ – Poor, inadequate

他**贫**于金钱，却富于知识。

tā **pín** yú jīn qián, què fù yú zhī shì.

He is **poor** in money, but rich in knowledge.

1360- 仁/rén/ – Kernel, humane

杏**仁**能吃吗？

xìng **rén** néng chī ma?

Are apricot **kernels** edible?

1361- 偶/ǒu/ – Accidental, pair

他们的结合是**偶**然的。

tā men de jié hé shì **ǒu** rán de.

Their marriage was quite **accidental**.

1362- 辑/jí/ – Edit

他认真编**辑**了一本诗集。

tā rèn zhēn biān **jí** le yī běn shī jí.

He carefully **edited** a book of poetry.

1363- 邦 /bāng/ – *Nation*

中国历来以礼仪之**邦**著称。

zhōng guó lì lái yǐ lǐ yí zhī **bāng** zhù chēng.

China has always been known as a **nation** of propriety.

1364- 恢 /huī/ – *To recover, resume*

预计很快能**恢**复交通。

yù jì hěn kuài néng **huī** fù jiāo tōng.

Traffic is expected to be **resumed** shortly.

1365- 赖 /lài/ – *To blame, depend on, disclaim*

都**赖**我。

dōu **lài** wǒ.

I'm to **blame**.

1366- 圈 /quān/ – *Loop*

他用绳子打了个**圈**。

tā yòng shéng zi dǎ le gè **quān**.

He made a **loop** in the string.

1367- 摸 /mō/ – *Touch*

别**摸**我。

bié **mō** wǒ.

Don't **touch** me.

1368- 仰 /yǎng/ – *Look up, admire, rely on*

亨利突然抬头**仰**望，发现天空中有一道彩虹。

hēng lì tú rán tái tóu **yǎng** wàng, fā xiàn tiān kōng zhōng yǒu yī dào cǎi hóng.

When **looking up** suddenly, Henry saw a rainbow in the sky.

1369- 润 /rùn/ – *Lubricate, moisten*

我需要**润润**嗓子。

wǒ xū yào **rùn rùn** sǎng zi.

My throat needs **lubricating**.

1370- 堆 /duī/ – *Pile*

他把落叶**堆**在院子一角。

tā bǎ luò yè **duī** zài yuàn zi yī jiǎo.

He **piled** up fallen leaves in a corner of the yard.

1371- 碰 /pèng/ – *Meet, bump*

很抱歉**碰**上你。

hěn bào qiàn pèng **shàng** nǐ.

I'm sorry to **bump** into you.

1372- 艇 /tǐng/ – *Vessel, boat*

水手们降下了救生**艇**。

shuǐ shǒu men jiàng xià le jiù shēng **tǐng**.

The sailors lowered a life**boat**.

1373- 稍 /shāo/ – *Slightly*

每所房子都**稍**有区别。

měi suǒ fáng zi dōu **shāo** yǒu qū bié.

Each of the houses is **slightly** different.

1374- 迟 /chí/ – *Late*

你**迟**到了。

nǐ **chí** dàole.

You're **late**.

1375- 辆 /liàng/ – *Measure word for vehicles*

他买了一**辆**车。

tā mǎi le yī **liàng** chē.

He bought **a car**.

1376- 废 /fèi/ – *Abolish*

我们应该**废**止死刑吗?

wǒ men yīng gāi **fèi** zhǐ sǐ xíng ma?

Should we **abolish** the death penalty?

1377- 净 /jìng/ – Clean; Purify

水不能**净**化空气。

shuǐ bù néng **jìng** huà kōng qì.

Water cannot **purify** the air.

1378- 凶 /xiōng/ – Fearful; vicious, fierce

他一脸**凶**相。

tā yī liǎn **xiōng** xiàng.

He has a **fierce** look on his face.

1379- 署 /shǔ/ – To sign

请在此**署**名。

qǐng zài cǐ **shǔ** míng.

Please **sign** your name here.

1380- 壁 /bì/ – Wall

他把墙**壁**刷成了绿色。

tā bǎ qiáng **bì** shuā chéng le lǜ sè.

He colored the **walls** green.

1381- 御 /yù/ – Resist, defend

他的防**御**能力比进攻能力强。

tā de fáng **yù** néng lì bǐ jìn gōng néng lì qiáng.

He's better at **defending** than attacking.

1382- 奉 /fèng/ – Present, offer (as a tribute)

请接受我们的供**奉**。

qǐng jiē shòu wǒ men de gòng **fèng**.

Please accept our **offer**.

1383- 旋 /xuán/ – Revolve

轮子慢慢开始**旋**转。

lún zi màn màn kāi shǐ **xuán** zhuǎn.

Wheels began to **revolve** slowly.

1384- 冬 /dōng/ – Winter

我不喜欢**冬**天。

wǒ bù xǐ huān **dōng** tiān.

I don't like **winter**.

1385- 矿 /kuàng/ – Mine

他父亲是个**矿**工。

tā fù qīn shì gè **kuàng** gōng.

His father is a **mine** worker.

1386- 抬 /tái/ – Lift

他虚弱地**抬**不起手。

tā xū ruò de **tái** bù qǐ shǒu.

He was too weak to **lift** his hand.

1387- 蛋 /dàn/ – Egg

那只母鸡每天生一个**蛋**。

nà zhī mǔ jī měi tiān shēng yī gè **dàn**.

The hen lays an **egg** a day.

1388- 晨 /chén/ – Morning

早**晨**好。

zǎo **chén** hǎo.

Good **morning**.

1389- 伏 /fú/ – Ambush

他怀疑有埋**伏**。

tā huái yí yǒu mái **fú**.

He suspected an **ambush**.

1390- 吹 /chuī/ – Blow

风扇正**吹**着。

fēng shàn zhèng **chuī** zhe.

The fan was **blowing**.

1391- 鸡/jī/ – Chicken

他有一个养鸡场。

tā yǒu yī gè yǎng **jī** chǎng.

He has a **chicken** farm.

1392- 倍/bèi/ – Multiply

我们成功的机会倍增。

wǒ men chéng gōng de jī huì **bèi** zēng.

Our chances of success **multiplied**.

1393- 糊/hú/ – Muddled, scorched; to paste

孩子们忙着剪裁和糊纸帽子。

hái zi men máng zhe jiǎn cái hé **hú** zhǐ mào zi.

The children were busy cutting and **pasting** paper hats.

1394- 秦/qín/ – Qin (a dynasty in history; surname)

他姓秦。

tā xìng **qín**.

His surname is **Qin**.

1395- 盾/dùn/ – Shield

剑掠过骑士的盾。

jiàn lüè guò qí shì de **dùn**.

The sword glanced off the knight's **shield**.

1396- 杯/bēi/ – Cup

这只杯子是不锈钢的。

zhè zhī **bēi** zi shì bù xiù gāng de.

This **cup** is made of stainless steel.

1397- 租/zū/ – Rent

我向她租了一个房间。

wǒ xiàng tā **zū** le yī gè fáng jiān.

I **rent** a room from her.

1398- 骑 /qí/ – Ride

你**骑**了多远？

nǐ **qí** le duō yuǎn?

How far did you **ride**?

1399- 乏 /fá/ – Short of, lack

他缺**乏**必要的能力。

tā quē **fá** bì yào de néng lì.

He **lacks** the necessary ability.

1400- 隆 /lóng/ – Prosperous

他的生意十分兴**隆**。

tā de shēng yì shí fēn xīng **lóng**.

His business is **prosperous**.

1401- 诊 /zhěn/ – Diagnose

医生**诊**断出麻疹。

yī shēng **zhěn** duàn chū má zhěn.

The doctor **diagnosed** measles.

1402- 奴 /nú/ – Slave

他的祖父曾为**奴**。

tā de zǔ fù céng wèi **nú**.

His grandfather used to be a **slave**.

1403- 摄 /shè/ – To take a photo, absorb, shoot

这个镜头可不容易拍**摄**。

zhè gè jìng tóu kě bù róng yì pāi **shè**.

This scene is not easy to **shoot**.

1404- 丧 /sàng/ – Die

他受火刑而**丧**命。

tā shòu huǒ xíng ér **sàng** mìng.

He **died** at the stake.

1405- 污 /wū/ – Filthy, dirty

你说这块**污**渍能去掉吗？

nǐ shuō zhè kuài **wū** zì néng qù diào ma?

Do you think that **dirty** mark will come out?

1406- 渡 /dù/ – To ferry

船在**渡**人。

chuán zài **dù** rén.

The boat is **ferrying** people.

1407- 旗 /qí/ – Flag, banner

旗子在风中飘扬。

qí zi zài fēng zhōng piāo yáng.

Flags are fluttering in the breeze.

1408- 甘 /gān/ – Sweet; willing

你**甘**愿帮忙吗？

nǐ **gān** yuàn bāng máng ma?

Are you **willing** to help?

1409- 耐 /nài/ – Patient; endure

我再也不**耐**烦听那一套了。

wǒ zài yě bù **nài** fán tīng nà yī tào le.

I can't **endure** listening to that any longer.

1410- 凭 /píng/ – Rely on; proof

你有什么**凭**证说这辆自行车是你的？

nǐ yǒu shén me **píng** zhèng shuō zhè liàng zì xíng chē shì nǐ de?

Have you got any **proof** that you own this bike?

1411- 扎 /zhā/ – Prick

她被针**扎**了一下。

tā bèi zhēn **zhā** le yī xià.

She **pricked** herself on a needle.

1412- 抢 /qiǎng/ – *Rob*

他们**抢**了那个女孩。

tā men **qiǎng** le nà gè nǚ hái.

They **robbed** the girl.

1413- 绪 /xù/ – *Clue*

我一点头**绪**都没有。 wǒ yī diǎn tóu **xù** dōu méi yǒu.

I don't have any **clue**.

1414- 粗 /cū/ – *Rough*

猫的舌头表面很**粗糙**。

māo de shé tóu biǎo miàn hěn **cū cāo**.

The cat had a **rough** tongue.

1415- 肩 /jiān/ – *Shoulder*

子弹打伤了他的**肩膀**。

zǐ dàn dǎ shāng le tā de **jiān bǎng**.

The bullet wounded his **shoulder**.

1416- 梁 /liáng/ – *Beam*

横**梁**是用来支撑屋顶的。

héng **liáng** shì yòng lái zhī chēng wū dǐng de.

Beams support the roof of a house.

1417- 幻 /huàn/ – *Fantasy*

这是一个**幻**想故事。

zhè shì yī gè **huàn** xiǎng gù shì.

This story is a **fantasy**.

1418- 菲 /fēi/ – *Abbreviation for 菲律宾 (the Philippines)*

菲律宾位于东南亚。

fēi lǜ bīn wèi yú dōng nán yà.

The **Philippines** is located in Southeast Asia.

1419- 皆 /jiē/ – *All*

四海之内**皆**兄弟。

sì hǎi zhī nèi **jiē** xiōng dì.

All men are brothers.

1420- 碎 /suì/ – *Break down, smash*

杯子掉下来摔**碎**了。

bēi zi diào xià lái shuāi **suì** le.

The cup fell and **smashed**.

1421- 宙 / zhòu/ – *Universe*

我们的地球是**宇宙**的一小部分。

wǒ men de dì qiú shì **yǔ zhòu** de yī xiǎo bù fèn.

Our earth is a small part of the **universe**.

1422- 叔 /shū/ – *Uncle (father's young brother)*

他是我**叔**。

tā shì wǒ **shū**.

He's my **uncle**.

1423- 岩 /yán/ – *Rock*

岩石是坚硬的。

yán shí shì jiān yìng de.

Rock is hard.

1424- 荡 /dàng/ – *Sway*

树叶在风中飘**荡**。

shù yè zài fēng zhōng piāo **dàng**.

The leaves of the trees were **swaying** in the wind.

1425- 综 /zōng/ – *Put together, combine*

你应该把这些因素**综合**起来分析。

nǐ yīng gāi bǎ zhè xiē yīn sù **zōng** hé qǐ lái fēn xī.

You should **combine** these factors into a single analysis.

1426- 爬/pá/ – *Crawl*

那个婴儿正在学习爬行。

nà gè yīng ér zhèng zài xué xí **pá** xíng.

The baby is just learning to **crawl**.

1427- 荷/hé/ – *Lotus*

荷叶是舒展的。

hé yè shì shū zhǎn de.

The **lotus** leaves are unfolding.

1428- 悉/xī/ – *Know*

我已获悉这个消息。

wǒ yǐ huò **xī** zhè gè xiāo xī.

I've **known** this news.

1429- 蒂/dì/ – *The base of a flower or fruit ; butt*

捡起那个烟蒂。

jiǎn qǐ nà gè yān **dì**.

Pick up the cigarette **butt**.

1430- 返/fǎn/ – *Return*

他返回了广场。

tā **fǎn** huí le guǎng chǎng.

He **returned** to the square.

1431- 井/jǐng/ – *Well*

警察在一口枯井里找到了丢失的财宝。

jǐng chá zài yī kǒu kū **jǐng** lǐ zhǎo dào le diū shī de cái bǎo.

The police found the lost treasure in an abandoned **well**.

1432- 壮/zhuàng/ – *Strong*

他很强壮。

tā hěn qiáng **zhuàng**.

He's **strong**.

1433- 薄/bó/ – _Thin_

山上空气很稀**薄**。

shān shàng kōng qì hěn xī **bó**.

The air on the mountain is very **thin**.

1434- 悄/qiāo/ – _Quietly_

他**悄悄**地走了。

tā **qiāo qiāo** de zǒu le.

He left **quietly**.

1435- 扫/sǎo/ – _Sweep_

她正在**扫**地。

tā zhèng zài **sǎo** dì.

She's **sweeping** the floor.

1436- 敏/mǐn/ – _Agile, nimble_

他是个**敏**捷的攀岩者。

tā shì gè **mǐn** jié de pān yán zhě.

He is a **nimble** rock-climber.

1437- 碍/ài/ – _Hinder, block_

别**碍**事！

bié **ài** shì!

Don't **hinder** me!

1438- 殖/zhí/ – _Reproduce_

兔子的繁**殖**速度很快。

tù zi de **fán zhí** sù dù hěn kuài.

Rabbits **reproduce** quickly.

1439- 详/xiáng/ – _Detail_

他告诉了我们故事的**详**情。

tā gào sù le wǒ men gù shì de **xiáng** qíng.

He told us the story in **detail**.

1440- 迪/dí/ – Enlighten

这本书会对读者有所启迪。

zhè běn shū huì duì dú zhě yǒu suǒ qǐ **dí.**

This book will **enlighten** the reader.

1441- 矛/máo/ – Spear

渔夫用矛做武器。

yú fū yòng **máo** zuò wǔ qì.

The fisherman used a **spear** as his weapon.

1442- 霍/huò/ – Huo (surname)

她姓霍。

tā xìng **huò.**

Her surname is **Huo.**

1443- 允/yǔn/ – Allow

不允许你这么做。

bù **yǔn** xǔ nǐ zhè me zuò.

You're not **allowed** to do this.

1444- 幅/fú/ – Measure word for painting, picture, etc.

她送了我一幅画。

tā sòng le wǒ **yī fú huà.**

She sent me **a painting.**

1445- 撒/sā/ – Let go

撒开我！

sā kāi wǒ!

Let go of me!

1446- 剩/shèng/ – Remain

树上还剩几个苹果。

shù shàng hái **shèng** jǐ gè píng guǒ.

A few apples **remained** on the tree.

1447- 凯 /kǎi/ – *Victorious*

我相信你一定会**凯**旋归来。

wǒ xiāng xìn nǐ yī dìng huì **kǎi** xuán guī lái.

I'm sure you will return **victorious**.

1448- 颗 /kē/ – *Measure word for pearls, corn grains, teeth, etc.*

这颗牙对冷敏感。

zhè **kē yá** duì lěng mǐn gǎn.

This tooth is sensitive to cold.

1449- 骂 /mà/ – *Abuse, scold*

谁知道他为什么在**骂**人？

shuí zhī dào tā wèi shén me zài **mà** rén?

Who knows why he was **scolding**?

1450- 赏 /shǎng/ – *Reward*

保护油田者有**赏**。

bǎo hù yóu tián zhě yǒu **shǎng**.

Those who protect the oil field will be **rewarded**.

1451- 液 /yè/ – *Liquid*

该**液**体的体积为 5 升。

gāi **yè** tǐ de tǐ jī wéi 5 shēng.

The **liquid** was 5 liters in volume.

1452- 番 /fān/ – *Measure word for occurrences of an action or deed*

为了项目过审，他真是费了**一番心思**。

wèi le xiàng mù guò shěn, tā zhēn shì fèi le **yī fān xīn sī**.

In order to finish the project, he really took **a lot of thoughts**.

1453- 箱 /xiāng/ – *Case, trunk, chest*

箱子里装着一个海员的私人物品。

xiāng zi lǐ zhuāng zhe yī gè hǎi yuán de sī rén wù pǐn.

The **chest** contained the personal belongings of a seaman.

1454- 贴/tiē/ – *Paste*

她把图片**贴**在笔记本上。

tā bǎ tú piàn **tiē** zài bǐ jì běn shàng.

She **pasted** the pictures into a notebook.

1455- 漫/màn/ – *Overflow; free*

厨房水槽的水**漫**到了地板上。

chú fáng shuǐ cáo de shuǐ **màn** dào le dì bǎn shàng.

Water from the kitchen sink **overflowed** onto the floor.

1456- 酸/suān/ – *Sour*

柠檬有股**酸**味。

níng méng yǒu gǔ **suān** wèi.

Lemons have a **sour** taste.

1457- 郎/láng/ – *Personal pronoun for male*

令郎可好？

lìng láng kě hǎo?

How is **your son**?

1458- 腰/yāo/ – *Waist*

他搂住了她的**腰**。

tā lǒu zhù le tā de **yāo**.

He put his arm around her **waist**.

1459- 舒/shū/ – *Comfortable*

他过着**舒**适的生活。

tā guò zhe **shū** shì de shēng huó.

He lives a **comfortable** life.

1460- 眉/méi/ – *Eyebrow*

她怀疑地挑起了**眉**。

tā huái yí de tiǎo qǐ le **méi**.

She raised a questioning **eyebrow**.

1461- 忧/yōu/ – Worried; to worry

别担**忧**。

bié dān **yōu**.

Don't **worry**.

1462- 浮/fú/ – Float

这些植物漂**浮**在水面上。

zhè xiē zhí wù piāo **fú** zài shuǐ miàn shàng.

These plants **float** on the surface of the water.

1463- 辛/xīn/ – Hard, laborious

她的工作很**辛**苦。

tā de gōng zuò hěn **xīn** kǔ.

Her work is a **laborious** task.

1464- 恋/liàn/ – Feel attached to

人们并不觉得依**恋**本地区域。

rén men bìng bù jué dé yī **liàn** běn dì qū yù.

People don't **feel attached to** their local region.

1465- 餐/cān/ – Meal

这是我所吃过的最好的一**餐**。

zhè shì wǒ suǒ chī guò de zuì hǎo de yī **cān**.

This is the best **meal** I had ever eaten.

1466- 吓/xià/ – To scare

你**吓**到我了。

nǐ **xià** dào wǒ le.

You **scared** me.

1467- 挺/tǐng/ – Stick out, straighten up; rather, quite

今天**挺**冷。

jīn tiān **tǐng** lěng.

It's **quite** cold today.

1468- 励/lì/ – Encourage

她的父母鼓**励**她好好学习。

tā de fù mǔ gǔ **lì** tā hǎo hào xué xí.

Her parents **encouraged** her in her studies.

1469- 辞/cí/ – Resign, take leave

他**辞**职了。

tā **cí** zhí le.

He **resigned**.

1470- 艘/sōu/ – Measure word for ships

他买了一**艘游艇**。

tā mǎi le **yī sōu yóu tǐng**.

He bought **a yacht**.

1471- 键/jiàn/ – Key, button

退出本页面按退出**键**。

tuì chū běn yè miàn àn tuì chū **jiàn**.

To exit from this page, press the ESC **key**.

1472- 伍/wǔ/ – Army, rank

彼得决定入**伍**。

bǐ dé jué dìng rù **wǔ**.

Peter decided to join the **army**.

1473- 峰/fēng/ – Peak

他正处于事业的巅**峰**。

tā zhèng chǔ yú shì yè de diān **fēng**.

He's at the **peak** of his career.

1474- 尺/chǐ/ – Ruler

在**尺**子上分厘米刻度。

zài **chǐ** zi shàng fēn lí mǐ kè dù.

The **ruler** is divided into centimetres.

1475- 昨/zuó/ – Yesterday

我**昨**天去医院了。

wǒ **zuó** tiān qù yī yuàn le.

I went to the hospital **yesterday**.

1476- 黎/lí/ – Dawn

戴安娜在**黎**明前唤醒了他们。

dài ān nà zài **lí** míng qián huàn xǐng le tā men.

Diana aroused them just before **dawn**.

1477- 辈/bèi/ – Generation

年轻一**辈**热望新奇的经历。

nián qīng yī **bèi** rè wàng xīn qí de jīng lì.

The younger **generation** is avid of new experiences.

1478- 贯/guàn/ – Run through, pass through

这种思想**贯**穿在她的多数作品之中。

zhè zhǒng sī xiǎng **guàn** chuān zài tā de duō shù zuò pǐn zhī zhōng.

This theme **runs through** most of her writings.

1479- 侦/zhēn/ – Detect, scout

一个小组被派去**侦**察。

yī gè xiǎo zǔ bèi pài qù **zhēn** chá.

A party was sent ahead to **scout**.

1480- 滑/huá/ – Slip; slippery

下雨之后道路很**滑**。

xià yǔ zhī hòu dào lù hěn **huá**.

The road was **slippery** after the rain.

1481- 券/quàn/ – Bond, coupon

请于下单前出示此**券**。

qǐng yú xià dān qián chū shì cǐ **quàn**.

The **coupon** must be presented when ordering.

1482- 崇 /chóng/ – *Worship*

她**崇**拜她的父亲。

tā **chóng** bài tā de fù qīn.

She **worshipped** her father.

1483- 扰 /rǎo/ – *Disturb*

很抱歉打**扰**你。

hěn bào qiàn dǎ **rǎo** nǐ.

I am sorry to **disturb** you.

1484- 宪 /xiàn/ – *Constitution*

总统宣誓维护**宪**法。

zǒng tǒng xuān shì wéi hù **xiàn** fǎ.

The President swore to uphold the **constitution**.

1485- 绕 /rào/ – *Move around, detour*

我们**绕**道走，避开繁忙的交通。

wǒ men **rào** dào zǒu, bì kāi fán máng de jiāo tōng.

We made a **detour** to avoid the heavy traffic.

1486- 趋 /qū/ – *Tend*

物价**趋**涨。

wù jià **qū** zhǎng.

Prices are **tending** upwards.

1487- 慈 /cí/ – *Merciful*

她对犯人很仁**慈**。

tā duì fàn rén hěn rén **cí**.

She was **merciful** to the prisoners.

1488- 乔 /qiáo/ – *Qiao (surname)*

他姓**乔**。

tā xìng **qiáo**.

His surname is **Qiao**.

1489- 阅/yuè/ – *Read*

她正在学习**阅**读。

tā zhèng zài xué xí **yuè** dú.

She is learning to **read**.

1490- 汗/hàn/ – *Sweat*

他浑身是**汗**。

tā hún shēn shì **hàn**.

He is covered with **sweat**.

1491- 枝/zhī/ – *Branch*

他将那树**枝**折下来。

tā jiāng nà shù **zhī** zhé xià lái.

He broke that **branch** off.

1492- 拖/tuō/ – *Drag, tow*

他们把倒下的树从路上**拖**走。

tā men bǎ dào xià de shù cóng lù shàng **tuō** zǒu.

They **towed** the fallen tree off the road.

1493- 墨/mò/ – *Ink*

他的红**墨**水用完了。

tā de hóng **mò** shuǐ yòng wán le.

He has run out of red **ink**.

1494- 肋/lèi/ – *Rib*

一个人有几条**肋**骨？

yī gè rén yǒu jǐ tiáo **lèi** gǔ?

How many **ribs** does a man have?

1495- 插/chā/ – *Insert*

她把钥匙**插**入锁中。

tā bǎ yào shi **chā** rù suǒ zhōng.

She **inserted** the key into the lock.

1496- 箭 /jiàn/ – *Arrow*

他抽出第二枝**箭**。

tā chōu chū dì èr zhī **jiàn**.

He discharged his second **arrow**.

1497- 腊 /là/ – *The last month of the lunar year*

我这辈子从未感到像**腊**月天这么寒冷。

wǒ zhè bèi zi cóng wèi gǎn dào xiàng **là** yuè tiān zhè me hán lěng.

I have never felt so cold in my life like **the last month of the lunar year**.

1498- 粉 /fěn/ – *Pink; powder*

粉色是她最喜欢的颜色。

fěn sè shì tā zuì xǐ huān de yán sè.

Pink is her favorite color.

1499- 泥 /ní/ – *Mud*

他去掉鞋上的**泥**。

tā qù diào xié shàng de **ní**.

He removed the **mud** from his shoes.

1500- 氏 /shì/ – *Family name, clan*

他们还保留了**氏**族社会的痕迹。

tā men hái bǎo liú le **shì** zú shè huì de hén jī.

They still kept traces of the **clan** society.

1501- 彭 /péng/ – *Peng (surname)*

他姓**彭**。

tā xìng **péng**.

His surname is **Peng**.

1502- 拔 /bá/ – *Pull out*

我昨天**拔**了一颗蛀牙。

wǒ zuó tiān **bá** le yī kē zhù yá.

I had a bad tooth **pulled out** yesterday.

1503- 骗/piàn/ – Cheat

骗人是不对的。

piàn rén shì bù duì de.

It is wrong to **cheat**.

1504- 凤凰/fèng huáng/ – Phoenix

凤凰其实并不存在。

fèng huáng qí shí bìng bù cún zài.

The **phoenix** is a nonexistent bird.

1505- 慧/huì/ – Wisdom

她经年累月造就了很高的智慧。

tā jīng nián lěi yuè zào jiù le hěn gāo de zhì **huì**.

She had acquired much **wisdom** during her long life.

1506- 媒/méi/ – Intermediary; matchmaker

那时，媒人安排我们在公园见面。

nà shí, **méi** rén ān pái wǒ men zài gōng yuán jiàn miàn.

At that time, the **matchmaker** arranged us to meet at a park.

1507- 佩/pèi/ – Admire

我佩服他的勇气。

wǒ **pèi** fú tā de yǒng qì.

I **admire** him for his courage.

1508- 愤/fèn/ – Indignant; anger

他的愤怒无关紧要。

tā de **fèn** nù wú guān jǐn yào.

His **anger** is an affair of no consequence.

1509- 扑/pū/ – Pounce on

那只鹰向猎物扑过去。

nà zhǐ yīng xiàng liè wù **pū** guò qù.

The hawk **pounced on** its prey.

1510- 龄 /líng/ – Age

你多大**年龄**？

nǐ duō dà **nián líng**?

What is your **age**?

1511- 驱 /qū/ – Banish, expel

他因说谎而被老婆**驱逐**出家门。

tā yīn shuō huǎng ér bèi lǎo pó **qū zhú** chū jiā mén.

His lies caused his wife to **banish** him from home.

1512- 惜 /xī/ – Cherish

我很**珍惜**我的自由。

wǒ hěn **zhēn xī** wǒ de zì yóu.

I **cherish** my freedom.

1513- 豪 /háo/ – Heroic

他是一位英**豪**。

tā shì yī wèi yīng **háo**.

He is a **heroic** man.

1514- 掩 /yǎn/ – Cover

掩护我。

yǎn hù wǒ.

Cover me.

1515- 兼 /jiān/ –Holding more than one post at the same time

他在我们公司**兼任**顾问。

tā zài wǒ men gōng sī **jiān rèn gù wèn**.

He's **also a consultant** in our company.

1516- 跃 /yuè/ – Jump

那匹马**跃**过了栅栏。

nà pǐ mǎ **yuè** guò le zhà lán.

The horse **jumped** over the fence.

1517- 尸/shī/ – *Corpse*

尸体躺在血泊中。

shī tǐ tǎng zài xuè bó zhōng.

The **corpse** lies down in a pool of blood.

1518- 肃/sù/ – *Solemn*

他表情严**肃**地望着她。

tā biǎo qíng yán **sù** de wàng zhe tā.

He looked at her with a **solemn** expression.

1519- 手帕/shǒu pà/ – *handkerchief*

我用**手帕**把钮扣擦亮。

wǒ yòng **shǒu pà** bǎ niǔ kòu cā liàng.

I polished my buttons with a **handkerchief**.

1520- 驶/shǐ/ – *Sail, pilot, drive*

你会驾**驶**船只吗？

nǐ huì jià **shǐ** chuán zhī ma?

Can you **sail** a boat?

1521- 堡/bǎo/ – *Castle*

幽灵常出没于古**堡**。

yōu líng cháng chū mò yú gǔ **bǎo**.

A spirit haunts the **castle**.

1522- 届/jiè/ – *Measure word for events, meetings, elections, etc.*

谁是**本届奥运会**的协办者？

shuí shì **běn jiè ào yùn huì** de xié bàn zhě?

Who is the assistant organizer of **the Olympic Games**?

1523- 欣/xīn/ – *Happy*

他**欣**然应约。

tā **xīn** rán yìng yuē.

He's **happy** to accept the invitation.

1524- 惠 /huì/ – *Favor; benefit*

新医院将**惠**及整个社区。

xīn yī yuàn jiāng **huì** jí zhěng gè shè qū.

The new hospital will **benefit** the entire community.

1525- 册 /cè/ – *Booklet*

把文章写在**册**子里就可以。

bǎ wén zhāng xiě zài **cè** zi lǐ jiù kě yǐ.

It is all right to write the essay in your **booklet**.

1526- 储 /chǔ/ – *To store, save*

有些食物不能**储**存。

yǒu xiē shí wù bù néng **chǔ** cún.

Some food won't **store**.

1527- 飘 /piāo/ – *Flutter*

蓝蓝的天上白云**飘**。

lán lán de tiān shàng bái yún **piāo**.

White clouds **flutter** in the blue sky.

1528- 桑 /sāng/ – *Mulberry*

蚕吃**桑**叶。

cán chī **sāng** yè.

Silkworms feed on the leaves of **mulberry**.

1529- 闲 /xián/ – *Not busy; leisure*

我很**闲**。

wǒ hěn **xián**.

I'm **not busy**.

1530- 惨 /cǎn/ – *Miserable, tragic*

我们过了一段悲**惨**的生活。

wǒ men guò le yī duàn bēi **cǎn** de shēng huó.

We have a **miserable** life.

1531- 洁/jié/ – Clean

你必须保持衣着整洁。

nǐ bì xū bǎo chí yī zhuó zhěng **jié**.

You must keep your clothes **clean**.

1532- 踪/zōng/ – Trace

洞穴里有人住过的踪迹。

dòng xué lǐ yǒu rén zhù guò de **zōng** jī.

There were **traces** of someone living in the cave.

1533- 勃/bó/ – Suddenly; burst into

他勃然大怒。

tā **bó** rán dà nù.

He **bursts into** anger.

1534- 宾/bīn/ – Guest

他对宾客照顾得很好。

tā duì **bīn** kè zhào gù dé hěn hǎo.

He looked after his **guest** very well.

1535- 频/pín/ –Frequency

事故发生得越来越频繁。

shì gù fā shēng dé yuè lái yuè **pín** fán.

Accidents are happening with increasing **frequency**.

1536- 仇/chóu/ – Hatred

他的话激起了我的仇恨。

tā de huà jī qǐ le wǒ de **chóu** hèn.

His words stirred up my **hatred**.

1537- 磨/mó/ – Grind

这种麦子很好磨。

zhè zhǒng mài zi hěn hǎo **mó**.

This wheat **grinds** well.

1538- 递/dì/ – *Hand over*

请把那本书**递**给我。

qǐng bǎ nà běn shū **dì** gěi wǒ.

Please **hand over** that book to me.

1539- 邪/xié/ – *Evil*

她是个**邪**恶的人。

tā shì gè **xié** è de rén.

She's an **evil** person.

1540- 撞/zhuàng/ – *Bump into, run into*

我不想见她，偏**撞**上她了。

wǒ bù xiǎng jiàn tā, piān **zhuàng** shàng tā le.

I tried to avoid her, but it was just my luck to **bump into** her.

1541- 拟/nǐ/ – *Imitate, to draft*

谁将草**拟**起诉状？

shuí jiāng cǎo **nǐ** qǐ sù zhuàng?

Who will **draft** the indictment?

1542- 滚/gǔn/ – *Roll*

圆的东西容易**滚**动。

yuán de dōng xī róng yì **gǔn** dòng.

Round things **roll** easily.

1543- 节奏/jié zòu/ – *Rhythm*

说英语时，重音和**节奏**是很重要的。

shuō yīng yǔ shí, zhòng yīn hé **jié zòu** shì hěn zhòng yào de.

Stress and **rhythm** are important in speaking English.

1544-巡/xún/ – *Patrol*

警察在街上**巡**逻。

jǐng chá zài jiē shàng **xún** luó.

Policemen **patrol** the streets.

1545- 颜/yán/ – Color, face

红色是她最喜欢的**颜色**。

hóng sè shì tā zuì xǐ huān de **yán** sè.

Red is her favorite **color**.

1546- 剂/jì/ – Dose

医生开了一**剂**口服药。

yī shēng kāi le yī **jì** kǒu fú yào.

The doctor prescribed an oral **dose** of medicine.

1547- 绩/jì/ – Accomplishment, merit

晋升应完全根据**功绩**。

jìn shēng yīng wán quán gēn jù **gōng jì**.

Promotion should be based on **merit** alone.

1548- 贡/gòng/ – Tribute

许多希腊城市不得不每年向雅典进**贡**。

xǔ duō xī là chéng shì bù dé bù měi nián xiàng yǎ diǎn jìn **gòng**.

Many Greek cities had to send yearly **tribute** to Athens.

1549- 疯/fēng/ – Insane

你**疯**了。

nǐ **fēng** le.

You're **insane**.

1550- 坡/pō/ – Slope

我们顺着草**坡**滑下去。

wǒ men shùn zhe cǎo **pō** huá xià qù.

We slid down the grassy **slope**.

1551- 瞧/qiáo/ – To look, see

走着**瞧**!

zǒu zhe **qiáo**!

Wait and **see**!

1552- 截/jié/ – Cut

他把甘蔗**截**成几节。

tā bǎ gān zhè **jié** chéng jǐ jié.

He **cut** the sugarcane into several pieces.

1553- 燃/rán/ – Burn

油在**燃**烧。

yóu zài **rán** shāo.

The oil is **burning**.

1554- 焦/jiāo/ – Burnt, anxious

我们一直**焦**虑着。

wǒ men yī zhí **jiāo** lǜ zhe.

We have had an **anxious** time.

1555- 殿/diàn/ – Palace

马车进入了**宫殿**的大门。

mǎ chē jìn rù le **gōng diàn** de dà mén.

The carriage passed through the **palace** gate.

1556- 伪/wěi/ – Fake

他**伪**造父亲的签字。

tā **wěi** zào fù qīn de qiān zì.

He **faked** his father's signature.

1557- 柳/liǔ/ – Willow

你最好把那棵**柳**树的枝丫砍掉。

nǐ zuì hǎo bǎ nà kē **liǔ** shù de zhī yā kǎn diào.

You'd better hack off the branch of that **willow**.

1558- 锁/suǒ/ – Lock

这箱子**锁**不上。

zhè xiāng zi **suǒ** bù shàng.

This trunk won't **lock**.

1559- 逼/bī/ – To force, compel

别**逼**我那么做。

bié **bī** wǒ nà me zuò.

Don't **force** me to do that.

1560- 颇/pō/ – Quite, rather

这里人**颇**多。

zhè lǐ rén **pō** duō.

There are **quite** a lot people here.

1561- 昏/hūn/ – To faint; twilight, dusk

一到黄**昏**灯就亮了。

yī dào huáng **hūn** dēng jiù liàng le.

The lights go on at **dusk**.

1562- 劝/quàn/ – Console, exhort

他经常**劝**勉玛丽要更加努力地工作。

tā jīng cháng **quàn** miǎn mǎ lì yào gèng jiā nǔ lì de gōng zuò.

He often **exhorts** Mary to work harder.

1563- 呈/chéng/ – Submit, assume (color, shape, etc.)

他向委员会**呈交**了一份报告。

tā xiàng wěi yuán huì **chéng** jiāo le yī fèn bào gào.

He **submitted** a report to the committee.

1564- 搜/sōu/ – Search

搜索引擎方便了用户。

sōu suǒ yǐn qíng fāng biàn le yòng hù.

Search engines are convenient for users.

1565- 勤/qín/ – Diligent, hardworking

他**勤**奋地学习俄语。

tā **qín** fèn de xué xí é yǔ.

He made a **diligent** attempt to learn Russian.

1566- 戒/jiè/ – Quit, guard against

我**戒**烟了。

wǒ **jiè** yān le.

I **quit** smoking.

1567- 驾/jià/ – Drive, sail

下个月我想学习**驾**驶。

xià gè yuè wǒ xiǎng xué xí **jià** shǐ.

I want to learn to **drive** next month.

1568- 漂/piāo/ – Float, drift

船顺水**漂**流而下。

chuán shùn shuǐ **piāo** liú ér xià.

The boat **drifted** down the river.

1569- 饮/yǐn/ – To drink

我为不**饮**酒的人准备了橘子汁。

wǒ wèi bù **yǐn** jiǔ de rén zhǔn bèi le jú zi zhī.

I've got orange juice for those who don't **drink**.

1570- 曹/cáo/ – Cao (surname)

他姓**曹**。

tā xìng **cáo**.

His surname is **Cao**.

1571- 朵/duǒ/ – Measure word for flowers, clouds, etc.

她头上戴了**一朵红花**。

tā tóu shàng dài le **yī duǒ hóng huā**.

She was wearing **a red flower** in her hair.

1572- 仔/zǎi/ – Personal pronoun for young male

再见了，**靓仔**。

zài jiàn le, **liàng zǎi**.

See you around, **handsome**.

1573- 柔 /róu/ – *Soft; gentle*

房间里充满了**柔**和的光。

fáng jiān lǐ chōng mǎnle **róu** hé de guāng.

The room was flooded with **soft** light.

1574- 俩 /liǎ/ – *Two*

我有**俩**秘密。

wǒ yǒu **liǎ** mì mì.

I have **two** secrets.

1575- 孟 /mèng/ – *Meng (surname)*

他姓**孟**。

tā xìng **mèng**.

His surname is **Meng**.

1576- 腐 /fǔ/ – *Rot, decay*

雨水使屋梁**腐**烂了。

yǔ shuǐ shǐ wū liáng **fǔ** làn le.

The rain has **rotted** the roof beams.

1577- 幼 /yòu/ – *Immature, young*

他还年**幼**。

tā hái nián **yòu**.

He's still **young**.

1578- 践 /jiàn/ – *Tread, trample, carry out*

他不小心**践**踏了草坪。

tā bù xiǎo xīn **jiàn** tà le cǎo píng.

He accidentally **trampled** on the lawn.

1579- 籍 /jí/ – *Book, record*

在我院图书馆里藏有许多典**籍**。

zài wǒ yuàn tú shū guǎn lǐ cáng yǒu xǔ duō diǎn **jí**.

There are many ancient codes and **records** in the library of our institute.

1580- 牧 /mù/ – *Herd*

狗常被训练来**牧**羊。

gǒu cháng bèi xùn liàn lái **mù** yáng.

Dogs are often trained to **herd** sheep.

1581- 凉 /liáng/ – *Cool*

今天很**凉**快。

jīn tiān hěn **liáng** kuai.

It is very **cool** today.

1582- 牲 /shēng/ – *Livestock*

他擅长蓄养**牲**畜。

tā shàn cháng xù yǎng **shēng** chù.

He is good at breeding **livestock**.

1583- 佳 /jiā/ – *Fine, good, well*

我今天状态不**佳**。

wǒ jīn tiān zhuàng tài bù **jiā**.

I'm not feeling **well** today.

1584- 娜 /nà/ – *Na (used in female names)*

她叫**娜娜**。

tā jiào **nà nà**.

Her name is **Nana**.

1585- 浓 /nóng/ – *Dense*

雾很**浓**。

wù hěn **nóng**.

The fog was very **dense**.

1586- 芳 /fāng/ – *Fragrant*

空气里弥漫着橘子花的芬**芳**。

kōng qì lǐ mí màn zhe jú zi huā de fēn **fāng**.

The air was **fragrant** with the smell of orange blossoms.

1587- 稿/gǎo/ – Manuscript, draft

我看过他小说的手稿。

wǒ kàn guò tā xiǎo shuō de shǒu gǎo.

I read his novel in **manuscript**.

1588- 竹/zhú/ – Bamboo

他常坐在竹椅上。

tā cháng zuò zài zhú yǐ shàng.

He often sits in his **bamboo** chair.

1589- 腹/fù/ – Abdomen

我的下腹有点痛。

wǒ de xià fù yǒu diǎn tòng.

I have a pain in the lower **abdomen**.

1590- 跌/diē/ – Fall over

我跳起来接球，结果跌了个跟头。

wǒ tiào qǐ lái jiē qiú, jié guǒ diē le gè gēn tóu.

I jumped up to catch a ball and **fell over**.

1591- 逻/luó/ – Patrol

营地被严加巡逻。

yíng dì bèi yán jiā xún luó.

The camp was carefully **patrolled**.

1592- 垂/chuí/ – Droop

她垂着头坐在那儿。

tā chuí zhe tóu zuò zài nà er.

She sat there with her head **drooping**.

1593- 遵/zūn/ – Obey, comply with

我们应当遵守法律。

wǒ men yīng dāng zūn shǒu fǎ lù.

We should **obey** the law.

1594- 脉 /mài/ – *Pulse*

这位病人**脉**搏很弱。

zhè wèi bìng rén **mài** bó hěn ruò.

The patient has a weak **pulse**.

1595- 貌 /mào/ – *Appearance*

她是一位年轻**貌**美的女子。

tā shì yī wèi nián qīng **mào** měi de nǚ zǐ.

She was a young woman of good **appearance**.

1596- 柏 /bǎi/ – *Cypress*

这棵**柏**树又高又细。

zhè kē **bǎi** shù yòu gāo yòu xì.

This **cypress** is tall and thin.

1597- 狱 /yù/ – *Prison*

城里有座大监**狱**。

chéng lǐ yǒu zuò dà jiān **yù**.

There is a large **prison** in this town.

1598- 猜 /cāi/ – *Guess*

我让你**猜**三次。

wǒ ràng nǐ **cāi** sān cì.

I'll give you three **guesses**.

1599- 怜 /lián/ – *To pity*

他不要被人可**怜**。

tā bù yào bèi rén kě **lián**.

He does not want to be **pitied**.

1600- 惑 /huò/ – *Confuse*

智者不**惑**。

zhì zhě bù **huò**.

A wise man is never **confused**.

1601- 陶/táo/ – *Pottery*

一些碗是用**陶**土和木头制成的。

yī xiē wǎn shì yòng **táo** tǔ hé mù tóu zhì chéng de.

Some bowls were made of **pottery** and wood.

1602- 兽/shòu/ – *Beast*

山中有野**兽**。

shān zhōng yǒu yě **shòu**.

There are wild **beasts** in the mountains.

1603- 帐/zhàng/ – *Tent*

他们在海滨附近搭起了一个**帐**篷。

tā men zài hǎi bīn fù jìn dā qǐ le yī gè **zhàng** péng.

They set up a **tent** near the seashore.

1604- 饰/shì/ – *Decorate*

我妈妈非常喜欢装**饰**房间。

wǒ mā mā fēi cháng xǐ huān zhuāng **shì** fáng jiān.

My mother likes to **decorate** rooms.

1605- 贷/dài/ – *Loan*

银行将向他提供一笔**贷**款。

yín háng jiāng xiàng tā tí gōng yī bǐ **dài** kuǎn.

The bank will accommodate him with a **loan**.

1606- 昌/chāng/ – *Prosperous*

该国任何时候都没有现在这样**昌**盛。

gāi guó rèn hé shí hòu dōu méi yǒu xiàn zài zhè yàng chāng **shèng**.

At no time has the country been more **prosperous** than at present.

1607- 叙/xù/ – *Narrate*

我把我的一次奇遇**叙述**一下好吗？

wǒ bǎ wǒ de yī cì qí yù **xù shù** yī xià hǎo ma?

Shall I **narrate** a strange experience of mine?

1608- 躺 /tǎng/ – To lie

那里**躺**着一个男孩。

nà lǐ **tǎng** zhe yī gè nán hái.

There **lay** a boy.

1609- 钢 /gāng/ – Steel

大多数工具是由**钢**做的。

dà duō shù gōng jù shì yóu **gāng** zuò de.

Most tools are made from **steel**.

1610- 沟 /gōu/ – Ditch, gutter

青蛙跳进了**沟**里。

qīng wā tiào jìn le **gōu** lǐ.

The frog jumped into the **ditch**.

1611- 寄 /jì/ – To send, post

我**寄**出了那封信。

wǒ **jì** chū le nà fēng xìn.

I **posted** the letter.

1612- 扶 /fú/ – To help sb. up

他**扶**她在床上坐起来。

tā **fú** tā zài chuáng shàng zuò qǐ lái.

He **helped** her sit **up** in bed.

1613- 铺 /pū/ – Pave

那条路是用鹅卵石**铺**成的。

nà tiáo lù shì yòng é luǎn shí **pū** chéng de.

The road was **paved** with cobblestones.

1614- 邓 /dèng/ – Deng (surname)

他姓**邓**。

tā xìng **dèng**.

His surname is **Deng**.

1615- 寿/shòu/ – Age, life

小事故会缩短汽车**寿**命。

xiǎo shì gù huì suō duǎn qì chē **shòu** mìng.

Minor accidents can shorten the **life** of a car.

1616- 惧/jù/ – Fear

他的眼睛里流露出恐**惧**。

tā de yǎn jīng lǐ liú lù chū kǒng **jù**.

There was a look of **fear** in his eyes.

1617- 询/xún/ – Inquiry

我对你的咨**询**无能为力。

wǒ duì nǐ de zī **xún** wú néng wéi lì.

I'm not able to help you with your **inquiry**.

1618- 汤/tāng/ – Soup

我给我丈夫做了一些肉**汤**。

wǒ gěi wǒ zhàng fū zuò le yī xiē ròu **tāng**.

I made some gravy **soup** for my husband.

1619- 盗/dào/ – Bandit

强**盗**头子已经被绞死。

qiáng **dào** tóu zi yǐ jīng bèi jiǎo sǐ.

The **bandit** chief has been hanged.

1620- 肥/féi/ – Fat, fertile

尼罗河三角洲土地**肥**沃。

ní luó hé sān jiǎo zhōu tǔ dì **féi** wò.

There are **fertile** fields in the Nile Delta.

1621- 尝/cháng/ – To taste

我**尝**了一口汤,看看是不是还要加点盐。

wǒ **cháng** le yī kǒu tāng, kàn kàn shì bù shì hái yào jiā diǎn yán.

I **tasted** the soup to see if it needed more salt.

1622- 匆 /cōng/ – *Hasty, hurried*

我**匆**忙吃完早饭就离开了。

wǒ **cōng** máng chī wán zǎo fàn jiù lí kāi le.

I ate a **hurried** breakfast and left.

1623- 辉 /huī/ – *Splendor*

要想剧院重拾昔日的**辉**煌，必须进行大规模整修。

yào xiǎng jù yuàn chóng shí xī rì de **huī** huáng, bì xū jìn xíng dà guī mó zhěng xiū.

It will take a lot of repair work before the theater regains its former **splendor**.

1624- 奈 /nài/ – *Bear, tackle ; but*

她**奈**不住纠缠不休。

tā **nài** bù zhù jiū chán bù xiū.

She couldn't **bear** the constant bother.

1625- 扣 /kòu/ – *Buckle, button*

他把裤带**扣**得紧紧的。

tā bǎ kù dài **kòu** dé jǐn jǐn de.

He **buckled** up his belt tightly.

1626- 廷 /tíng/ – *Court*

他们家族在宫**廷**中无疑颇受敬重。

tā men jiā zú zài gōng **tíng** zhōng wú yí pō shòu jìng zhòng.

Their family was certainly well regarded at **court**.

1627- 澳 /ào/ – *Abbreviation for 澳门 (Aomen) or 澳大利亚 (Australia)*

中**澳**两国的关系是怎样的？

zhōng **ào** liǎng guó de guān xì shì zěn yàng de?

What is the relationship between China and **Australia**?

1628- 嘛/ma/ – Particle expressing a hope or giving advice

有意见就提嘛！

yǒu yì jiàn jiù tí **ma!**

Make a comment if you want!

1629- 董/dǒng/ – Dong (surname) ; director

他姓董。

tā xìng **dǒng.**

His surname is **Dong.**

1630- 迁/qiān/ – To shift, move

他们现在的办公室太小了,所以决定搬迁。

tā men xiàn zài de bàn gōng shì tài xiǎo le, suǒ yǐ jué dìng bān **qiān.**

Their present office is too small, so they've decided to **move.**

1631- 凝/níng/ – Congeal

血液已经开始凝结。

xuě yè yǐ jīng kāi shǐ **níng** jié.

The blood had started to **congeal.**

1632- 慰/wèi/ – Comfort, console

我试着去安慰她。

wǒ shì zhe qù ān **wèi** tā.

I tried to **console** her.

1633- 厌/yàn/ – Loathe, dislike

我讨厌大城市。

wǒ tǎo **yàn** dà chéng shì.

I **dislike** the big cities.

1634- 脏/zāng/ – Dirty

游客抱怨说房间太脏了。

yóu kè bào yuàn shuō fáng jiān tài **zàng** le.

The tourist complained that the room was too **dirty.**

1635- 腾 /téng/ – *Prance, vacate*

房间很快**腾**了出来。

fáng jiān hěn kuài **téng** le chū lái.

The room **vacated** very quickly.

1636- 幽 /yōu/ – *Secluded, dim; imprison*

你可以**幽**禁我的身体，却束缚不了我的心灵。

nǐ kě yǐ **yōu** jìn wǒ de shēn tǐ, què shù fù bù liǎo wǒ de xīn líng.

You can **imprison** my body but not my mind.

1637- 怨 /yuàn/ – *Complain, blame*

他总是抱**怨**。

tā zǒng shì bào **yuàn**.

He is always **complaining**.

1638- 鞋 /xié/ – *Shoe*

我买了一双新**鞋**。

wǒ mǎi le yī shuāng xīn **xié**.

I bought a new pair of **shoes**.

1639- 丢 /diū/ – *Lose, throw*

我昨天**丢**了钱包。

wǒ zuó tiān **diū** le qián bāo.

I **lost** my wallet yesterday.

1640- 埋 /mái/ – *Bury*

敌人将他活**埋**了。

dí rén jiāng tā huó **mái** le.

The enemy **buried** him alive.

1641- 泉 /quán/ – *Spring*

这里的**泉**水含有丰富的矿盐。

zhè lǐ de **quán** shuǐ hán yǒu fēng fù de kuàng yán.

The **springs** here are rich in mineral salts.

1642- 涌 /yǒng/ – Gush

油从断裂的管道中**涌**出。

yóu cóng duàn liè de guǎn dào zhōng **yǒng** chū.

Oil **gushed** out from the broken pipe.

1643- 辖 /xiá/ – Govern

管**辖**一个州的人是州长。

guǎn xiá yīgè zhōu de rén shì zhōuzhǎng.

A man who **governs** a state is a governor.

1644- 躲 /duǒ/ – Hide

他**躲**在哪儿呢?

tā **duǒ** zài nǎ er ne?

Where is he **hiding**?

1645- 晋 /jìn/ – Move forward, promote

他已**晋**升为副经理。

tā yǐ **jìn** shēng wēi fù jīng lǐ.

He has been **promoted** to deputy manager.

1646- 紫 /zǐ/ – Purple

我最喜欢的颜色是**紫**色。

wǒ zuì xǐ huān de yán sè shì **zǐ** sè.

My favorite color is **purple**.

1647- 艰 /jiān/ – Hardship

他不会因任何**艰**难而畏缩。

tā bù huì yīn rèn hé **jiān** nán ér wèi suō.

He will not shrink from any **hardship**.

1648- 魏 /wèi/ – Wei (surname)

他姓**魏**。

tā xìng **wèi**.

His surname is **Wei**.

1649- 吾/wú/ – I

吾十有五而志于学。

wú shí yǒu wǔ ér zhì yú xué.

I have been interested in learning since fifteen.

1650- 慌/huāng/ – Panic

别**慌**!

bié **huāng**!

Don't **panic**!

1651- 祝/zhù/ – To wish

祝你一路平安。

zhù nǐ yī lù píng ān.

I **wish** you a good journey.

1652- 邮/yóu/ – To mail

她**邮**了本书给我。

tā **yóu** le běn shū gěi wǒ.

She **mailed** a book to me.

1653- 吐/tù/ – Vomit

我喝了混合饮料后**吐**了起来。

wǒ hē le hùn hé yǐn liào hòu **tù** le qǐ lái.

The mixture of drinks made me **vomit**.

1654- 狠/hěn/ – Fierce, vicious

他是一个残忍凶**狠**的人。

tā shì yī gè cán rěn xiōng **hěn** de rén.

He was a cruel and **vicious** man.

1655- 鉴/jiàn/ – Reflection; reflect

水清可**鉴**。

shuǐ qīng kě **jiàn**.

The water is so clear that you can see your **reflection** in it.

1656- 曰/yuē/ – Say

孙权**曰**："此金玉之论也！"

sūn quán **yuē**:"cǐ jīn yù zhī lùn yě!"

"This advice is most valuable," **said** Sun Quan.

1657- 械/xiè/ – Appliance

这些器**械**是用不锈钢制成的。

zhè xiē qì **xiè** shì yòng bù xiù gāng zhì chéng de.

These **appliances** are made of stainless steel.

1658- 咬/yǎo/ – Bite

它**咬**了我。

tā **yǎo** le wǒ.

It **bit** me.

1659- 邻/lín/ – Neighbor; adjacent

那花园与高尔夫球场相**邻**。

nà huā yuán yǔ gāo ěr fū qiú chǎng xiāng **lín**.

The garden is **adjacent** to the golf course.

1660- 赤/chì/ – Red; absolute

41%的巴西人生活在**赤**贫中。

41% de bā xī rén shēng huó zài **chì** pín zhōng.

41% of Brazilians live in **absolute** poverty.

1661- 挤/jǐ/ – Squeeze

他给她**挤**了些鲜牛奶。

tā gěi tā **jǐ** le xiē xiān niú nǎi.

He **squeezed** her some fresh milk.

1662- 弯/wān/ – Bend

树枝被风吹**弯**了。

shù zhī bèi fēng chuī **wān** le.

The branches **bent** in the wind.

1663- 椅/yǐ/ – Chair

他坐在靠门的一把**椅**子上。

tā zuò zài kào mén de yī bǎ **yǐ** zi shàng.

He sat in a **chair** near the door.

1664- 陪/péi/ – Accompany

她要求我**陪**她到机场去。

tā yāo qiú wǒ **péi** tā dào jī chǎng qù.

She asked me to **accompany** her to the airport.

1665- 割/gē/ – Cut

别让碎玻璃**割**伤你的手。

bié ràng suì bō lí **gē** shāng nǐ de shǒu.

Don't **cut** your finger on the broken glass.

1666- 揭/jiē/ – Unmask, expose

是时候**揭**开真相了。

shì shí hòu **jiē** kāi zhēn xiàng le.

It's time for us to **unmask** the truth.

1667- 韦/wéi/ – Wei (surname)

她姓**韦**。

tā xìng **wéi**.

Her surname is **Wei**.

1668- 悟/wù/ – Comprehend

我无法领**悟**他的意思。

wǒ wú fǎ lǐng **wù** tā de yì si.

I did not **comprehend** his meaning.

1669- 聪/cōng/ – Clever, wise

你真**聪**明。

nǐ zhēn **cōng** míng.

You're so **clever**.

1670- 雾 /wù/ – Fog, mist

雾将整夜不散。

wù jiāng zhěng yè bú sàn.

Fog will persist throughout the night.

1671- 锋 /fēng/ – Vanguard; sharp

先**锋**部队昨晚已经出发。

xiān **fēng** bù duì zuó wǎn yǐ jīng chū fā.

The **vanguard** units started off last night.

1672- 梯 /tī/ – Ladder

这架**梯**子不牢靠。

zhè jià **tī** zi bù láo kào.

This **ladder** isn't very stable.

1673- 猫 /māo/ – Cat

我不喜欢**猫**。

wǒ bù xǐ huān **māo**.

I don't like **cats**.

1674- 祥 /xiáng/ – Auspicious

这个时候开张不吉**祥**。

zhè ge shí hòu kāi zhāng bù jí **xiáng**.

It was not an **auspicious** time to start a new business.

1675- 阔 /kuò/ – Wide, broad

亚洲的平原非常广**阔**。

yà zhōu de píng yuán fēi cháng guǎng **kuò**.

The Asiatic plains are very **wide**.

1676- 誉 /yù/ – Reputation

他在学识方面享有盛**誉**。

tā zài xué shì fāng miàn xiǎng yǒu shèng **yù**.

He earned a high **reputation** for his learning.

1677- 筹/chóu/ – Raise (money)

我们办这个俱乐部作为一种**筹**资的途径。

wǒ men bàn zhè ge jù lè bù zuò wéi yī zhǒng **chóu** zī de tú jìng.

We began this club as a way of **raising** money.

1678- 丛/cóng/ – Bush

树**丛**里有些冰。

hù **cóng** lǐ yǒu xiē bīng.

There is some ice in the **bush**.

1679- 牵/qiān/ – Hold

请**牵**住我的手。

qǐng **qiān** zhù wǒ de shǒu.

Please **hold** my hand.

1680- 鸣/míng/ – Chirp of birds or insects

很快他就听见了外面的虫**鸣**声。

hěn kuài tā jiù tīng jiàn le wài miàn de chóng **míng** shēng.

Very soon he heard insects **chirp** outside.

1681- 沈/shěn/ – Shen (surname)

她姓**沈**。

tā xìng **shěn**.

Her surname is **Shen**.

1682- 阁/gé/ – Pavilion

山腰有一座楼**阁**。

shān yāo yǒu yī zuò lóu **gé**.

A **pavilion** is halfway up the hill.

1683- 穆/mù/ – Mu (surname)

她姓**穆**。

tā xìng **mù**.

Her surname is **Mu**.

1684- 屈 /qū/ – *Feel wronged*

她觉得受了委屈。

tā jué dé shòu le wěi **qū**.

She **felt** she'd been **wronged**.

1685- 旨 /zhǐ/ – *Aim*

本会议旨在达成共识。

běn huì yì **zhǐ** zài dá chéng gòng shí.

The meeting **aims** to reach a consensus.

1686- 袖 /xiù/ – *Sleeve*

她用袖子拭眼泪。

tā yòng **xiù** zi shì yǎn lèi.

She wiped away her tears with her **sleeve**.

1687- 猎 /liè/ – *Hunt*

他们在猎狐。

tā men zài **liè** hú.

They are **hunting** the foxes.

1688- 臂 /bì/ – *Arm*

他在事故中折断了手臂。

tā zài shì gù zhōng zhé duàn le shǒu **bì**.

He broke his **arm** in an accident.

1689- 蛇 /shé/ – *Snake*

他被蛇咬了。

tā bèi **shé** yǎo le.

He was bitten by a **snake**.

1690- 贺 /hè/ – *Congratulate*

请允许我向您道贺。

qǐng yǔn xǔ wǒ xiàng nín dào **hè**.

Let me **congratulate** you.

1691- 柱/zhù/ – *Pillar*

强盗把他捆在**柱**子上。

qiáng dào bǎ tā kǔn zài **zhù** zi shàng.

The robber tied him to a **pillar**.

1692- 抛/pāo/ – *Toss*

孩子们互相**抛**球。

hái zi men hù xiāng **pāo** qiú.

The children **tossed** the ball to each other.

1693- 鼠/shǔ/ – *Rat, mouse*

这老**鼠**很大。

zhè lǎo **shǔ** hěn dà.

This **mouse** is very big.

1694- 瑟瑟/sè sè / – *Rustle, shiver*

他**瑟瑟**发抖。

tā **sè sè** fā dǒu.

He's **shivering** because of cold.

1695- 戈/gē/ – *Dagger-axe*

这看起来不像是矛，更像**戈**。

zhè kàn qǐ lái bù xiàng shì máo, gèng xiàng **gē**.

It doesn't look like a lance, but a **dagger-axe**.

1696- 牢/láo/ – *Jail*

两名犯人从**牢**中脱逃。

liǎng míng fàn rén cóng **láo** zhōng tuō táo.

Two prisoners escaped from the **jail**.

1697- 逊/xùn/ – *To suck; modest, inferior*

你太**逊**了。

nǐ tài **xùn** le.

You **suck**.

1698- 迈 /mài/ – *Take a step*

请向前迈一步。

qǐng xiàng qián **mài** yī bù.

Please **take a step** forward.

1699- 欺 /qī/ – *Deceive*

欺骗他们是不光彩的。

qī piàn tā men shì bù guāng cǎi de.

It's not honorable to **deceive** them.

1700- 吨 /dūn/ – *Ton*

这头大象重多少**吨**？

zhè tóu dà xiàng zhòng duō shǎo **dūn**?

How many **tons** does this elephant weigh?

1701- 琴 /qín/ – *Lute; musical instrument*

她会弹古**琴**。

tā huì dàn gǔ **qín**.

She knows how to play the Chinese **lute**.

1702- 衰 /shuāi/ – *Wane*

帝国经过全盛以后逐渐**衰**落。

dì guó jīng guò quán shèng yǐ hòu zhú jiàn **shuāi** luò.

The empire was on the **wane** after its period of prosperity.

1703- 瓶 /píng/ – *Bottle*

瓶子从他的手中滑落。

píng zi cóng tā de shǒu zhōng huá luò.

The **bottle** slipped out of his hand.

1704- 恼 /nǎo/ – *Annoy*

她看样子很烦**恼**。

tā kàn yàng zi hěn fán **nǎo**.

She looked **annoyed**.

1705- 燕/yàn/ – Swallow

天空中有许多**燕**子。

tiān kōng zhōng yǒu xǔ duō **yàn** zi.

There are many **swallows** flying in the sky.

1706- 仲/zhòng/ – Intermediate; arbitrate

得有一个人在他们当中进行**仲**裁。

děi yǒu yī gè rén zài tā men dāng zhōng jìn xíng **zhòng** cái.

Someone must **arbitrate** between them.

1707- 诱/yòu/ – Tempt

饥饿**诱**使他偷窃。

jī è **yòu** shǐ tā tōu qiè.

Hunger **tempted** him to steal.

1708- 狼/láng/ – Wolf

这匹**狼**咬住猎人的手。

zhè pǐ **láng** yǎo zhù liè rén de shǒu.

The **wolf** snapped at the hunter's hand.

1709- 池/chí/ – Pond, pool

池塘里有些芦苇。

chí táng lǐ yǒu xiē lú wěi.

There are some reeds in the **pond**.

1710- 疼/téng/ – Sore

他的脚**疼**。

tā de jiǎo **téng**.

He had a **sore** on his foot.

1711- 卢/lú/ – Lu (surname)

她姓**卢**。

tā xìng **lú**.

Her surname is **Lu**.

1712- 仗 /zhàng/ – *Battle; depend on*

我们必须赢得这一**仗**。

wǒ men bì xū yíng dé zhè yī **zhàng**.

We must win this **battle**.

1713- 冠 /guàn/ – *Champion*

他成为世界**冠**军。

tā chéng wéi shì jiè **guàn** jūn.

He became the world **champion**.

1714- 粒 /lì/ – *Granule*

她在用勺往杯子里舀咖啡颗**粒**。

tā zài yòng sháo wǎng bēi zi lǐ yǎo kā fēi kē **lì**.

She was spooning coffee **granules** into cups.

1715- 遥 /yáo/ – *Far*

古巴离中国很**遥**远。

gǔ bā lí zhōng guó hěn **yáo** yuǎn.

Cuba is **far** apart from China.

1716- 吕 /lǚ/ – *Lǚ (surname)*

她姓**吕**。

tā xìng **lǚ**.

Her surname is **Lǚ**.

1717- 玄 /xuán/ – *Mysterious*

这真是件很**玄**的事情。

zhè zhēn shì jiàn hěn **xuán** de shì qíng.

This really is a **mysterious** event.

1718- 尘 /chén/ – *Dust*

他的衣服上落满了**尘**埃。

tā de yī fú shàng luò mǎn le **chén** āi.

His clothes were covered with **dust**.

1719- 冯/féng/ – Feng (surname)

她姓**冯**。

tā xìng **féng**.

Her surname is **Feng**.

1720- 抚/fǔ/ – Stroke, console

猫喜欢让人**抚**摸。

māo xǐ huān ràng rén **fǔ** mō.

The cat likes being **stroked**.

1721- 浅/qiǎn/ – Shallow

他在游泳池的**浅**水区下水。

tā zài yóu yǒng chí de **qiǎn** shuǐ qū xià shuǐ.

He got in at the **shallow** end of the swimming pool.

1722- 敦/dūn/ – Urge

我们将**敦**促他们遵守巴黎协议。

wǒ men jiāng **dūn** cù tā men zūn shǒu bā lí xié yì.

We will **urge** them to adhere to the Paris Agreement.

1723- 纠/jiū/ – To correct, gather together

如果下列句子中有错，请**纠**正。

rú guǒ xià liè jù zi zhōng yǒu cuò, qǐng **jiū** zhèng.

Correct the errors in the following sentences if any.

1724- 钻/zuàn/ – Diamond

这是人造**钻**石。

zhè shì rén zào **zuàn shí**.

It's a synthetic **diamond**.

1725- 晶/jīng/ – Crystal

盐会结**晶**。

yán huì jié **jīng**.

Salt forms **crystals**.

1726- 岂 /qǐ/ – *How*

岂能由你胡来？

qǐ néng yóu nǐ hú lái?

How can I allow you to misbehave?

1727- 峡 /xiá/ – *Gorge*

你去过长江三峡吗？

nǐ qù guò cháng jiāng sān **xiá** ma?

Have you been to the Yangtze **Gorges**?

1728- 苍 /cāng/ – *Blue*

苍空就像深海。

cāng kōng jiù xiàng shēn hǎi.

The **blue** sky looks like the deep sea.

1729- 喷 /pēn/ – *Spray, spout*

水正从管子里喷出来。

shuǐ zhèng cóng guǎn zi lǐ **pēn** chū lái.

Water is **spouting** out of the pipe.

1730- 耗 /hào/ – *Consume*

他的破车很耗油。

tā de pò chē hěn **hào** yóu.

His old car **consumed** much gasoline.

1731- 凌 /líng/ – *Insult; rise high*

他感觉深受凌辱。

tā gǎn jué shēn shòu **líng** rù.

He feels deeply **insulted**.

1732- 敲 /qiāo/ – *Knock*

有人在敲门。

yǒu rén zài **qiāo** mén.

Someone is **knocking** at the door.

1733- 菌/jūn/ – Germ

细**菌**会侵入有机体。

xì **jūn** huì qīn rù yǒu jī tǐ.

Germs may invade the organism.

1734- 赔/péi/ – Indemnify

他们提出要**赔**偿我们的损失。

tā men tí chū yào **péi** cháng wǒ men de sǔn shī.

They offered to **indemnify** us for our losses.

1735- 涂/tú/ – Smear, scrawl

你该把双手**涂**上油脂。

nǐ gāi bǎ shuāng shǒu **tú** shàng yóu zhī.

You should **smear** your hands with grease.

1736- 粹/cuì/ – Essence; pure; completely

纯粹是他的错。

chún cuì shì tā de cuò.

It is **completely** his fault.

1737- 扁/biǎn/ – Flat

有些人仍硬说地球是**扁**的。

yǒu xiē rén réng yìng shuō dì qiú shì **biǎn** de.

Some people still maintain that the Earth is **flat**.

1738- 亏/kuī/ – Deficit

我们今年有很大**亏**损。

wǒ men jīn nián yǒu hěn dà **kuī** sǔn.

We have a great **deficit** this year.

1739- 寂/jì/ – Silent

这所旧房子非常**寂**静。

zhè suǒ jiù fáng zi fēi cháng **jì** jìng.

The old house was quite **silent**.

1740- 煤/méi/ – *Coal*

再往火里加点**煤**。

zài wǎng huǒ lǐ jiā diǎn **méi**.

Put some more **coal** on the fire.

1741- 熊/xióng/ – *Bear*

猎人挥刀向**熊**猛烈砍去。

liè rén huī dāo xiàng **xióng** měng liè kǎn qù.

The hunter slashed at the **bear** with his knife.

1742- 恭/gōng/ – *Respectful*

我希望你对父亲**恭**敬些。

wǒ xī wàng nǐ duì fù qīn **gōng** jìng xiē.

I wish you were more **respectful** to your father.

1743- 湿/shī/ – *Wet*

雨后地上是**湿**的。

yǔ hòu dì shàng shì **shī** de.

The ground is **wet** after the rain.

1744- 循/xún/ – *Follow, abide by*

所有的人都应遵**循**法律。

suǒ yǒu de rén dōu yīng **zūn xún** fǎ lǜ.

Everyone must **abide by** the law.

1745- 暖/nuǎn/ – *Warm*

天气转**暖**了。

tiān qì zhuǎn **nuǎn** le.

The weather has **warmed** up.

1746- 糖/táng/ – *Sugar, candy*

她吃**糖**太多了。

tā chī **táng** tài duō le.

She eats too much **candy**.

1747- 赋/fù/ – Endow with

法官享有国家**赋**予的权力。

fǎ guān xiǎng yǒu guó jiā **fù** yǔ de quán lì.

A judge is **endowed with** the authority of the state.

1748- 抑/yì/ – Repress, restrain

他的童年是压**抑**而孤独的。

tā de tóng nián shì yā **yì** ér gū dú de.

His childhood was **repressed** and solitary.

1749- 秩/zhì/ – Order

有些老师觉得维持课堂**秩**序不容易。

yǒu xiē lǎo shī jué dé wéi chí kè táng **zhì** xù bù róng yì.

Some teachers find it difficult to maintain **order** in classroom.

1750- 帽/mào/ – Hat

这**帽**子是最新式的。

zhè **mào** zi shì zuì xīn shì de.

This **hat** is in the latest style.

1751- 哀/āi/ – Grief; grieve for

她的去世实在令人**哀**伤。

tā de qù shì shí zài lìng rén **āi** shāng.

Her death was a real **grief**.

1752- 宿/sù/ – Lodge for the night

你能让我们借**宿**一晚吗？

nǐ néng ràng wǒ men jiè **sù** yī wǎn ma?

Can you **lodge** us **for the night**?

1753- 踏/tà/ – Step on

我梦想着某一天能**踏**上南极洲。

wǒ mèng xiǎng zhe mǒu yī tiān néng **tà** shàng nán jí zhōu.

I dreamed to **step on** the Antarctic one day.

1754- 烂/làn/ – Rot, decay

卷心菜已经开始烂了。

juǎn xīn cài yǐ jīng kāi shǐ **làn** le.

The cabbages had already started to **decay**.

1755- 袁/yuán/ – Yuan (surname)

她姓袁。

tā xìng **yuán**.

Her surname is **Yuan**.

1756- 侯/hóu/ – Hou (surname)

他姓侯。

tā xìng **hóu**.

His surname is **Hou**.

1757- 抖/dǒu/ – Tremble

他气得发抖。

tā qì dé fā **dǒu**.

He was **trembling** with rage.

1758- 夹/jiā/ – Clip

在信背面夹着一张支票。

zài xìn bèi miàn **jiā** zhe yī zhāng zhī piào.

There was a cheque **clipped** to the back of the letter.

1759- 昆虫/kūn chóng/ – Insect

这个地区有许多种昆虫。

zhè ge dì qū yǒu xǔ duō zhǒng **kūn chóng**.

There are many kinds of **insects** in this area.

1760- 肝/gān/ – Liver

他的肝不好。

tā de **gān** bù hǎo.

He has a weak **liver**.

1761- 擦/cā/ – Wipe

她**擦**掉了眼泪。
tā **cā** diào le yǎn lèi.
She **wiped** her tears away.

1762- 猪/zhū/ – Pig

猪是一种家畜。
zhū shì yī zhǒng jiā chù.
A **pig** is a domestic animal.

1763- 炼/liàn/ – Refine, smelt

这些石油将被精**炼**。
zhè xiē shí yóu jiāng bèi jīng **liàn**.
The oil will be **refined**.

1764- 恒/héng/ – Permanent, constant

这是**恒**久不变的。
zhè shì **héng** jiǔ bù biàn de.
It is unchangeable and **permanent**.

1765- 慎/shèn/ – Cautious

她很谨**慎**，不会泄露秘密。
tā hěn jǐn **shèn**, bù huì xiè lòu mì mì.
She is **cautious** of telling secrets.

1766- 搬/bān/ – Move

我下个月就**搬**走。
wǒ xià gè yuè jiù **bān** zǒu.
I will **move** away next month.

1767- 纽扣/niǔ kòu/ – Button

她的衬衣掉了一粒**纽扣**。
tā de chèn yī diào le yī lì **niǔ kòu**.
One of the **buttons** has come off her shirt.

1768- 纹/wén/ – Mark, trace, grain

切肉时顺着**纹**路切最容易。

qiē ròu shí shùn zhe **wén** lù qiē zuì róng yì.

It is easiest to cut meat in the direction of the **grain**.

1769- 玻璃/bō lí/ – Glass

玻璃易碎。

bō lí yì suì.

Glass breaks easily.

1770- 渔/yú/ – To fish

授人以鱼不如授人以**渔**。

shòu rén yǐ yú bù rú shòu rén yǐ **yú**.

Giving a man a fish is not as good as teaching a man **to fish**.

1771- 磁/cí/ – Magnetic

通电时线圈就会有**磁**性。

tōng diàn shí xiàn quān jiù huì yǒu **cí** xìng.

The loop becomes **magnetic** when the current is switched on.

1772- 铜/tóng/ – Copper

铜是电的良导体。

tóng shì diàn de liáng dǎo tǐ.

Copper conducts electricity well.

1773- 齿/chǐ/ – Tooth

梳子和锯子的尖锐部分叫作**齿**。

shū zi hé jù zi de jiān ruì bù fèn jiào zuò **chǐ**.

The sharp parts of a comb or a saw are called **teeth**.

1774- 跨/kuà/ – Straddle, stride

孩子太小**跨**不过这条沟。

hái zi tài xiǎo **kuà** bù guò zhè tiáo gōu.

The kid is too young to **stride** the ditch.

1775- 押 /yā/ – *Mortgage*

银行拒绝接受任何土地抵**押**。

yín háng jù jué jiē shòu rèn hé tǔ dì dǐ **yā**.

The bank refused to accept any **mortgage** on land.

1776- 怖 /bù/ – *Terror*

那个政府实行恐**怖**统治。

nà gè zhèng fǔ shí xíng kǒng **bù** tǒng zhì.

The government rules by **terror**.

1777- 漠 /mò/ – *Desert; unconcerned*

广大的地区均已沦为荒**漠**。

guǎng dà de dì qū jūn yǐ lún wéi huāng **mò**.

Vast areas of land have become **desert**.

1778- 疲 /pí/ – *Weary*

她易**疲**劳。

tā yì **pí** láo.

She **wearies** easily.

1779- 叛 /pàn/ – *Betray, rebel*

他背**叛**了他的国家。

tā bèi **pàn** le tā de guó jiā.

He **betrayed** his country.

1780- 遣 /qiǎn/ – *Dispatch*

一名通讯员被**遣**去给前线士兵送信。

yī míng tōng xùn yuán bèi **qiǎn** qù gěi qián xiàn shì bīng sòng xìn.

A messenger was **dispatched** to take the news to the soldiers at the front.

1781- 兹 /zī/ – *This, now*

兹事体大。

zī shì tǐ dà.

This is indeed a serious matter.

1782- 祭 /jì/ – *Sacrifice*

他们献**祭**了牛、羊和猪。

tā men xiàn **jì** le niú, yáng hé zhū.

They **sacrificed** cattle, sheep and pigs.

1783- 醉 /zuì/ – *Drunk*

他显然是**醉**了。

tā xiǎn rán shì **zuì** le.

He was obviously **drunk**.

1784- 拳 /quán/ – *Fist*

他用**拳**头砸门。

tā yòng **quán** tou zá mén.

He was banging on the door with his **fist**.

1785- 弥 /mí/ – *Make up, fill*

她的美貌不能**弥**补她的愚蠢。

tā dì měi mào bù néng mí bǔ tā de yú **chǔn**.

Her beauty can't **make up** for her stupidity.

1786- 斜 /xié/ – *Incline, tilt*

不要**斜**着戴帽子。

bù yào **xié** zhe dài mào zi.

Don't **tilt** your hat sideways.

1787- 档 /dàng/ – *Record, file*

请把这些信件存**档**。

qǐng bǎ zhè xiē xìn jiàn cún **dàng**.

Please **file** those letters.

1788- 稀 /xī/ – *Rare, watery*

服务员给他端来一杯**稀**咖啡。

fú wù yuán gěi tā duān lái yī bēi **xī** kā fēi.

A waiter brought him a **watery** coffee.

1789- 捷 /jié/ – *Prompt; victory*

这支军队赢得了第一场大**捷**。

zhè zhī jūn duì yíng dé le dì yī chǎng dà **jié**.

The army had won the first **victory**.

1790- 肤 /fū/ – *Skin*

他的皮**肤**是棕色的。

tā de pí **fū** shì zōng sè de.

He had brown **skin**.

1791- 疫 /yì/ – *Plague*

那时一场大瘟**疫**正在该城肆虐。

nà shí yī chǎng dà wēn **yì** zhèng zài gāi chéng sì nüè.

A great **plague** was then raging in the city.

1792- 肿 /zhǒng/ – *Swell*

受伤的脚踝开始**肿**了。

shòu shāng de jiǎo huái kāi shǐ **zhǒng** le.

The injured ankle began to **swell**.

1793- 豆 /dòu/ – *Bean*

你喜欢吃**豆**子吗？

nǐ xǐ huān chī **dòu** zi ma?

Do you like to eat **beans**?

1794- 削 /xuē/ – *Pare, reduce*

她正在**削**苹果。

tā zhèng zài **xuē** píng guǒ.

She is **paring** the apple.

1795- 岗 /gǎng/ – *Post*

经理的**岗位**仍然空缺。

jīng lǐ de **gǎng** wèi réng rán kòng quē.

The **position** of manager is still open.

1796- 晃/huàng/– Sway

他稍许**晃**了一下,并未跌倒。

tā shāo xǔ **huàng** le yī xià, bìng wèi diē dǎo.

He didn't fall but **swayed** a little.

1797- 吞/tūn/ – Swallow

他**吞**下一口面包。

tā **tūn** xià yī kǒu miàn bāo.

He **swallowed** a mouthful of bread.

1798- 宏/hóng/ – Grand

这座宫殿很**宏**大。

zhè zuò gōng diàn hěn **hóng** dà.

This palace is **grand**.

1799- 癌/ái/ – Cancer

他患了**癌**症。

tā huàn le **ái** zhèng.

He was afflicted with **cancer**.

1800- 肚/dù/ – Belly

我**肚**子饿了。

wǒ **dù** zi è le.

My **belly** is empty.

1801- 隶/lì/ – Attached to; slave

他的祖母曾是奴**隶**。

tā de zǔ mǔ céng shì nú **lì**.

His grandmother used to be a **slave**.

1802- 履/lǚ/ – Shoe; carry out

我一丝不苟地**履**行我的职责。

wǒ yī sī bù gǒu de **lǚ** xíng wǒ de zhí zé.

I **carried out** my duties conscientiously.

1803- 涨/zhǎng/ – *Increase, rise*

物价又上**涨**了。

wù jià yòu shàng **zhǎng** le.

Prices have **risen** again.

1804- 耀/yào/ – *Sparkle, shine*

她眼里闪**耀**着激动的光芒。

tā yǎn lǐ shǎn **yào** zhe jī dòng de guāng máng.

There was a **sparkle** of excitement in her eyes.

1805- 扭/niǔ/ – *Twist, sprain*

他**扭**断一根树枝。

tā **niǔ** duàn yī gēn shù zhī.

He **twisted** a twig and broke it.

1806- 坛/tán/ – *Altar*

牧师在圣**坛**前行鞠躬礼。

mù shī zài shèng **tán** qián xíng jū gōng lǐ.

The priest bowed down before the **altar**.

1807- 拨/bō/ – *Dial, set aside, allocate*

您**拨**打的电话忙。

nín **bō** dǎ de diàn huà máng.

The number you **dialed** is busy.

1808- 沃/wò/ – *Fertile*

植物在肥**沃**的土壤里长势良好。

zhí wù zài féi **wò** de tǔ rǎng lǐ cháng shì liáng hǎo.

Plants grow well in **fertile** soil.

1809- 绘/huì/ – *To draw*

他**绘**画比班上任何人都好。

tā **huì** huà bǐ bān shàng rèn hé rén dōu hǎo.

He **draws** pictures better than any student in his class.

1810- 伐/fá/ – Cut down

他们在**伐**木。

tā men zài **fá** mù.

They are **cutting down** trees.

1811- 堪/kān/ – Endure

他那傲慢无礼的行为令我不**堪**。

tā nà ào màn wú lǐ de xíng wéi lìng wǒ bù **kān**.

I could not **endure** the insolence of his behaviour.

1812- 仆/pú/ – Servant

他是个恭顺的**仆**人。

tā shì gè gōng shùn de **pú** rén.

He is a humble and submissive **servant**.

1813- 郭/guō/ – Guo (surname)

他姓**郭**。

tā xìng **guō**.

His surname is **Guo**.

1814- 牺/xī/ – Sacrifice

她为事业**牺**牲了家庭。

tā wèi shì yè **xī** shēng le jiā tíng.

She **sacrificed** family life for her career.

1815- 歼/jiān/ – Annihilate

我们必须聚敌而**歼**之。

wǒ men bì xū jù dí ér **jiān** zhī.

We must herd the enemy troops together and **annihilate** them.

1816- 墓/mù/ – Tomb, grave

一些古**墓**被掘开了。

yī xiē gǔ **mù** bèi jué kāi le.

Some ancient **tombs** were opened.

1817- 雇/gù/ – Hire

他们**雇**用了很多人。

tā men **gù** yòng le hěn duō rén.

They **hired** many people now.

1818- 廉/lián/ – Inexpensive

我们存有多种**廉**价酒。

wǒ men cún yǒu duō zhǒng **lián** jià jiǔ.

We stocked a wide range of **inexpensive** wines.

1819- 契/qì/ – Deed

这是约翰农场的**契**约。

zhè shì yuē hàn nóng chǎng de **qì** yuē.

This is the **deed** to John's plantation.

1820- 拼/pīn/ – Piece together; adventurous

我在设法把碎片**拼**起来。

wǒ zài shè fǎ bǎ suì piàn **pīn** qǐ lái.

I was trying to **piece together** those fragments.

1821- 惩/chéng/ – Punish

危险驾驶应受严**惩**。

wēi xiǎn jià shǐ yīng shòu yán **chéng**.

Dangerous driving should be severely **punished**.

1822- 捉/zhuō/ – Grab, capture

他们活**捉**了敌人的军官。

tā men huó **zhuō** le dí rén de jūn guān.

They **captured** the enemy officer alive.

1823- 覆/fù/ – Cover

雪**覆**盖了地面。

xuě **fù** gài le dì miàn.

Snow **covered** the ground.

1824- 刷/shuā/ – Brush

他用**刷**子涂墙。

He painted the wall with a **brush**.

1825- 劫/jié/ – Plunder, rob

他们**劫**掠了宫殿的财宝。

tā men **jié** lüè le gōng diàn de cái bǎo.

They **plundered** a palace of its treasures.

1826- 嫌/xián/ – Suspicion; dislike

大家都**嫌**他脾气太急。

dà jiā dōu **xián** tā pí qì tài jí.

Everybody **disliked** him because of his hot temper.

1827- 瓜/guā/ – Melon

这个**瓜**怕有十几公斤吧。

zhè gè **guā** pà yǒu shí jǐ gōng jīn ba.

This **melon** weighs more than ten kilograms.

1828- 歇/xiē/ – Rest

我想**歇**一会。

wǒ xiǎng **xiē** yī huǐ.

I want to take a **rest**.

1829- 雕/diāo/ – To carve, engrave

在大理石上**雕**刻是困难的。

zài dà lǐ shí shàng **diāo** kè shì kùn nán de.

It is difficult to **engrave** in marble.

1830- 闷/mèn/ – Bored

我好**闷**啊。

wǒ hǎo **mèn** a.

I'm so **bored**.

1831- 乳/rǔ/ – Milk

什么也替代不了母乳。

shén me yě tì dài bù liǎo mǔ **rǔ**.

Nothing could replace mother's **milk**.

1832- 串/chuàn/ – String

他们把这些珍珠串得太紧了。

tā men bǎ zhè xiē zhēn zhū **chuàn** dé tài jǐn le.

They **strung** these pearls too tightly.

1833- 娃/wá/ – Baby, doll

她要我给她的娃娃做些衣服。

tā yào wǒ gěi tā de **wá wá** zuò xiē yī fú.

She asked me to make some clothes for her **doll**.

1834- 缴/jiǎo/ – Hand in, turn in

时至今日只上缴了少数几支枪。

shí zhì jīn rì zhǐ shàng **jiǎo** le shǎo shù jǐ zhī qiāng.

Only a few guns have been **turned in** so far.

1835- 唤/huàn/ – To call

远处有人在呼唤我们。

yuǎn chù yǒu rén zài hū **huàn** wǒ men.

Somebody is **calling** us in the distance.

1836- 赢/yíng/ – Win

他要赢了。

tā yào **yíng** le.

He's **winning**.

1837- 莲/lián/ – Lotus

我希望像莲花一样，出淤泥而不染。

wǒ xī wàng xiàng **lián** huā yī yàng, chū yū ní ér bù rǎn.

May I live like the **lotus**, at ease in muddy water.

1838- 霸 /bà/ – Despot

他是当地一霸。

tā shì dāng dì yī **bà**.

He is a local **despot**.

1839- 桃 /táo/ – Peach

桃是又甜又多汁的水果。

táo shì yòu tián yòu duō zhī de shuǐ guǒ.

The **peach** is a sweet and juicy fruit.

1840- 妥 /tuǒ/ – Appropriate; ready; settled

一切都办妥了。

yī qiè dōu bàn **tuǒ** le.

Everything is **settled**.

1841- 瘦 /shòu/ – Thin

她真瘦。

tā zhēn **shòu**.

She's really **thin**.

1842- 搭 /dā/ – To build, join together

小鸟们在忙着搭窝。

xiǎo niǎo men zài máng zhe **dā** wō.

The birds are busy **building** their nests.

1843- 赴 /fù/ – Go, attend

我会准时赴会。

wǒ huì zhǔn shí **fù** huì.

I'll **attend** the meeting in time.

1844- 岳 /yuè/ – Yue (surname); mountain

他姓岳。

tā xìng **yuè**.

His surname is **Yue**.

1845- 嘉/jiā/ – Cite

那位下士因作战英勇而受到**嘉**奖。

nà wèi xià shì yīn zuò zhàn yīng yǒng ér shòu dào **jiā** jiǎng.

The corporal was **cited** for bravery in battle.

1846- 舱/cāng/– Cabin

请帮我在船上订个**舱**。

qǐng bāng wǒ zài chuán shàng dìng gè **cāng**.

Please book me a **cabin** on the ship.

1847- 俊/jùn/ – Handsome

我喜欢那个英**俊**的男子。

wǒ xǐ huān nà gè yīng **jùn** de nán zǐ.

I like that **handsome** man.

1848- 址/zhǐ/ – Site

新厂的地**址**尚未选定。

xīn chǎng de dì **zhǐ** shàng wèi xuǎn dìng.

The **site** for the new factory has not been decided yet.

1849- 庞/páng/ – Enormous

这栋建筑非常**庞**大。

zhè dòng jiàn zhú fēi cháng **páng** dà.

The building is **enormous**.

1850- 耕/gēng/ – Plow

这块田地容易**耕**。

zhè kuài tián dì róng yì **gēng**.

This field **plows** easily.

1851- 锐/ruì/ – Acute, sharp

她有很敏**锐**的听力。

tā yǒu hěn mǐn **ruì** de tīng lì.

She has **acute** hearing.

1852- 缝/féng/ – *To sew, stitch*

他正在**缝**制一件新外套。

tā zhèng zài **féng** zhì yī jiàn xīn wài tào.

He was **sewing** a new coat.

1853- 悔/huǐ/ – *Regret*

你会后**悔**的。

nǐ huì hòu **huǐ** de.

You'll **regret** this.

1854- 邀/yāo/ – *Invite*

他们**邀**请你了吗?

tā men **yāo** qǐng nǐ le ma?

Did they **invite** you?

1855- 玲/líng/ – *Ling (used in female names)*

她叫**张玲**。

tā jiào **zhāng líng**.

Her name is **Zhang Ling**.

1856- 惟/wéi/ – *Only*

惟手熟尔。

wéi shǒu shú ěr.

It is **only** because of experience.

1857- 斥/chì/ – *To scold*

你们为何**斥**责他?

nǐ men wèi hé **chì** zé tā?

Why did you **scold** him?

1858- 宅/zhái/ – *Residence*

他们在北方有一幢夏季住**宅**。

tā men zài běi fāng yǒu yī chuáng xià jì zhù **zhái**.

They have a summer **residence** in the north.

1859- 添/tiān/ – Add

他**添**了些柴，使火更旺。

tā **tiān** le xiē chái, shǐ huǒ gèng wàng.

He **added** some wood to increase the fire.

1860- 挖/wā/ – Dig

他们**挖**了一个坑。

tā men **wā** le yī gè kēng.

They **dug** a hole.

1861- 呵/hē/ – Ah, oh

呵，这字写得真漂亮！

hē, zhè zì xiě dé zhēn piào liàng!

Oh, what beautiful handwriting!

1862- 讼/sòng/ – Litigation

有些商业争端需提出诉**讼**。

yǒu xiē shāng yè zhēng duān xū tí chū sù **sòng**.

Some business disputes require **litigation**.

1863- 氧/yǎng/ – Oxygen

氢和**氧**是气体。

qīng hé **yǎng** shì qì tǐ.

Hydrogen and **oxygen** are gases.

1864- 浩/hào/ – Grand

这是个**浩**大的场景。

zhè shì gè **hào** dà de chǎng jǐng.

This is a **grand** scene.

1865- 羽/yǔ/ – Feather

垫子里充满了**羽**毛。

diàn zi lǐ chōng mǎn le **yǔ** máo.

The cushion is filled with **feathers**.

1866- 斤/jīn/ – Catty

我要买一**斤**茄子。

wǒ yāo mǎi yī **jīn** qié zi.

I want to buy a **catty** of eggplant.

1867- 酷/kù/ – Ruthless

残**酷**的敌人杀害了那位老太太。

cán **kù** de dí rén shā hài le nà wèi lǎo tài tài.

The **ruthless** enemy killed the old lady.

1868- 掠/lüè/ – Plunder

帝国主义列强**掠**夺了许多珍贵的艺术品。

dì guó zhǔ yì liè qiáng **lüè** duó le xǔ duō zhēn guì de yì shù pǐn.

The imperialists **plundered** many valuable works of art.

1869- 妖/yāo/ – Goblin, monster

穿着那些衣服的他看上去就像个小**妖**。

chuān zhuó nà xiē yī fú de tā kàn shàng qù jiù xiàng gè xiǎo **yāo**.

He looked like a **goblin** in those clothes.

1870- 祸/huò/ – Misfortune

祸不单行。

huò bù dān xíng.

One **misfortune** followed hard on another.

1871- 侍/shì/ – Serve

服务员正**侍**候另一位客人。

fú wù yuán zhèng **shì** hòu lìng yī wèi kè rén.

The waiter is **serving** another customer.

1872- 乙/yǐ/ – Party B (in a legal contract)

甲方违反了合同中规定的条款，必须对**乙**方进行赔偿。

jiǎ fāng wéi fǎn le hé tóng zhōng guī dìng de tiáo kuǎn, bì xū duì **yǐ** fāng jìn xíng péi cháng.

The Party A has violated the contract, so it is obliged to compensate the **Party B**.

1873- 妨 /fáng/ – Hinder

不要**妨**碍他的进步。

bù yào **fáng** ài tā de jìn bù.

Don't **hinder** him on his progress.

1874- 贪 /tān/ – Greedy

他是个**贪**婪的资本家。

tā shì gè **tān** lán de zī běn jiā.

He is a **greedy** capitalist.

1875- 挣 /zhèng/ – Make (money), struggle, strive

我通过卖衣服**挣**钱。

wǒ tōng guò mài yī fú **zhèng** qián.

I **make** money by selling clothes.

1876- 汪 /wāng/ – Wang (surname)

她姓**汪**。

tā xìng **wāng**.

Her surname is **Wang**.

1877- 尿 /niào/ – Urine; urinate

膀胱储存**尿**。

páng guāng chǔ cún **niào**.

The bladder collects **urine**.

1878- 莉 /lì/ – Li (used in female names)

她叫**莉莉**。

tā jiào **lì lì**.

Her name is **Lily**.

1879- 悬 /xuán/ – Unresolved

这件事还**悬**着呢。

zhè jiàn shì hái **xuán** zhe ne.

This matter is still **unresolved**.

1880- 唇/chún/ – Lip

他吻了她的嘴唇。

tā wěn le tā de zuǐ **chún**.

He kissed her on the **lips**.

1881- 翰/hàn/ – Writing brush

他挥翰写下一首诗。

tā huī **hàn** xiě xià yī shǒu shī.

He wielded his **writing brush** and wrote down a poem.

1882- 仓/cāng/ – Barn, granary

这个谷仓能放五吨粮食。

zhè gè gǔ **cāng** néng fàng wǔ dūn liáng shí.

The **barn** will store five tons of grain.

1883- 轨/guǐ/ – Rail, track

电车正被移至另外一条轨道上。

diàn chē zhèng bèi yí zhì lìng wài yī tiáo **guǐ** dào shàng.

The tram is being switched on to another **track**.

1884- 枚/méi/ – Measure word for coins, rings, badges, etc.

这枚硬币听声音是真的。

zhè méi yìng bì tīng shēng yīn shì zhēn de.

This **coin** rings true.

1885- 盐/yán/ – Salt

水溶解盐。

shuǐ róng jiě **yán**.

Water dissolves **salt**.

1886- 览/lǎn/ – Read

这个人博览群书。

zhè ge rén bó **lǎn** qún shū.

This guy has **read** lots of books.

1887- 傅 /fù/ – *Fu (surname); teacher, master*

她姓**傅**。

tā xìng **fù**.

Her surname is **Fu**.

1888- 帅 /shuài/ – *Handsome*

他真是个**帅**小伙。

tā zhēn shì gè **shuài** xiǎo huǒ.

He is really a **handsome** guy.

1889- 庙 /miào/ – *Temple*

那儿有座孔**庙**。

nà er yǒu zuò kǒng **miào**.

There is a **temple** to Confucius there.

1890- 芬 /fēn/ – *Fragrance*

薰衣草有淡淡的**芬**芳。

xūn yī cǎo yǒu dàn dàn de **fēn** fāng.

Lavender has a delicate **fragrance**.

1891- 屏 /píng/ – *Screen*

今天，我们买了一个更大的电视**屏**。

jīn tiān, wǒ men mǎi le yī gè gèng dà de diàn shì **píng**.

Today, we bought a larger TV screen.

1892- 寺 /sì/ – *Temple*

寺院里有一幅很大的壁画。

sì yuàn lǐ yǒu yī fú hěn dà de bì huà.

There is a large mural in the **temple**.

1893- 胖 /pàng/ – *Fat*

她有一个**胖**儿子。

tā yǒu yī gè **pàng** ér zi.

She has a **fat** son.

1894- 玻璃/**bō lí**/ – *Glass*

这家工厂生产**玻璃**。

zhè jiā gōng chǎng shēng chǎn **bō lí**.

This factory makes **glass**.

1895- 愚/**yú**/ – *Stupid; to cheat*

真是个**愚**蠢的白痴！

zhēn shì gè **yú** chǔn de bái chī!

What a **stupid** idiot!

1896- 滴/**dī**/ – *Drop; to drip*

一**滴**都不剩了。

yī **dī** dōu bù shèng le.

There is not a **drop** left.

1897- 疏/**shū**/ – *Neglect; sparse*

这是个人口稀**疏**的国家。

zhè shì gè rén kǒu xī **shū** de guó jiā.

This is a country of **sparse** population.

1898- 萧/**xiāo**/ – *Bleak, desolate*

秋天是一个**萧**瑟的季节。

qiū tiān shì yī gè **xiāo** sè de jì jié.

Autumn is **bleak**.

1899- 姿/**zī**/ – *Pose*

他在那儿摆了一小时**姿**势。

tā zài nà er bǎi le yī xiǎo shí **zī** shì.

He **posed** an hour there.

1900- 颤/**chàn**/ – *Tremble, shiver*

她浑身**颤**了一下。

tā hún shēn **chàn** le yī xià.

A **shiver** ran down her spine.

1901- 丑 /chǒu/ – Ugly

他真丑。

tā zhēn **chǒu**.

He is **ugly**.

1902- 劣 /liè/ – Inferior

那家商店卖劣等货。

nà jiā shāng diàn mài **liè** děng huò.

They sell **inferior** goods at that store.

1903- 柯 /kē/ – Ke (surname)

她姓柯。

tā xìng **kē**.

Her surname is **Ke**.

1904- 寸 /cùn/ – Cun (Chinese inch)

她把衬衫截短了一寸。

tā bǎ chèn shān jié duǎn le yī **cùn**.

She shortened the shirt by one **cun**.

1905- 扔 /rēng/ – Throw

不要扔石子。

bù yào **rēng** shí zǐ.

Don't **throw** stones.

1906- 盯 /dīng/ – Stare at, gaze at

盯着人看是不礼貌的。

dīng zhe rén kàn shì bù lǐ mào de.

It's impolite to **stare at** people.

1907- 辱 /rǔ/ – Insult

我没有侮辱你的意思。

wǒ méi yǒu wǔ **rǔ** nǐ de yì si.

I don't mean to **insult** you.

1908- 匹/pǐ/ – Measure word for horses, cloth, etc.

这匹马很听从他的指挥。

zhè pǐ mǎ hěn tīng cóng tā de zhǐ huī.

The horse responded well to his control.

1909- 俱/jù/ – All, together; entirely

他万念俱灰。

tā wàn niàn jù huī.

All of his thoughts are blasted.

1910- 辨/biàn/ – Distinguish

我们应明辨是非。

wǒ men yīng míng **biàn** shì fēi.

We should **distinguish** between right and wrong.

1911- 饿/è/ – Hungry

我饿了。

wǒ è le.

I'm **hungry**.

1912- 蜂/fēng/ – Bee

蜜蜂蜇人。

mì **fēng** zhē rén.

Bees sting.

1913- 哦/ò/ – Oh

明白了吗？—哦。

míng bái le ma?—ò.

Understand? —**Oh**.

1914- 腔/qiāng/ – Accent of speech; cavity of body

胚胎在羊膜腔中发育。

pēi tāi zài yáng mó **qiāng** zhōng fā yù.

The embryo lives in the amniotic **cavity**.

1915- 郁/yù/ – *Melancholy*

她的温柔话语驱散了他的忧**郁**。

tā de wēn róu huà yǔ qū sàn le tā de yōu **yù**.

Her sweet words dispersed his **melancholy**.

1916- 溃/kuì/ – *To fester, ulcerate, break down; collapse*

千里之堤，**溃**于蚁穴。

qiān lǐ zhī dī, **kuì** yú yǐ xué.

One ant hole may cause the **collapse** of a great dyke.

1917- 谨/jǐn/ –*Cautious*

我**谨**防得罪人。

wǒ **jǐn** fáng dé zuì rén.

I am **cautious** of giving offence.

1918- 糟/zāo/ – *Mess, too bad*

你把事情弄**糟**了。

nǐ bǎ shì qíng nòng **zāo** le.

You have made a **mess** of the matter.

1919- 葛/gě/ – *Ge (surname)*

她姓**葛**。

tā xìng gě.

Her surname is **Ge**.

1920- 苗/miáo/ – *Sprout, seedling*

幼**苗**通常都会放在冷床里越冬。

yòu **miáo** tōng cháng dōu huì fàng zài lěng chuáng lǐ yuè dōng.

The young **seedlings** are usually wintered in a cold frame.

1921- 肠/cháng/ – *Bowel, intestine*

他得了**肠**癌。

tā dé le **cháng** ái.

He had **bowel** cancer.

1922- 忌 /jì/ – Fear, scruple; abstain from

她会肆无忌惮地说谎。

tā huì sì wú **jì** dàn de shuō huǎng.

She will tell lies without **scruple**.

1923- 溜 /liū/ – Slip away, skate

这回你溜不掉了。

zhè huí nǐ **liū** bù diào le.

You can't **slip away** this time.

1924- 鸿 /hóng/ – Swan; great

贫富的鸿沟始终存在。

pín fù de **hóng** gōu shǐ zhōng cún zài.

There is always a **great** chasm between rich and poor.

1925- 爵 /jué/ – Rank or title of nobility

长子将继承爵位。

zhǎng zǐ jiāng jì chéng **jué** wèi.

The eldest son will inherit the **title**.

1926- 鹏 /péng/ – Roc

大鹏是中国一种传说中的鸟。

dà **péng** shì zhōng guó yī zhǒng chuán shuō zhōng de niǎo.

The **roc** is a legendary bird in China.

1927- 鹰 /yīng/ – Eagle

那只鹰向兔子猛扑下来。

nà zhī **yīng** xiàng tù zǐ měng pū xià lái.

The **eagle** dived down on the rabbit.

1928- 笼 /lóng/ – Cage

老人想买一个鸟笼。

lǎo rén xiǎng mǎi yī gè niǎo **lóng**.

The old man wants to buy a **cage** for birds.

1929- 丘/qiū/ – *Mound, hillock*

孩子们正在小土**丘**上玩。

hái zi men zhèng zài xiǎo tǔ **qiū** shàng wán.

The children are playing on the **hillock**.

1930- 桂/guì/ – *Cassia, cinnamon; laurel*

胜利者获得一**桂**冠。

shèng lì zhě huò dé yī **guì** guàn.

The winner received a **laurel** crown.

1931- 滋/zī/ – *Nourish; taste*

他们需要好食品**滋**养身体。

tā men xū yào hǎo shí pǐn **zī** yǎng shēn tǐ.

They needed good food to **nourish** their bodies.

1932- 聊/liáo/ – *Chat*

他们在角落里闲**聊**。

tā men zài jiǎo luò lǐ xián **liáo**.

They were **chatting** in the corner.

1933- 挡/dǎng/ – *To block*

别**挡**路！

bié **dǎng** lù!

Don't **block** my way!

1934- 纲/gāng/ – *Outline, principle*

这不是**纲**领性问题。

zhè bù shì **gāng** lǐng xìng wèn tí.

This is not a matter of **principle**.

1935- 肌/jī/ – *Muscle*

运动强健**肌**肉。

yùn dòng qiáng jiàn **jī** ròu.

Physical exercises develop **muscle**.

1936- 茨/cí/ – A house built with thatch and reeds

我在山上建了座茅**茨**。

wǒ zài shān shàng jiàn le zuò máo **cí**.

I build a house with thatch and reeds on the mountain.

1937- 壳/ké/ – Shell

他们砸开坚果，剥去硬**壳**。

tā men zá kāi jiān guǒ, bō qù yìng **ké**.

They cracked the nuts and removed the **shells**.

1938- 痕/hén/ – Trace

乡村留有战争的**痕**迹。

xiāng cūn liú yǒu zhàn zhēng de **hén** jī.

War had left its **traces** on the countryside.

1939- 碗/wǎn/ – Bowl

我每天早晨吃一**碗**麦片粥。

wǒ měi tiān zǎo chén chī yī **wǎn** mài piàn zhōu.

I have a **bowl** of cereal every morning.

1940- 穴/xué/ – Cave

他们把熊从**穴**中引出。

tā men bǎ xióng cóng **xué** zhōng yǐn chū.

They lured the bear out of its **cave**.

1941- 膀/bǎng/ – Arm

他们抓住了我的臂**膀**。

tā men zhuā zhù le wǒ de bì **bǎng**.

They took me by the **arm**.

1942- 卓/zhuó/ – Outstanding

他曾是个**卓**越的学生。

tā céng shì gè **zhuó** yuè de xué shēng.

He was an **outstanding** student.

1943- 贤/xián/ – Virtuous

叔叔一直为娶到一位**贤**惠的妻子而骄傲。

shū shū yī zhí wèi qǔ dào yī wèi xián huì de qī zi ér jiāo ào.

My uncle is always proud of having a **virtuous** wife.

1944- 卧/wò/ – Lie, (animals) crouch

我们躺**卧**在树丛里。

wǒ men tǎng **wò** zài shù cóng lǐ.

We were **lying** in the bushes.

1945- 膜/mó/ – Membrane

耳**膜**的振动帮助声音传送到大脑。

ěr **mó** de zhèn dòng bāng zhù shēng yīn chuán sòng dào dà nǎo.

A vibrating **membrane** in the ear helps to convey sounds to the brain.

1946- 毅/yì/ – Staunch

他们是坚**毅**的战士。

tā men shì jiān **yì** de zhàn shì.

They are **staunch** soldiers.

1947- 锦/jǐn/ – Brocade

这种织**锦**看上去很漂亮。

zhè zhǒng zhī **jǐn** kàn shàng qù hěn piào liàng.

This kind of **brocade** looks very beautiful.

1948- 欠/qiàn/ – Owe

我**欠**你一个人情。

wǒ **qiàn** nǐ yī gè rén qíng.

I **owe** you one.

1949- 哩/li/ – Final particle indicating exclamation

我还没到**哩**！

wǒ hái méi dào **lī**!

I haven't arrived yet!

284

1950- 函/hán/ – *Envelope, letter*

我收到了你的邀请**函**。

wǒ shōu dào le nǐ de yāo qǐng **hán**.

I've received your invitation **letter**.

1951- 茫/máng/ – *Confused*

这问题太难，我们感到**茫**然。

zhè wèn tí tài nán, wǒ men gǎn dào **máng** rán.

The question is so hard, and we're getting **confused**.

1952- 昂/áng/ – *Raise (One's head); high spirit*

那匹马**昂**起头来。

nà pǐ mǎ **áng** qǐ tóu lái.

The horse **raised** its head.

1953- 薛/xuē/ – *Xue (surname)*

她姓**薛**。

tā xìng **xuē**.

Her surname is **Xue**.

1954- 皱/zhòu/ – *Wrinkle*

那老人的脸上有**皱**纹。

nà lǎo rén de liǎn shàng yǒu **zhòu** wén.

The old man's face has **wrinkles**.

1955- 夸/kuā/ – *Exaggerate, praise*

人们不会相信老是**夸**大的人。

rén men bù huì xiāng xìn lǎo shì **kuā** dà de rén.

People will not believe a man who always **exaggerates**.

1956- 犹豫/yóu yù/ – *Hesitate*

他犹**豫**了一会才选了一本书。

tā yóu **yù** le yī huǐ cái xuǎn le yī běn shū.

He **hesitated** before choosing a book.

1957- 胃 /wèi/ – Stomach

忧虑可能会引起胃不适。

yōu lǜ kě néng huì yǐn qǐ **wèi** bù shì.

Anxiety may disorder the **stomach**.

1958- 舌 /shé/ – Tongue

舌是发声器官之一。

shé shì fā shēng qì guān zhī yī.

The **tongue** is one of the vocals.

1959- 剥 /bō/ – Peel, flay

油漆剥落了。

yóu qī **bō** luò le.

The paint was **peeling**.

1960- 傲 /ào/ – Proud, arrogant

我以你为傲。

wǒ yǐ nǐ wèi **ào**.

I'm **proud** of you.

1961- 拾 /shí/ – Pick up

他从地上拾起了刀叉。

tā cóng dì shàng **shí** qǐ le dāo chā.

He **picked up** the knife and fork from the ground.

1962- 窝 /wō/ – Nest

这是个贼窝。

zhè shì gè zéi **wō**.

This is a thief's **nest**.

1963- 睁 /zhēng/ – Open (one's eyes)

他终于睁开了眼睛。

tā zhōng yú **zhēng** kāi le yǎn jīng.

He finally **opened** his eyes.

1964- 携/xié/ – *Carry, bring along*

这些袋子便于**携**带。

zhè xiē dài zi biàn yú **xié** dài.

These bags are easy to **carry**.

1965- 陵/líng/ – *Tomb*

那座**陵**上散放着几朵红玫瑰。

nà zuò **líng** shàng sàn fàng zhe jǐ duǒ hóng méi guī.

A few red roses were scattered on the **tomb**.

1966- 哼/hēng/ – *Hum*

她在**哼**一支小曲。

tā zài **hēng** yī zhī xiǎo qǔ.

She is **humming** a little tune.

1967- 棉/mián/ – *Cotton*

该国家出产大量的**棉**花。

gāi guó jiā chū chǎn dà liàng de **mián** huā.

This country abounds with **cottons**.

1968- 晴/qíng/ – *Clear*

这天几日内不大可能放**晴**。

zhè tiān jǐ rì nèi bù dà kě néng fàng **qíng**.

The weather is not likely to **clear** up within a few days.

1969- 铃/líng/ – *Bell*

铃响了。

líng xiǎng le.

The **bell** is ringing.

1970- 填/tián/ – *Fill*

根据本单元学的单词和短语**填**空。

gēn jù běn dān yuán xué de dān cí hé duǎn yǔ **tián** kòng.

Fill in the blanks with the words and phrases you have learned in this unit.

1971- 饲/sì/ – Feed

母鸡的**饲**料不够了。

mǔ jī de **sì** liào bù gòu le.

There isn't enough **feed** left for the hens.

1972- 渴/kě/ – Thirsty

我**渴**了。

wǒ **kě** le.

I'm **thirsty**.

1973- 吻/wěn/ – Kiss

他们热烈地**吻**着。

tā men rè liè de **wěn** zhe.

They **kissed** passionately.

1974- 扮/bàn/ – Dress up, play (a role)

他们都打**扮**得漂漂亮亮。

tā men dōu dǎ **bàn** dé piào piào liàng liàng.

They are all **dressed up** beautifully.

1975- 逆/nì/ – Inverse; betray

减法是加法的**逆**运算。

jiǎn fǎ shì jiā fǎ de **nì** yùn suàn.

Subtraction is the **inverse** operation of addition.

1976- 脆/cuì/ – Fragile, crisp

这种纸太**脆**。

zhè zhǒng zhǐ tài **cuì**.

This kind of paper is too **fragile**.

1977- 喘/chuǎn/ – Gasp; asthma

我朋友有哮**喘**。

wǒ péng yǒu yǒu xiāo **chuǎn**.

My friend has **asthma**.

1978- 罩 /zhào/ – *Cover*

用大小合适的盖子**罩**住砂锅。

yòng dà xiǎo hé shì de gài zi **zhào** zhù shā guō.

Cover the casserole with a lid of the right size.

1979- 卜 /bǔ/ – *To divine*

他声称能预**卜**未来。

tā shēng chēng néng yù **bǔ** wèi lái.

He claimed that he could **divine** the future.

1980- 炉 /lú/ – *Stove, furnace*

这屋子热得像火**炉**。

zhè wū zi rè dé xiàng huǒ **lú**.

This room is like a **furnace**.

1981- 柴 /chái/ – *Firewood*

木**柴**太湿，点不着。

mù **chái** tài shī, diǎn bù zháo.

The **firewood** was so wet that we couldn't light it.

1982- 愉 /yú/ – *Happy*

这是我一生中最**愉**快的日子。

zhè shì wǒ yī shēng zhōng zuì **yú** kuài de rì zi.

It was the **happiest** day in my life.

1983- 绳 /shéng/ – *Rope*

他用**绳**子把猴子拴住。

tā yòng **shéng** zi bǎ hóu zi shuān zhù.

He tied the monkey with a **rope**.

1984- 胎 /tāi/ – *Embryo, fetus*

此为中期妊娠的**胎**儿及子宫。

cǐ wéi zhōng qí rèn shēn de **tāi** ér jí zǐ gōng.

This is a second trimester **fetus** and uterus.

1985- 蓄/xù/ – To store

这个水库是用来为我们小镇**蓄**水的。

zhè ge shuǐ kù shì yòng lái wèi wǒ men xiǎo zhèn **xù** shuǐ de.

This reservoir is used to **store** water for our town.

1986- 眠/mián/ – Sleep

最近我睡**眠**不足。

zuì jìn wǒ shuì **mián** bù zú.

I haven't had enough **sleep** lately.

1987- 竭/jié/ – To exhaust

资金已告**竭**。

zī jīn yǐ gào **jié**.

The capital has been **exhausted**.

1988- 喂/wèi/ – To feed

帮我**喂**下猫好吗？

bāng wǒ **wèi** xià māo hǎo ma?

Will you **feed** my cat for me?

1989- 傻/shǎ/ – Silly

我太**傻**了。

wǒ tài **shǎ** le.

How **silly** of me.

1990- 慕/mù/ – Admire

没有人不羡**慕**他。

méi yǒu rén bù xiàn **mù** tā.

There is no man who does not **admire** him.

1991- 浑/hún/ – Muddy

别把溪水弄**浑**。

bié bǎ xī shuǐ nòng **hún**.

Don't **muddy** the water of the stream.

1992- 奸 /jiān/ – Wicked, evil ; traitor

有一些**奸**恶之徒从一开始就打算要舞弊。

yǒu yī xiē **jiān** è zhī tú cóng yī kāi shǐ jiù dǎ suàn yào wǔ bì.

There are **evil** people who set out to commit frauds.

1993- 扇 /shàn/ – Fan

请打开电**扇**。

qǐng dǎ kāi diàn **shàn**.

Please turn the electric **fan** on.

1994- 柜 /guì/ – Cabinet, cupboard

我把盘子放到**柜**子里。

wǒ bǎ pán zi fàng dào **guì** zi lǐ.

I put the dishes in the **cupboard**.

1995- 悦 /yuè/ – Delight

他用表演使观众喜**悦**。

tā yòng biǎo yǎn shǐ guān zhòng xǐ **yuè**.

He **delighted** the audience with his performance.

1996- 拦 /lán/ – To block, stop someone from doing

我被警察**拦**了下来。

wǒ bèi jǐng chá **lán** le xià lái.

I was **blocked** by the police.

1997- 诞 /dàn/ – Birth

耶稣的**诞**生是世界历史上一个重要纪元的开端。

yē sū de **dàn** shēng shì shì jiè lì shǐ shàng yī gè zhòng yào jì yuán de kāi duān.

The **birth** of Jesus was the beginning of a major epoch of world history.

1998- 饱 /bǎo/ – To be full

我**饱**了。

wǒ **bǎo** le.

I'm **full**.

1999- 乾/qián/ – Qian (one of the Eight Diagrams)

乾卦是中国古代文化中的八卦之一。

qián guà shì zhōng guó gǔ dài wén huà zhōng de bā guà zhī yī.

The Qian Diagram is one of the Eight Trigrams in ancient Chinese culture.

2000- 泡/pào/ – Bubble, soak

锅里的水开始起**泡**。

guō lǐ de shuǐ kāi shǐ qǐ **pào**.

The water in the pan was beginning to **bubble**.

CONCLUSION

And thus, we've finally reached the very end of this wonderful list of the *2000 Most Common Words in Chinese*! Be glad - your vocabulary has been greatly increased. Just remember: don't be too harsh on yourself! Learning a language is a gradual process - you have to keep at it. To be honest, Chinese is one of the hardest languages to learn, so take your time. Once you feel comfortable with the basics of Chinese speech, consider taking a trip to China.

We are happy to have helped you with your practice of Chinese and hope to see you again soon; we'll surely meet again in future books and learning materials.

So, take care and study hard, and don't forget the tips we gave you at the beginning if you want to become a Chinese pro!

1. Repetition
2. Concentration
3. Application
4. Movement
5. Associations

With that said, we've covered every single thing. Now go out and learn some more Chinese — you're already more than halfway there!

PS: Keep an eye out for more books like this one; we're not done teaching you Chinese! Head over to www.LingoMastery.com and read our free articles, sign up for our newsletter and check out our **Youtube channel**. We give away so much free stuff that will accelerate your Chinese learning and you don't want to miss that!

If you liked the book, we would really appreciate a little review wherever you bought it.

THANKS FOR READING!

CPSIA information can be obtained
at www.ICGtesting.com
Printed in the USA
LVHW050359020222
709976LV00014B/605